TEXAS A&M UNIVERSITY
95
MILITARY HISTORY SERIES

TALES OF A COLD WAR SUBMARINER

TEXAS
A&M
UNIVERSITY
PRESS
COLLEGE
STATION

DAN SUMMITT

TALES OF A COLD WAR
SUBMARINER

The paper used in this book meets the minimum requirements
of the American National Standard for Permanence of Paper for
Printed Library Materials, z39.48-1984.

∞

Binding materials have been chosen for durability.

Library of Congress Cataloging-in-Publication Data
Summitt, C. D., 1924–
   Tales of a Cold War submariner / C. D. Summitt. — 1st ed.
      p. cm. — (Texas A & M University military history series ;
· 95)
   Includes index.
   ISBN 1-58544-360-3 (cloth : alk. paper)
   1. Summitt, C. D., 1924– 2. United States. Navy—Officers—
Biography. 3. Admirals—United States—Biography. 4. Cold
War. 5. United States. Navy—Submarine forces—History—
20th century. I. Title. II. Series.
  V63.S85A3 2004
  359'.0092—dc22

                              2004004327

To all those who asked, "What did you do in the navy?" and "What was it like in the navy?"; to all my many shipmates through the years; and to my wonderful, beautiful wife, June, who never knew me during this chapter of my life.

CONTENTS

PREFACE

I joined the navy as an apprentice seaman in a college training program in 1942 and retired as a captain in 1974. I enjoyed just about every minute of it and felt very privileged in being able to associate with some of the finest people on the face of the earth — and equally fortunate to be able to fulfill my desire to see most of the world and have many exciting and wonderful adventures.

I often have been asked the questions, "What was it like being in the navy?" and "What did you do in the navy?" It is impossible to answer these questions in a few short words.

Now in my late retirement years, I realized that I wanted to write about my more interesting experiences to pass along to my children, their offspring, and my close friends. I also thought it possible that people not in my family might enjoy these tales, commonly called "sea stories" in the navy.

Terrorism now threatens our way of life. The Cold War came about early in mine and continued beyond my retirement. Our country and our way of life are worth whatever it takes to preserve them. I am proud to have served my country to the best of my ability.

TALES OF A COLD WAR SUBMARINER

1

HOW IT ALL STARTED

In the early 1930s I was impressed with how many toys bore the inscription "Made in China." One day I asked my father, "Where is China?" To my puzzlement, he pointed straight down. "You mean down there?" He then tried to explain how absolutely huge the world was. It had many oceans, many countries, and China was a big country on the far side of the big, round world. This made a deep impression on me that gave me many things to ponder for quite a while. He fed my interest by showing me pictures in *National Geographic* from time to time, and relating tales now and then about exploration, ships, wars, battles, and so forth. I developed a real desire to see the world and have my own adventures.

My father read a great deal and wanted to get me interested in reading books. One of the first books he gave me was *Treasure Island*. It was difficult to put it down. I wanted to be like Jim.

I had a normal boyhood, but travel and adventure were always in the back of my mind. One day I noticed a sticker in the back window of a car ahead of us. It read "U.S. Naval Academy." I asked my sister who was driving, "What's the U.S. Naval Academy?" She explained it was a college in Annapolis, Maryland, where you went to become a navy officer. "That's what I want to do!" I exclaimed. She then explained that I could not just go because I wanted to, but that I would have to gain an appointment from one of our U.S. senators or our congressman. I was determined to try. First, however, I would have to complete grammar school and then high school.

In 1939, after completing my freshman year in high school, I set out to request an appointment from our U.S. representative, the Honorable J. Percy Priest. He maintained an office in Nashville during the congressional summer break.

He said he was very pleased that I had come to him. He explained that quite a few young men wanted appointments to the Naval Academy and to the U.S. Military Academy whom he would have to consider ahead of me, but that I should be patient and he would do all he could to oblige me. In the meantime, he wanted me to send my report cards to him to help prove my interest and my scholastic ability. I assured him that I would pass along my grade reports and do the best I could in all my classes.

I liked this man from the very beginning and through the years I became more and more impressed with his honesty, sincerity, and capability. Quite a fine gentleman!

I had already applied to Vanderbilt University when the attack on Pearl Harbor occurred. I could not enlist or register for the draft until my birthday late that next summer. My parents pleaded with me to continue with my plans to attend Vanderbilt that fall. Classes at Vanderbilt had barely started when all engineering students were told to convene in the assembly hall for a presentation. A group of naval officers explained that the navy wanted engineering students to join a navy training program that would accelerate our studies. We would then be commissioned upon graduation. Since I wanted to serve my country and to join the navy, the program was just what I wanted. It assured me of a commission even if I did not go to the Naval Academy. Most all of us who were physically fit enrolled and were told to continue as we were and await further orders. It could be months, probably the end of our freshman year, before we heard anything.

Sure enough, just when we were about to complete freshman year, we received our orders. Vanderbilt became an army school, so we were sent to colleges all over the United States. I, along with most of my friends, was ordered to Georgia Tech.

After a year at Georgia Tech I received a telegram from Representative

Priest giving me a principal appointment to the U.S. Naval Academy. I was truly excited. A few days later I received all of the required paperwork from the Navy Department. After studying the papers I went to my company officer to see how it would all be handled. The date I was to report to the Naval Academy was such that I could complete my current term at Georgia Tech and go directly to Annapolis. On the train I met Paul Early, who also was going to the Naval Academy from Georgia Tech. He was a member of the Navy Reserve Officer Training Corps (NROTC) unit rather than the V-12 Program, in which I was enrolled. We stuck together and ended up in the same company at the Naval Academy. Through the years we kept crossing paths. We both became submariners. We roomed together while attending the Prospective Commanding Officers Course at Adm. Hyman Rickover's office. We both took command of our submarines on the same day at Pearl Harbor. We both commanded Polaris submarines at the same time, working out of Holy Loch, Scotland. He was a very fine friend.

We spent the first few days at the Naval Academy undergoing the entrance physical and filling out forms. Since I was already in the military, I was permitted to live in the "Visiting Team" dormitory in Bancroft Hall. I had to take my meals aboard a Civil War ship, the *Cumberland*. Within a couple of days I was discharged from the Naval Reserve and immediately sworn into the regular navy as a midshipman along with about a thousand classmates. In no time at all we received our initial issue of uniforms and bedding. By that evening we all had settled in our assigned rooms with our assigned roommates.

Only a portion of the upper-class midshipmen was at the Naval Academy for summer classes. The rest were at sea on cruise or at home on leave.

My class spent the summer training in sailing, rowing cutters, athletics, obstacle courses, swimming, infantry drill, and on the rifle range. There were constant personnel inspections. We could not help but get shaped up to be proper midshipmen in very short order.

As you can imagine, plebe year was pretty rough. I did my best, but by either ignorance or carelessness I was put on report quite a few times. It seemed that practically all my hours of extra duty were served rowing cutters. A cutter was about eighteen feet long and propelled by ten or twelve oars. We rowed from the landing up to the bridge across the Severn River and back again. You knew you had a workout. I was required to repeat most of my academics. No matter how much education you had received before entering the Naval Academy, you had to start at the beginning. Of course, there were things I had never taken, such as navigation, seamanship, gunnery, military justice, and rifle marksmanship. Everything was accelerated except plebe year. It stayed a year. However, at the end of World War II, schedules were rearranged to go back to a four-year program. My class was informed that it would be split: Half would graduate in three years; the other half would complete the program in four years. I was pleased to be a member of the three-year group.

One could write an entire book about life at the Naval Academy, but there is only one story I want to tell. During my summer cruise, after completing my first year, we pulled into Guantanamo Bay, Cuba, where we were to spend several days.

On the second day it was announced, much to our surprise, that the group of midshipmen aboard the *Raleigh* (my ship) would be guests at a tea dance at the Officers' Club so we could see what an Officers' Club looked like, sort of an indoctrination. The midshipmen on the other cruise ships were to go on succeeding days. The uniform was dress whites, our formal uniform, with high collar, gold buttons, shoulder boards, and white shoes and socks — really dressy.

At the appointed hour we loaded on buses and off we went. The club was very attractive. It was a rambling one-story building located on a point of land overlooking the bay and had a white sand beach. It was also quite attractive inside. We were led to the ballroom. It was very impressive. Windows and French doors lined the walls of the room overlooking the bay. The doors opened out onto a good-sized terrace about six or eight feet above the sandy beach. A low stone wall bordered the terrace to prevent someone from accidentally falling off the terrace. The wall had purposely been built low so that those sitting on the terrace would have an unobstructed view of the bay. Several long, white tables — on which waiters were already setting out large punchbowls and cups — bordered the dance floor. It was a very hot day and there was no air-conditioning, so most of us were anxious to get a cup of ice-cold fruit punch as soon as the bowls were filled. We expected fruit punch because that was all we midshipmen were ever offered at any party.

As the waiters went about their work, girls started arriving. They had come from Havana. Each was accompanied by a proper, matronly chaperone. The Cubans were very strict with their young ladies. There were a good number of punchbowls, and the waiters were filling all of them to the brim. We wanted to get with the girls but did not know how to go about doing it. In the meantime, we headed for the serving tables to get some ice-cold punch. It was very good punch. It was the best we had come across in our brief midshipman experience. You could not help but get a couple of refills. Several of us wandered out on the terrace to get a better view of the scenery before the dance got organized. It was very relaxing on the terrace. We all agreed that the setting was perfect: beautiful scenery, warm fellowship, and very good punch. Soon we were laughing as various midshipmen told of their more humorous escapades during the cruise. We really were a very jovial group. A few of us were standing by the wall bordering the terrace, howling in laughter at a story just completed by one of the fellows. The fellow next to him was so carried away that he slapped him on the back and over the wall he went. We rushed to the edge, looked down, and there he was — flat on this back on the beach below, still laughing. He apparently was not hurt. We could not figure out how to get to him quickly, so we carried on as though nothing had happened. Slowly it dawned on me that we were not acting quite normally. I know I felt a little woozy. I figured I would walk around a bit and see more of the club. Maybe I would feel better.

I left the terrace and entered a large party room next to the ballroom. I could hear laughter and girlish squeals coming from the ballroom. From there I started down a large hallway and spotted a midshipman ahead of me going the same way. He turned into another room ahead. As I reached the room, I was impressed with its deep, red carpet and stately furnishings. Inside were the admiral, the captains of the four cruisers, and several other captains and commanders. They were standing in a large circle enjoying their cocktails. I stood there watching the other midshipman walk into the center of the circle. What in the world was he doing? He finally stopped in the middle and started turning about slowly. His open-mouthed expression showed he did not know what he was doing there either. He abruptly threw up all over the beautiful red carpet. I made a hasty departure.

What in the world was happening to everybody? I saw a door to the men's room at the end of the hall and headed for it, thinking that it was a good place to go to figure all of this out. I could hear a good bit of noise inside the men's room as I approached the door. In I went. I was astonished to see a midshipman in each of the four shower stalls. The showers were running full blast, drenching the midshipmen, who were still in uniform. A couple of others were waiting in line for their turn. I stood there a moment and then decided to get out of there, get out of the club.

Once outside, I found my bus and climbed aboard. I sat there thinking that all of us had gotten ourselves in a lot of trouble. There was no other answer. That punch had to have been spiked, heavily spiked. There was no way a midshipman, or even a group of midshipmen, could have done it. I wondered how the girls had fared. They must have had some punch, too. Soon others joined me on the bus. Everyone else was as mystified as I. No one had detected anything strange tasting about the punch. Everyone agreed it was simply great punch. How were we to know? No one ever served midshipmen alcohol. We had simply done it to ourselves unwittingly. In pretty short order everyone was loaded back on the buses and that was the end to a very short party. Back to the ship we went, laughing about all the unusual things that had happened. What a party!

The next day we learned that the Bacardi Rum plant had furnished its finest, smoothest rum as a promotional effort. The club staff had simply made that splendid punch, not knowing that midshipmen were not permitted to have alcohol. The parties for the rest of the midshipmen were canceled. They did not give a specific reason, but I bet it was because they could not find any more girls whose mothers would let them come.

Enough with the humorous stories. The end of the war came as a complete surprise. I had a guilty feeling, as though I had planned all along to avoid the fighting. I reconciled myself with the knowledge that I had always intended to make the navy my career, and who knew what the future would hold.

Of course, we were all surprised and mystified when news of the existence of the atomic bomb broke. That such a powerful weapon existed was mind-boggling. You simply could not comprehend that such a powerful weapon was possible.

For the most part, my three years at the Naval Academy passed rather quickly. In our final parade I carried my grandfather's Civil War sword. Finally, graduation: June 6, 1947. Many war heroes attended the ceremony. I was off for a couple of weeks before having to return for duty, along with about a dozen of my classmates, to serve as instructors for the incoming plebe class. In September, I was slated to join a destroyer being overhauled in Bremerton, Washington. We were not permitted to transfer to submarines or aviation until we had spent at least a year at sea and qualified to serve as officer of the deck on a surface ship. I considered myself quite fortunate to have attended the Naval Academy. It was a distinct privilege that I greatly appreciated.

At the beginning of the fall term, our task of training the incoming plebe class at the Naval Academy was complete and I started my drive to the West Coast via Nashville for a brief stay with my parents. I had bought a brand-new dark blue Ford convertible with all the trimmings for the all-inclusive price of $1,600. I only made about $180 a month, so my family loaned me the money, to be paid back over a period of time.

Driving along in the beautiful countryside in my very own car gave me a new sense of freedom. I had left Annapolis in the afternoon and spent the rest of that day and most of the next driving to Nashville.

It was great to be back home again. By this time there was no more food or gasoline rationing. Life seemed to be back to normal. I got to see quite a few friends and learn of their experiences during the war. One had been a German prisoner for several years. A few never made it back.

After a few days it was time for me to hit the road to report to my first ship, a destroyer, the USS *Stickell* (DD-888), which was undergoing overhaul in the Bremerton Naval Shipyard, across from Seattle, Washington. It was a long way to go, and I wanted to push on and go as far as reasonable each day. I estimated I would arrive in Seattle several days ahead of my reporting date. I wanted to allow for some extra time in case I had any problems. The last thing I wanted was to start my career reporting late. I left home with a bag of sandwiches so I could have lunch whenever I wanted to by simply pulling off the road. I did not want to waste time searching for a place to eat. I planned to spend the nights in cities where I could expect to find a hotel room. Motels were quite rare at that time; those you did find usually did not look like the sort of place you would want to spend the night. The marvelous interstate road system did not exist then either. All the highways went through the center of each town. The more towns you went through, the more time you lost snarled in city traffic. The roads had only two lanes, one in each direction. On hills and curves you might wind up going at a snail's pace, waiting for a chance to pass a slowpoke. You had to watch for people jumping in front of you from hidden roads and driveways. Expressways were almost nonexistent.

My scheme of getting a sack of sandwiches at breakfast to eat later for lunch was a good idea. I enjoyed being able to stop and eat whenever I desired. It was surprising how few cars I encountered in the open country. One day I stopped for lunch, and only one car passed during that roughly twenty-minute period. It sure was lonesome. I do not know why people worry so much about the world becoming overcrowded.

I eventually reached Seattle after traveling about twenty-seven hundred miles coast to coast by myself and checked into a hotel where I planned to spend a couple of days. I called the shipyard and learned that my destroyer was indeed there and would not be going anywhere for a couple of months. I then spent a couple of very relaxed days eating, sleeping, and going to movies. After all of that driving, I needed the rest.

My reporting date finally arrived. I caught the ferry and eventually arrived in Bremerton. It was a short drive to the shipyard. After getting some directions, I found my ship moored to the seawall. A messenger led me from the quarterdeck to the executive officer. He welcomed me, introduced me to a few officers, and had me shown to my stateroom, which was up forward, under the main deck. One of the stewards helped me unload my car. I had time to unpack and get moved into my stateroom before lunch. There were three staterooms up forward. One could accommodate two officers and the other two staterooms three officers each. The wartime complement of officers was nineteen, but we had only nine, so everyone had his own private stateroom.

I went up to the wardroom a little early and met a few more of the officers. A door flew open and flattened me against the bulkhead. I heard the exec say, "Captain, I want you to meet the Ensign who just reported aboard, but you have him trapped behind the door."

The door eased away from me, and there was the captain.

"Hi, George," he said.

"My name is Dan, Sir."

"No, your name is George," he said as he shook my hand.

I did not argue. Still, I wondered why he could not get my name straight. After lunch, one of the officers explained that it was a long-standing tradition to call the junior officer aboard ship "George." There was no doubt I was "George"— and I remained so for quite some time.

2

MY DESTROYER DAYS

I remember very clearly how pleased I was to have finally reported aboard my first ship. I soon got over my disappointment that the ship was not yet seaworthy as I slowly realized how much I was learning from seeing all the various jobs being brought to completion. I needed to learn everything I could about the *Stickell*.

Upon completion of our overhaul, we sailed to San Diego for a week of training under a special team of officers and men. Our transit to Hawaii and the time we spent there provided me with even more training. I finally became qualified to stand officer of the deck watches on our way to China. This was very important to me because it meant I was capable of handling the ship by myself.

Although every day was a new adventure for me, I will relate here only those events that I think were most unusual or instructive.

We had been operating in the China Sea for about five months. I had been serving long enough to feel that I really belonged aboard my destroyer, that I was at last an integral member of the crew. My interest in China had not waned a bit. I was still interested in seeing all of China that I could, and in learning as much about the people, their customs and traditions, their food, their dress, and so on. However, lately I was becoming more preoccupied with how these people around me would be affected by the imminent Communist takeover.

The Communists controlled the majority of China, with only pockets of Nationalists still holding their ground — mainly in the areas of the major seaports. We sailed about the East and South China Sea quite a bit but spent most of our in-port time in Tsingtao, located to the north in the Yellow Sea, particularly in the later months. Tsingtao therefore provided us the best study of what was probably happening at China's other ports as well.

Tsingtao's population was steadily swelling with the arrival of more and more refugees from inland. The demand for food and shelter had become unmanageable. The streets had always held bands of children begging for food or money, but now there were more and more adults begging for help. I no longer meandered aimlessly around, sightseeing as I went. Now I went ashore only when I had a purpose. I made straight for where I needed to go and, after accomplishing what I had come ashore to do, returned directly to the ship. I had heard that people were camping in the hills outside the city. Even from a distance you could see trees that had been stripped of their bark. Apparently people used the bark for food and for making tea of sorts.

So many people thronged the streets that it was almost impossible to drive through in a jeep with any speed. You made headway by pushing ahead slowly and honking the horn almost steadily. Walking from one place to another was also difficult, as might be expected.

The Communists were holding four or five U.S. military personnel captive. I knew that a couple of them had been captured when their plane had been forced down inside Communist territory. I did not know how the others had been captured. The U.S. government was trying desperately to get them released, but the Communists refused.

Orders had already come down for us to be ready to evacuate Americans as and when directed. We had drawn up plans detailing how many we could carry, where they would be berthed, how we would feed them, and so forth. There were U.S. citizens in just about every port and they would eventually have to get out somehow.

It was a Monday morning. We had spent the weekend at anchor in port, and now it was time to get under way and carry out our scheduled operations. However, at quarters, we were told we would not depart as scheduled and that we would receive new instructions later. All of us wondered what was happening. We could see all the other ships preparing to get under way and then sailing off, leaving us still at anchor. This was most unusual. The crew offered a wide range of guesses, but none of them proved correct.

About midmorning word was passed to prepare to get under way. We headed for the open sea. As soon as we were well clear of the regular sea-lanes, we turned in a northerly direction and paralleled the shoreline, which was well beyond the horizon. Just before the noon meal, the exec called the officers together and explained that we were on a special mission directed verbally by the admiral. The captain was to meet with the authorities at certain ports all the way to the northern extremity of the China coast. He was to ask them how much longer they thought it would be before the Communists took control of their areas. We welcomed the idea of doing something different. I was particularly pleased with the prospect of seeing even more of China.

We reached the first port we were to visit in midafternoon. As we were mooring in the berth assigned to us by the harbormaster, the exec told me I was to go ashore and make an appointment for the captain to meet with whoever was in charge. I was the most junior officer aboard, so such tasks normally fell to me. In further discussion it became obvious that no one knew if the Nationalists still held the ports we were to visit or if they had already fallen into Communist hands. My adrenaline started running pretty high as I realized that I might just become the next U.S. military person to be detained by the Communists.

I had already spotted a small building close to shore a short distance to the left of our pier. It had a yardarm for displaying signal flags and I could see a large spyglass on a tripod though a large window, but there was no flag flying anywhere to indicate whether Nationalists or Communists were in charge. I figured the small building must be the harbormaster's office, so I headed for it.

It was a very quiet place. Only a couple of small merchant ships were in port, and I saw only a couple of people here and there. I walked into the small building, but no one was there. I figured this office was my best bet for contacting someone who could help me, so I went back outside and waited. A few minutes later, a jeeplike vehicle appeared. The driver was an Englishman who also turned out to be the harbormaster. I had expected to be dealing with a Chinaman who hopefully could speak a little bit of broken English. After learning what I wanted, he assured me he would contact the proper person and get word back to the captain regarding what arrangements had been made for the two to meet. I had not told him the purpose of the meeting, only that my captain desired to meet at the earliest convenient time with the local person in charge.

I returned to the ship, relieved that the proper wheels were in motion. Sure enough, the harbormaster drove up in his jeep a short time later and took the captain to his meeting. Thank goodness things had gone smoothly. Within a few hours we were under way again, headed for our next port of call.

During the next couple of days we visited several more ports. In each case, I had been lucky in setting up the meetings very readily. Sometimes the captain would go to them and sometimes they would come to the ship.

One of the ports we visited was most unusual. On the chart, the port appeared to be man-made. A breakwater enclosed a good-sized bay except for an entranceway near its south end. Upon arriving we could see a couple of large merchant ships moored along the breakwater inside the port. We were directed to moor beyond the ships toward the entrance. As we neared our berth, we could see that the ships were being loaded with coal. A train hauling many coal cars was parked atop the breakwater alongside the ships. Hundreds of coolies with baskets of coal on their heads were carrying the coal aboard the ships, dumping it in the ships' holds, and returning to the train with their empty baskets to get another load. It was obvious that they were dumping the coal on one side of the ships only, because both were beginning to list toward the pier. It later became obvious that their reason for doing this was to get the inboard side of the ships lower to the pier so they would not have such a steep climb to get aboard. After the ships had listed as far as their crews would permit, the coolies started loading the outboard side. Pretty good thinking on their part, I thought. It appeared that they were not permitted to rest until the train had been unloaded and left to get more loaded coal cars.

As soon as we tied up I had to go ashore to make arrangements for the captain's next visit. That gave me a chance to see this coal-loading operation up close. The coolie effort was awesome. I do not think the modern conveyor belt system of loading could have done it much faster.

At the base of the pier I headed for a likely looking office and once again dealt with an Englishman. He invited me to ride with him in his jeeplike vehicle and off we went. After about five minutes we emerged from some woods into a cleared area and a little bit below us saw a magnificent Chinese manor. It was near the edge of a cliff overlooking the sea, which was about a hundred feet below. A tall, ornamented wall with a large iron gate at the entrance enclosed the building and its beautiful formal gardens and paths. The portion of the wall running along the edge of the cliff was low because I am sure no one wanted to obscure the wonderful view of the sea.

The Englishman asked me to please wait in the jeep. He did not think it would take him but a few minutes. Time passed quickly because I was busy trying to take it all in while I sat there. Back he came, reporting that it was all set up. He would meet the captain at his office a little before four and drive him to that same place. As I headed back out the pier I could see that the coolies had a fresh trainload of coal and were busy as ants loading it on the two ships.

Back aboard ship, I passed on the pertinent information to the captain and tried to describe the beautiful home he was going to visit. After that I became immersed in my normal work and duties. At about five o'clock we received word from the captain that all officers except those on watch were invited to the mansion for cocktails and dinner. The Englishman brought us this word and said he would pick us up a little before six at the ship.

A couple of officers had to remain aboard ship, but five or six of us were ready and waiting a few minutes before six o'clock. To our surprise, the Englishman showed up not with a car, but with the locomotive that earlier had been pulling the coal cars. The coal-loading operation had been completed sometime earlier and both ships were gone. It was an old coal-fired steam engine. We climbed up into the cab trying not to get dirty and then off we went, chugging along with a couple of blasts of the whistle now and then. A few minutes after we left the pier, we stopped, climbed down, and loaded into a couple of automobiles. Within minutes we were through the gate and in front of the mansion's entrance. We were welcomed not by Chinese dignitaries but by Englishmen. It was quite a surprise to all of us.

Later in the evening we learned that the coal mines had been engineered by Herbert Hoover, who later became president of the United States. This meant that the mines had been in operation since at least the very early 1900s. The mines were jointly owned by an English company with the Chinese and were managed and operated by the British. The Japanese overran this part of China in the 1930s, but the Englishmen had stayed on and continued operating the mines during the occupation. Their wives and children had been evacuated prior to the Japanese takeover. Now the wives, except for one, and children had been evacuated again in anticipation of the imminent Communist takeover. The one wife not yet evacuated joined us in the manor and we learned that she was to leave the next day. Knowledge of the evacuation of the wives and children brought the point home quite clearly to us that the Communist takeover was indeed imminent.

From the main entrance hall we were invited into a large room that gave us an excellent view of the sea. We were standing in almost a large circle and a steward moved from person to person taking drink orders. Our host walked over and turned on a "wireless," saying he always listened to an English-language news broadcast at this time of day. I overheard the steward apologizing to someone, saying that they had no bourbon but they did have scotch. I had not developed a taste for scotch; being from Tennessee, my drink was bourbon. Maybe I would just not have a drink.

The news program came on but nothing caught my interest. The program droned on for several minutes, then the commentator paused and announced he had just received information that several U.S. fighters had shot down three British aircraft. All conversation stopped. The host broke the silence saying something to the effect that we had heard enough news for the day and switched off the radio. He then continued conversing very normally, as before. The steward was by my elbow asking for my drink order. Without hesitation, I ordered scotch and soda. As the opportunity presented itself, the other officers and I were asking each other, "What's going on?" No one had the foggiest notion and we did our best to continue as if no one had heard the news flash.

The dinner was delightful. Very good food and wine, served beautifully, and the conversation was very interesting. The "last wife" looked upon the drinks and dinner as a wonderful going away party. The attitude of the English was remarkable. They took the loss of their wives and children, and whatever else the future might hold for them, as part of the job and stuck to it. They had our respect and admiration.

Not long after dinner, with the captain leading the way, we expressed our appreciation for a wonderful evening, wished them well, and were driven back to the locomotive for the final leg of our journey back to the ship.

As soon as we were back aboard ship we dug through all of the incoming radio traffic and questioned the officers and men who might have information on the news we had heard about a U.S. attack on British planes. There were no messages; no one knew anything.

For months we tried to get information about the air attack, but we never did learn anything. No one else knew what we were talking about. The story might have been a local propaganda effort. Maybe our host had played a trick on us with a taped presentation by one of his own people. We will never know.

The next morning we were under way, headed farther north in the Gulf of Pohai for the port of Chingwantao. By noontime we had arrived and, finding no piers, we anchored not too far from the only boat landing we could spot. There were no other ships in the harbor. There were no buildings in sight. For some reason known only to the captain, there was to be no meeting here. However, he understood that Chingwantao was a reasonable liberty port, which meant that it was supposed to be able to provide enough things to make it worthwhile to let the crew go ashore for some relaxation.

They had not gone ashore in the other ports because there was nothing for them to enjoy. The exec detailed me and another junior officer to go ashore to find out if this was indeed still a reasonable place for the crew to visit.

Into the boat and off we went. We could see six or eight rickshaws waiting at the boat landing, so there probably was a town of some size beyond the trees. As soon as we landed, the rickshaw drivers went wild. Each of them wanted one of us to hire him. They were pushing and shoving each other and grabbing for us, trying to pull us into their rickshaws. We realized that we had to jump into a rickshaw in order to stop the ruckus. There was no time to think about our choices. Once we were seated in our rickshaws, the ruckus subsided and off we trotted along a dirt road through the trees. It was a dismal day — cloudy, dark, misty, and drizzly. The town appeared as we came out of the trees. Its dingy and dismal wooden buildings matched the weather. People went about their business, not really noticing us even though we were the only ones in rickshaws. The town looked rather poor. Nothing worthy of sightseeing was obvious.

Then I spotted a man who had noticed us. He wore a long coat and a dark felt Humphrey-Bogart-type hat. He had emerged from an alley and was trotting toward my friend's rickshaw ahead of me. Soon he was trotting alongside the rickshaw, showing my friend something he was carrying beneath his coat. My friend glanced at whatever it was and waved him aside. Then he started trotting alongside me. Beneath his coat he revealed two statues. I understood from his gestures that he wanted to sell them. I had the rickshaw driver stop so I could examine them. The statues were about eighteen inches tall and mirrored each other. They were black and appeared to be made of wood. There was a horse, reared up a bit, carrying a Chinese woman. A dwarf with a ferocious expression stood on the horse's rump wielding a war club. There were many, many strips of silver beaten into the wood, giving the horse a mail coat and giving intricate designs to the clothes worn by the woman and the dwarf. Small, polished black stones served as the eyes of the horse, woman, and dwarf. The workmanship was exquisite and must have taken a long time to accomplish. They were definitely very old. He wanted $50 for the pair. You never accepted the first price in China. You were expected to haggle. Besides, I only made $180 a month, so that was a pretty steep price for me. I directed the rickshaw driver to continue. The man came trotting along, still trying to get me to buy the statues. I offered him $25, which he accepted. I held out the money and he wrapped them quickly in newspaper and gave them to me. I was sure my mother would treasure the statues. Almost immediately we stopped in front of a store where the rickshaw drivers probably figured we wanted to go. The store turned out to be a restaurant and bar, but it was also a gift shop. As we entered, the biggest

Chinaman I had ever seen greeted us. He must have been at least six-foot-four and was well built, very dignified, and wore a long, black robe with a black skullcap. He looked like the character "Big Stoop" in the *Terry and the Pirates* comic strip. He spoke very clear English and graciously welcomed us to his establishment. First there was a large barroom with many tables and chairs. Then there was a restaurant area with the gift shop off to one side. He insisted we have some Chinese beer with him. While enjoying the beer, I wandered about the bar looking at framed photographs on the walls. They were pictures of American and English warships. The pictures looked old and, from the looks of the ships, the pictures dated back before World War II. Pen-and-ink handwriting on the pictures offered expressions of thanks and well wishes to the big Chinaman. Each was signed by the ship's captain. They were very good endorsements of the proprietor, T. T. Wang, and his establishment. Apparently ours was the first U.S. warship to visit since those days long ago.

After we explained our mission to him, he told us our crew would be safe in town, that he would be very pleased for them to visit his place, and that there were several other places to go — although none, of course, was as good as his.

He was showing us around his shop when I unwrapped the statues I had bought and asked what he thought of them. He said they were very fine pieces and wanted to know where I got them. I told him my story and he became quite concerned. He asked me for a description of the man who sold them. I described him as well as I could. He turned and in Chinese called for a couple of his men. They instantly appeared. He jabbered at them a bit and they quickly disappeared into the street. A short time later they reappeared with the man in tow. Mr. Wang started speaking very sternly to the man. He made the man give me $12 and explained that I had paid too much. After the man left he said they were very fine pieces but that must have been stolen.

We said our good-byes, thanking him for his help and telling him that we wanted to stay, but that we needed to get back and make our report to the executive officer. We promised to return later.

Of course, the crew was happy to be going ashore at last. After supper, I returned to T. T. Wang's establishment and presented him with a picture of our ship bearing an expression of good wishes and dated and signed by the captain.

The next day we were headed for what was probably the last port we would visit on this mission. Along the way we were able to see the Great Wall of China. I had already visited the Great Wall near Peking, but that was a close-up view. This long-distance view was spectacular. The Wall ran from the shore on up a mountain ridge and snaked its way out of sight along one ridge after another. I estimated that we saw at least thirty or forty miles of the Wall before it finally disappeared.

The following morning we entered the last port we were supposed to visit. There were no other ships, not even any boats, in sight. It was not an industrial or commercial port because none of the required buildings or warehouses was anywhere to be seen. The only place to make a boat landing was alongside a long seawall made of stone that protected a very large, very flat field. Hundreds of soldiers were spread around this wide expanse being drilled and instructed. A few buildings, apparently barracks, were located at the far side of the field. There was no building resembling a headquarters or administration building. None of us could spot a boat landing anywhere. I went to the bridge to see if there was a boat landing depicted on the chart. The captain said none could be found on the chart and that no one else had been able to spot a place to land a boat. The seawall appeared to be about eight feet above the water. The field beyond was level with the top of the seawall.

I asked the captain if the soldiers we could see drilling were Nationalist troops, but he had no information and there were no obvious clues to be seen, such as a flag.

We were anchored several hundred yards from shore and a motor whaleboat was already at the quarterdeck, so off I went. We made a pass along a good portion of the wall but could find no landing. I headed back to the area where the troops had been seen near the wall. However, being so close to the wall, we were unable to see the field. I had the coxswain bring the boat alongside the wall. By standing on the side of the boat and jumping I was able to grab the top of the wall. I pulled myself up until I had my arms on top of the wall and could see what was on the other side. I was looking at a big gathering of soldiers, with six or eight of them about three feet away, their bayonets pointed at me. By now the boat had drifted away from the wall. I figured I had two choices. I could drop into the water, swim to the boat, and lose face completely if these were Nationalists, or I could keep climbing. If they were Communists, I probably would become U.S. captive number six or seven. Up I went, hoping for the best. My uniform was pretty messy from climbing over the wall. I quickly brushed myself off while trying to identify someone in authority. Such a person was not obvious. I spoke my intentions to the swelling group. Someone in back started talking loudly in Chinese. The soldiers in front relaxed their bayonets and the crowd parted to allow the person who had barked the orders to approach. These soldiers were not like the youngsters I had seen in the other ports. They were experienced men and much better dressed. The person approaching me was very smartly dressed. He was wearing the same rank insignia worn by U.S. colonels. I had never seen any Chinese wearing our type of insignia, so I concluded I must be among Communists. He motioned for me to follow him. We headed for a jeep. He motioned for me to sit in the back and off we headed toward the woods. I wondered what I had gotten myself into. After traveling about a mile through the trees, we came to what looked like a guard shack. He barked some more orders and a couple of soldiers came bolting out of the shack to join the single soldier standing duty outside. He motioned me to follow him into the shack. It was empty. He pointed to a wooden bench and I sat down. He then spent ten to fifteen minutes on the phone — talking, I think, to several different people. When he finished, he motioned me out and back into the jeep. We continued along the same dirt road. Eventually, to my surprise, we ended up back at the drill field and drove to the seawall. We stopped at a boat landing! It was a good stone structure. Waiting there were my boat and crew. He turned to me and, in perfect English, said that his commanding general would meet with my captain at his convenience. I was pretty angry with him for not talking English earlier, but I held my temper and assured him that my captain would be ashore shortly. After clearing the landing, we looked back to make sure we could find the unnoticeable entrance for the captain's visit.

I reported it all to the captain and learned that they had been watching us through binoculars and had been quite concerned. I knew they could not have been as concerned as I was. I was relieved that we had no more ports to visit and that maybe we would return to more normal operations.

It was a beautiful morning. We lay at anchor in the Yellow Sea, well off the coast of China not far from Tsingtao. A bit of land could barely be seen here and there to the northwest. The sea was very calm, no waves, no white caps, but there was a slight swell that gave our destroyer an easy, lazy, rolling and rocking motion that was hardly noticeable. About all of our time at sea in this area had been in rough or stormy weather. We had ridden out numerous typhoons over the past several months. Some storms were very bad, some not so bad. All aboard were enjoying this beautiful, calm day.

At quarters this morning (quarters is a muster of the crew by division in designated areas on the weather decks, for accountability, inspection, and announcing the orders of the day) I had relayed to my division that we would be at anchor here until the next day, when the other three ships in our destroyer division rejoined us for scheduled operations. Our mission of visiting the various Chinese ports in the region complete, we were to relax and enjoy this respite — but not until all necessary items of work had been accomplished. My men knew what had to be done and I could count on them

My first ship, the USS Stickell *(DD-888).*

to do it. Meanwhile, I strolled around the deck talking to crewmen who were standing around. It was a day to be enjoyed and I was making the most of it.

My enjoyment of the weather and the view was interrupted by a messenger who relayed the word that the exec wanted to see all officers in the wardroom. I wondered what was up. We gathered and were told that a typhoon was headed our way and that we were to prepare for heavy weather and be ready to get under way in one hour. So much for spending a beautiful day in the sun. Nevertheless, I was all for doing our best to avoid at least the worst part of the storm bearing down on us. It is hard to outwit Mother Nature, but you need to do your best to stay out of trouble. Everything that was not already well secured needed to be properly stowed or lashed down. Once you get into heavy weather it is too late to prevent damage or destruction to or by loose gear.

The chief engineer raised a good head of steam, got the plant on line, and we were under way within the hour, headed at best speed along our escape route. Meanwhile, the swell had become more noticeable, which was an indication that the storm was indeed heading our way.

I need to explain that the weather information we were afforded at that point in time was very meager compared to that which is available today with the help of satellites, hurricane-hunting aircraft, weather ships, sensor buoys, and so forth. All the information available to weather forecasters at that time was information furnished to them by individual ships at sea, which was simply the data collected by a ship in its immediate location. If there were no ships, or very few ships, then the information was quite sketchy. We had a barometer, but a storm is pretty well on you before you get readings that warn you of its existence. We learned of this approaching typhoon by radio message, but a good deal of time already had passed from its last known position — and hurricanes and typhoons have a way of changing directions pretty quickly. We were using the best information available and hoping for the best.

It was nearly time for our noon meal, so I headed for the wardroom. This might be our last chance for a relatively calm, sit-down meal. The other officers seemed to have the same thought, because in pretty short order everyone except the officer of the deck, who had the bridge watch, was on hand, ready to eat. As I recall, everything went pretty well. The sea was noticeably building with waves and whitecaps, but this was the sea state we normally were accustomed to, so with unconscious effort we held our plates and water glasses at the right moment to prevent losing them. All in all, the meal was quite enjoyable.

I had the next watch. It was uneventful; there was nothing in sight, nothing on the radarscope, and we were able to stand and move about with reasonable effort and caution. The sea continued to build and the wind continued to increase, but it was not yet more than what we normally experienced. At any rate, we could hold our footing and not be thrown about.

Later, after being relieved, I spent my time rather aimlessly. The only event to look forward to was our evening meal, which I think was about six o'clock. I checked on things in the Combat Information Center (CIC), wandered around the ship to see what was going on (by this time no one ventured out on the main weather deck), and passed the time of day with others over a cup of coffee. We drank loads of coffee because there was nothing else to drink but water and tea.

At dinnertime, upon arriving in the wardroom, I was somewhat surprised to see that fiddle boards had been rigged. Fiddle boards were mahogany pieces with brass fittings that fenced off the area on the table at each chair to contain the plate, silverware, and glassware of each setting to prevent them from sliding around out of reach. The wood pieces were about half an inch thick and about two inches high. The chairs had been lashed to the deck. The steel deck had threaded sockets to hold threaded eyebolts, thus furnishing a means of running a line from the chairs, through an eye, back to the chair, through another eye, and so on until the chairs were held snugly in place. Chairs had to be completely tied down or a chair and its occupant could flip over during a heavy roll or pitch. This was the first time fiddle boards had been rigged during my time on board. The weather had always been either too bad or not bad enough. Today, the exec thought the fiddle boards were needed and that with them we could still have a sit-down dinner. It was better than having a sandwich, which you could eat only by holding on tight to something with your free hand.

The captain sat down and we followed his lead, but not without difficulty. With the chairs lashed in place you more or less had to climb into them. The stewards commenced serving as usual, presenting a plate or serving bowl of food to each one of us in turn. We served our plates as they passed around. Immediately we realized that, even with the fiddle boards, there were to be disasters of food slamming off the plates as they slid into the fiddle boards. Water sloshed out of the glasses. We had barely gotten started when the captain flipped head over heels. His chair had not been properly secured. A few of us grabbed what food we could in one hand, climbed out of the chairs and hung on to whatever was handy. After regaining his feet, the captain ordered a reduction in speed because we had begun slamming into the waves with such force that the ship shook and shuddered each time the crest of a wave passed and the bow dipped into the trough and hit the next wave. Although the commotion subsided somewhat after the ship slowed down, we were still being thrown about pretty heavily. We had to keep going to get clear of the storm track, at least the track we thought it was following, but we did not want to tear up the ship in the process.

When I had finished eating what I could by hand, I made my way to the bridge to see how things looked. It was already pretty dark, but you could still see the waves and feel the wind. The wind was whistling loudly as it blew past the superstructure, masts, and signal halyards. The weather was bad and getting worse. I had the midwatch, from midnight to four in the morning, so I headed for my stateroom to try to get some rest, and hopefully sleep, before assuming the watch. My stateroom was forward, on the starboard side, just below the main deck. My bunk was within a foot of the hull and I could clearly hear the sound of the sea rushing down the side of the ship and over the deck above. I could also feel the jolt and shudder of the ship slamming into each oncoming wave. I wedged myself in my bunk as well as I could to keep from being thrown out and hoped that my unblemished record for never being thrown out of my bunk would remain intact.

It seemed as though a very short time had passed when the messenger woke me to get ready to take the watch. I must have slept pretty well after all. We were regularly awakened twenty to twenty-five minutes ahead of time so that we could properly dress for the weather, get a cup of coffee to help us wake up good, and have enough time with the officer of the deck to learn what was going on, read the night orders from the captain, and take over the watch right on the hour. At night it was important to get to the bridge early enough to accustom your eyes to the darkness before assuming the watch.

I dressed so that I would have a fair chance of staying warm and dry, yet still be able to move around well. I then set out for the wardroom to get my coffee. Shortly after leaving my stateroom, I had to climb a ladder. Ship ladders are somewhat like steps, but much steeper. The steps are like ladder rungs but are deeper, about four or five inches, which gives better footing. Climbing a ladder in a heavy sea is not easy. If you try to go up when the ship is heaving up you feel like you weigh four hundred pounds. If you step up when it is going down you feel like a light gazelle. The trick is to time your movements. After reaching the deck above, I headed for the wardroom, ricocheting from one bulkhead to another, sometimes climbing uphill, sometimes downhill. I finally made it to the coffee pot in the wardroom and managed to pour about half a mug. I stayed right there to drink it rather than try to make it to the bridge with only one hand free. The coffee did wonders to make me feel alive and ready.

I had to climb two more ladders to get to the bridge. The pilothouse (the enclosed part of the bridge) seemed darker than normal. I felt around for something to hang on to until my eyes decided to let me see where I was going. After four or five minutes I was able to make out the figures of the officer of the deck and a few others. The doors on either side of the pilothouse were closed and dogged. In reasonable weather they were fastened wide open. It was completely overcast, so there was no help from the moon or stars. There was, however, an eerie, weak illumination a short distance in front of the ship produced by the masthead lights used to warn other ships of our presence. This enabled us to see the sea, which we could already appreciate from its affect on the ship. We were quite alone; nothing was visible on the radarscope. We were making the best headway possible without pushing our luck. The officer of the deck reported that all was well except that the storm was steadily intensifying. We proceeded together onto the open wing of the bridge that was best protected from the wind to have a clearer look around. The wind was howling so loud that it was difficult to talk to each other. We had to yell into each other's ear in order to communicate. Everything appeared to be well, so we struggled back inside and shut and dogged the door.

The helmsman, the two lookouts, the messenger, and the quartermaster had all been relieved, so I relieved the officer of the deck. He wished me well and headed for his bunk.

The lookouts were normally stationed on each wing of the open bridge, but it was impossible for them to see well looking into this stinging rain and spray. Inside the pilothouse they could see much better by peering through the portholes, which faced forward and on both sides. There was no clear view aft without stepping outside.

The lookouts, the helmsman, and the messenger routinely rotated about every half-hour for a change of pace. The messenger got coffee for the others when approved by the officer of the deck. Our talk that night was mainly about the weather. It was difficult to make yourself heard over the noise of the wind, even inside the pilothouse. Everyone was rating it as one of the worst storms they had ever experienced and marveled at the fact that it was still building. The engine room, radio room, CIC, and our roving damage control watchman all reported that things were going as well as could be expected.

As time passed, I could see even more clearly. The rain and spray roared by horizontally. The wind was very strong. The messenger had given up trying to bring coffee to the bridge because the sea was just too rough. Other than trying to hang on in one spot or trying to move from one place to another without flying aimlessly around the pilothouse, things were rather dull. We were all by ourselves: nothing on radar, no course or speed changes to execute, no tactical communications, and no visitors on the bridge. All our attention was on the storm. It was getting ferocious, almost as though the world was coming to an end.

I just happened to be looking out a porthole at the side when I noticed something small flying from the ship and disappearing in the distance rather than falling. It happened again! The best I could make out was that the objects were small antennas about a foot in length (several pieces together gave it an upside-down tripod look) that had been mounted on our yardarm to serve our electronic countermeasure system (ECM). Unbelievable! Pieces were being ripped off the ship!

Next, I sensed something unnatural happening. It finally dawned on me that the sea was subsiding. The wind was worse. It was literally screaming by us, but the sea was becoming flat! There was no more pitching or rolling of any consequence, however the ship had listed to one side and was staying there! Our list was probably about fifteen degrees. The helmsman had to carry a good amount of rudder in order to maintain a steady heading. It was unbelievable; the wind was so strong that it flattened the waves! I do not remember anyone uttering a word. We just stood there in disbelief. Of course, it was very hard to be heard over the sound of the wind.

I worried that there was something I should be doing, but we were riding steady and, although we were heeled over, I knew from experience that we could go over a lot farther and still recover. If the list increased I would head closer into the wind or out of it. Should I call the captain? What would I report? Should I report that the waves had disappeared? If I did, he would think, "Great, why wake me to tell me that?" I considered calling a couple of officers to come to the bridge for a look, but thought better of it. They would probably think I had lost my mind.

I have no idea how long the flat sea lasted. We were all so stunned that no one noted the exact time. My best guess is that it lasted about ten minutes, maybe more. Once the flatness started to break it took little time for the sea to regain its former ferocity.

It was definitely not the eye of the storm passing. When that happens, the wind dies down to a calm but the sea continues to run heavy. When the eye passes, the wind comes roaring back in, but from the opposite direction. In this case, the wind never changed direction and it certainly never slacked off while the sea was running flat. If anything, it peaked.

The rest of the watch was uneventful. We just hung on as well as we could.

When my relief arrived, I estimated the wind and sea to be just about what it had been when I first took over the watch. I briefed him on how things had been going and related our experience with the flattened sea. It was too dark to see the expression on his face, but his reply had a note of disbelief and was rather patronizing. I was the most junior officer aboard. All the others had more sea time than I did and he probably thought I was exaggerating or that I thought I had seen something that I really had not. I was too tired to hang around, so I headed for my bunk.

Again I slept pretty soundly, but around seven o'clock I struggled out of my bunk to go see if I could find something I could manage to eat for breakfast. The weather was still bad, but not as bad as it had been. I forget what I had for breakfast, but it was still so rough that the cooks were preparing only things that could be eaten while standing. There were two or three officers in the wardroom and I related my experience with the flattened sea. Once again there was polite rejection of what I said had happened. Later on I related my story to a couple of other officers and received the same polite brush-off. I finally gave up telling anyone else. If I persisted, they probably would think I was out of my mind.

Years passed and I related that incident very rarely and very cautiously. Then one day, while I was commanding a Polaris submarine, we were on patrol well north of England. The weather was usually bad in that region, and a couple of officers were sitting in the wardroom debating the definitions of various sea states and wind forces. They were pretty consistent in calling the sea states, but there seemed to be disagreement as to what the wind force was called. One might say four and another three. I suggested that someone go get a book that contained the definitions and we could all benefit from the review. In the meantime, I reached into a cabinet containing a set of encyclopedias and started searching. I found what I was looking for pretty quickly. I started studying and, to my amusement, found that the strongest wind to be experienced was described as being "so strong that waves are blown flat, no waves can exist, winds are 200 miles an hour or greater." I had never dwelled on that definition before because the wind was far above any normally experienced. I imagine very few had ever observed such an event. The officers looked at me quizzically, probably because they could not imagine what had caused me to get so excited. I told them my story and said the reason I was so happy was that what I had read in the encyclopedia confirmed I had actually seen what I thought I saw. Thank goodness I never saw it again.

I was truly enjoying my duty with the destroyer force. I felt very fortunate to be aboard this particular ship with its officers and crew, whom I greatly admired and respected. Everyone seemed interested in helping me learn all that I could and gave me the opportunities to learn through experience. The art of ship handling was probably my foremost interest. I not only wanted to learn all that I could to enable me to be good in my present job, but I also wanted to observe and learn all the tricks and procedures that would someday make me a good captain. If I was not on watch when some special evolution was taking place, I made a point of being where I could see what was going on and all that needed to be done to carry out that evolution. At that moment I felt very confident of handling anything I needed to do as officer of the deck.

Operating with a task force brought on many challenges for an officer of the deck. A task force was composed of a main body of large ships such as aircraft carriers, cruisers, tankers, and supply ships, all screened by destroyers. The arrangement of these ships in formation depended on what was trying to be done, moving from one location to another, refueling, replenishing, guarding against air attack, guarding against probable submarine attack, or any combination of those efforts.

A task force commander controlled the movement and arrangement (formation) of his ships simply by making his intentions known by issuing brief coded signals by radio, signal flags, or flashing lights. Radio and signal flags were generally employed in daylight and radio and flashing lights at night.

Officers and crew of the USS Stickell *in China during the summer of 1948. I am at the left end of the front row, the only officer not seated but squatting.*

After a brief period of one or two minutes he would "execute" his signal and then all ships except the one that had been designated to serve as "guide" would quickly move to their ordered positions relative to the guide.

From the time the task force commander made known his intentions to the time he said "Execute" was very brief and each officer of the deck had a lot to do in that short period. The orders sent by radio would be addressed with one word, which was the call sign for all of the ships in the task force. The signal would follow, composed of just a few letters and numbers. One or two specific ships would be instructed to "acknowledge" the message. The acknowledgment by those specifically designated ships gave the task force commander confidence that all of the ships had received his message.

As soon as the signal was received, the officer of the deck would have to grab the signal book and look to see what it meant. Although we knew the signals by memory, it was an absolute requirement that they be looked up in the signal book to insure there was no mistake. Once you knew what you were supposed to do, where you were to end up relative to the guide in the next formation, you had to figure out what course and speed was needed to get there. You figured all this out on a maneuvering board. The maneuvering board was a printed sheet of paper with a circle covering nearly all of it.

The circle was divided into thirty-six pie-shaped pieces, ten degrees in each piece. Concentric circles radiating from the center at regular intervals were used to determine the range from the center. You could mark them as being one hundred yards, two hundred yards, or a thousand yards apart — whatever scale you chose. You plotted your present position from the guide (located at the center of the circle) and the new position you needed to get to relative to the guide. The line joining the two points was the line of movement from one point to the other relative to the guide. By choosing the speed you intended to make, you could, by vectors, come up with the course you had to steer. Hopefully you had all this figured out by the time the task force commander transmitted the order to execute. If any other qualified officers happened to be on the bridge, they would usually jump in and start looking up the signal in the signal book and setting up the maneuvering board problem, just to help you out. I prided myself in being able to do it all with no help if necessary.

We had recently undergone a change of command. We greatly admired and respected our previous skipper, but the new one seemed to be well qualified and we figured he would prove to be a skipper we could admire and respect. However, during the three or four days he was aboard getting to know the ship prior to taking command, he did several things that were not in character for a commanding officer.

One morning I was on the after part of the bridge in the area where the signal flags are stored when another ship started calling us by flashing light. The signalman I was talking with also spotted it and immediately headed for our signal light in order to respond. Before he got there, however, the prospective commanding officer (PCO) jumped to it and started answering. In fact, he kept at it until the business was completed. He did a good job of it, but it was most unusual for anyone other than the signalman to perform the task. A little while later, the flagship started running up signal flags and here came the PCO, running up our answering (matching) hoist. Once again the signalman stood back, a bit dismayed. The next couple of days this happened time and again, but sometimes the PCO did not take over, which threw the signalman off balance. The confusion became apparent when we failed to respond as rapidly as we should. Several officers of the deck told similar tales about the PCO stepping in and doing what they should have been doing and, as a result, causing confusion when he did not step in and perform the task. We all hoped that this was just a passing thing and that when he finally took over we would be left to do the jobs we were supposed to do.

A few days after he formally took command we were operating with a task force composed of two cruisers, a tanker, a supply ship, and several other destroyers. We were all pretty excited to be operating with this task force because we stayed pretty busy and had many opportunities to prove just how well and professionally our ship performed.

I assumed the watch as officer of the deck at noon that day. For several hours the task force commander had been sending first one destroyer and then another alongside the tanker to be refueled. Each destroyer was being permitted to stay alongside the tanker to take on all the fuel it could in about forty-five minutes. Therefore, about every forty-five minutes the destroyer screen would have to be reoriented as one would leave for its turn alongside the tanker and the refueled destroyer returned to its original spot in the screen. I knew I was going to be busy moving the ship from one position to another each time the order was given. I was really looking forward to it all. Shortly after I took over, the captain came up from the noon meal and took his place in the captain's chair. The captain's chair reminded me of a throne. It was rigidly mounted on the starboard side of the open bridge, upholstered comfortably with a waterproof cover, and had a comfortable footrest because the chair was mounted high to enable the captain to have a clear view above the protective bulwark of the bridge. It was positioned to not only give a good view of the sea but also a good view inside the pilothouse through one of the portholes. There were many times that those of us standing watch as officer of the deck would have liked to sit in that chair (when the captain was not around), but doing so was absolutely forbidden. Once, when we were anchored and there was no one else on the bridge, I sat in it briefly just to see what it felt like. None of us would ever have dared to sit in that chair while we were under way. It was absolutely forbidden to anyone except the captain.

At that moment, the captain was in his chair enjoying his view of the task force and I was anxiously awaiting the anticipated orders from the task force commander to reorient the destroyer screen. Sure enough, the radio started barking the orders. I reached for the phone mike to be ready to acknowledge if required. In no time, the captain was there and took the phone from me. I backed off and headed for the signal book, but he beat me to it. I took the maneuvering board to start solving the problem and he took it from me as well. When we received the "Execute" signal he gave course and speed orders to the helmsman and went back to his chair, leaving me to take the ship to its new position. I was a bit miffed by his stepping in; it was as though he did not think I was capable of doing my job. I maintained my calm, though. After all, he was the captain and could do what he wanted.

Time passed and it was now time to expect another reorientation of the screen. Sure enough, here came the orders and here came the captain. Once again, he had all the fun while I tried to get involved, but to no avail. Once again he went back to his chair while I was left to get the ship to its new station. I was upset, but I tried not to let it bother me.

Time continued to pass and soon it was once again time to expect new screen assignments. Here came the signals and again, here came the captain. This time, however, a strange spell came over me. I was completely under its control. Like comedian Flip Wilson, the devil made me do it. I calmly walked to the open bridge and sat down in the captain's chair! I settled back, propped my feet up, and enjoyed the view. This was the life. Upon receiving the "Execute" order, we turned to the designated course and speeded up. In a moment the captain appeared and demanded to know what I was doing. I was still under the spell. I turned and said calmly, "Since you were playing officer of the deck, I thought I might as well play captain." I then got up and went back into the pilothouse. Apparently the captain was speechless, because nothing else was said.

After I got off watch I told my story to several officers and each had a series of reactions: first horror, then amazement, then laughter, then concern for my future. I was a bit concerned about my future, too, but nothing happened except that from that point on the captain stuck strictly to his job description and left the rest of us to do what we were supposed to do.

I may be the only person in the navy to have ever pulled such a stunt and survived to tell about it.

By chance I learned of a regular navy flight from Tsingtao to Peiping (Beijing). They carried navy personnel back and forth for brief leave periods in Peiping on a "space available" basis. There was no effort to advertise this service, so it was generally no problem to make the flight. I was granted permission to take leave for five or six days to make this trip during an inport upkeep period. It was sometime during the spring or summer and the weather was beautiful.

I was driven to the airport in the ship's jeep and with little difficulty we found the small "terminal" building used by the navy. I was the only person from my ship making the trip. I had passed around the information on the flight and had expected more people to participate, but no one else seemed interested. There were seven or eight sailors from other ships waiting to make the flight. It turned out that even though I was only an ensign, I was the senior passenger, which meant I had to sign papers making me responsible for the leave party. I was introduced to an American civilian who had received permission from the navy to make the fight. He was a correspondent for the *Saturday Evening Post* and had just spent several weeks in Tsingtao writing an article about the navy in China. He had spent quite a few years in the country, spoke Chinese, and had a goodly number of friends in Peiping who were also correspondents for various American and British publications.

Our plane was a twin-engine DC-3 configured to carry paratroopers. The passenger seats ran side by side along each side, facing the center of the aircraft, and were made of metal and canvas. There was some cargo piled in the center of the plane and strapped snugly to the deck. The primary mission of this regularly scheduled flight was to carry diplomatic pouches back and forth between our embassy in Peiping and the outside world. Most of it was over Communist-held territory. I was very relieved when we finally touched down at the Peiping airport. One of the most prominent news items at the time was our continuing effort to gain the release of Americans who had been forced to land in Communist territory.

A Chinese bus, ancient by American standards, was waiting to take us to our hotel. The ride to town was very interesting. The countryside was beautiful, with much of the land under cultivation. Traffic was light, but a fair number of people were walking or riding bicycles along the side of the road. Eventually I spotted a huge brick wall up ahead. In pretty short order we passed through a massive gate in the wall and entered the city. The number of people in the road greatly increased. It was rare to see a car; most of the rolling traffic was composed of a few trucks. Thousands of people were on bicycles and thousands more were walking. We soon came upon another huge wall. It was several stories high and continued for several blocks. The correspondent explained that behind that wall was the Forbidden City, which he had visited many times. He promised to give me a guided tour before I went back to my ship.

A short time later, we arrived at the hotel where we had reservations. It was nothing to write home about, but it was clean and fairly comfortable. It was noontime, so after checking into my room I had lunch in the hotel's very plain dining room. The food was good; nothing exceptional, but still very satisfactory. I enjoy Chinese food.

I was anxious to see the sights, so after lunch I headed out, not knowing what I was trying to see. Outside the front door, many rickshaws waited. They were really "pedicabs." The front was like a bicycle so that the driver peddled it rather than running on the ground, pulling it behind him. The rest was like a rickshaw: a seat over two wheels. One rickshaw stood out like a flower amongst the thorns. All of its brass parts were brightly shined; the rest of the frame was neatly painted and shiny clean. The seat and armrests were upholstered in clean, white macramé. I had never seen such a truly first-class rickshaw. The driver was very neat and clean. He was young, but appeared to be mature, with plenty of sense and a pleasant personality. I immediately chose him! He was obviously pleased with my choice. I explained, as best I could, that I wanted to see the more interesting parts of the city. Luckily for me he spoke a little English. He nodded, indicating that he understood, and off we went.

I was fascinated by Chinese architecture. Generally, the buildings were quite colorful. An unusual, very attractive shade of red seemed to be the favorite color. Most roofs were made of heavy tile with extended eves. At the corner of each eve several figures were lined up along the ridge. I later learned that the figures symbolized various animals keeping the bad spirit at the very edge of the corner from gaining entry into the building.

Bicycles and rickshaws were everywhere. Now and then we would encounter a parade of ten or fifteen costumed people playing various unusual instruments. The driver said they were either funeral or wedding parties. I could not tell the difference.

We went down a narrow side street that entered a complex of dingy buildings. It was a marketplace with hundreds of small stalls. He suggested I walk through and investigate while he waited outside. Some stalls catered to tourists, but most offered clothes for the local people or items for their homes. It was all very interesting, but I saw nothing I cared to buy.

We continued our tour of the city. Although I saw a lot of the city that day, I was pretty sure I did not get to see what I really wanted to see of Peiping. I decided to look up the magazine correspondent who had spent so much time in the city when I got back to the hotel and take him up on his offer to show me around.

Late in the afternoon we returned to the hotel. I paid my driver and thanked him for his good service. Inside the lobby I encountered the correspondent. He had just started looking for me. He said he was attending a dinner party that evening being given by his English-speaking friends and they had invited me to come along. I gladly accepted and we agreed on a time to meet in the lobby.

I met him at the appointed hour. As we went outside, I was pleased to see that it was still daylight and I would be able to see more of the city. I was also pleased to see the same rickshaw I had used previously. He had seen me first and had come right up to take me. In about fifteen minutes we arrived at the gate of a walled enclosure. An old man, apparently a security guard, opened the gate and waved us inside. There were about a dozen nice one-story homes backed up to the wall all around the rectangular enclosure, facing what looked like a parade ground in the center. A road ran around the parade ground, passing in front of each home. I had already been told that all the families living there were those of English-speaking correspondents representing publishers and newspapers in America, England, Australia, and a couple of other countries. My friend knew them all, from days past. They had all gathered at one home for drinks and dinner. I found them to be very friendly, pleasant, and interesting. Several volunteered information about the sights that I needed to see during my visit.

Dinner was most unusual. Round tables with settings for four or six people were arranged in the dining room. In the center of each table was an inverted, cone-shaped, copper utensil with burning charcoal inside at the bottom. It was open at the top like an Indian tepee to provide ventilation to keep the charcoal burning. A copper trough encircled the cone about midway up. The trough was about two inches wide and filled with water. There were two sets of chopsticks at each place. One set was normal in length, and the other was almost three times as long. A platter of thinly sliced raw meat and vegetables was passed to each person. After taking what you desired, you held the raw pieces in the boiling water with the long chopsticks and cooked them to suit your taste. You then returned the cooked pieces to your plate and ate them with the normal-size chopsticks. When everyone had finished cooking all they wanted, a servant added some other meat, vegetables, and spices to the boiling water and prepared a soup that was then ladled into your soup bowl. I enjoyed this meal very much. It was a Mongolian dish.

Soon after we arrived in China, the captain invited a couple of other officers and me to go with him to a Chinese home for dinner. The head of the household was an old friend he had met in the United States some years before. Although it was a Chinese home, it had an American touch. I was unusually hungry that night, so when we sat down to dinner I was a little horrified to see chopsticks rather than forks. These were unusual chopsticks. They were silver, completely round, with no flat surfaces, and connected at the top by a two-inch-long chain. The first course was green peas; that was it. I had not mastered chopsticks at that time, but I sure learned fast.

A couple of other evenings, I had dinner in other homes in the compound and each meal featured a different Chinese dish. One was Peking duck. It was very good. I had seen cooked ducks hanging in restaurants. They had been inflated like a balloon and had a crisp, shiny skin. You were served what looked like a tortilla. You placed slices of duck on the tortilla, added hot gravy, rolled it up, and ate it. *Very* good!

One evening, I invited a group of people to dinner at what must have been the nicest hotel in Peiping to try to pay back my obligations.

The third day of my stay in Peiping was set for my visit to the Forbidden City. The correspondent and I were admitted at about nine o'clock in the morning. The two of us and two or three others were the only visitors I saw. Some years later I heard that the Forbidden City was opened to visitors in 1949, but this was 1948. I do not know what strings the correspondent pulled to get us in, but we were pretty much by ourselves.

The pavement was made of big blocks of stone. After passing through a huge gate we were in a large open area that probably served as a parade ground. Buildings made of wood and brick ran along either side. Ahead was a large building that was probably used as an assembly hall. Stone steps flanked by stone statues of lions led to each building. A strange fence with posts and rails made of carved stone bordered the flat area and several elevated bridges leading to the assembly hall. My friend showed me where one stone post had been hollowed out and served as a trumpet that probably was used in the assembly and control of troops and guards. Through and beyond the assembly hall were a large courtyard and then a more elaborate building that contained the throne room. Beyond that building were more and more buildings of various shapes and sizes. We saw only a small portion of this huge walled area. Most of our time was spent going through buildings that served as museums, displaying many interesting works of art grouped by ages. We first saw the oldest pieces, which were grand and beautiful. No doubt some of them took years to complete. Starting in about the early 1900s, the pieces seemed to have a New World influence and to me lost their beauty because they were influenced by the outside world. How very sad. Throughout the visit I was overwhelmed by the realization that I was seeing things that had existed even before Columbus. I was very fortunate to have seen all this.

I was gradually seeing most all of the unusual and remarkable sights in Peiping. Each day I hired the same rickshaw. No matter where I went, day or night, the driver was always waiting for me, ready to go to the next place or to return to the hotel. Thank goodness he understood and spoke English quite well. Several times, while rolling along, I spotted acquaintances from the English compound riding in rickshaws. I would intercept them and ride alongside for a few minutes to pass the time of day. One day I was chatting with one of the wives. She was on her way to a hotel that had a very good gift shop. I accompanied her and indeed found some very good souvenirs. While shopping there, I noticed a very pretty girl who looked to be my age, shopping with her mother. I tried to talk to her, but her mother maintained a pretty tight rein.

That evening, the English correspondents invited me to accompany them to a fancy charity function at one of the better hotels. Most everyone was formally dressed. Of course, my uniform was the best I could do, but it was quite acceptable. The pretty young lady I had seen in the gift shop was there with her parents. Somehow I managed to get introduced and then we spent the rest of the party together. Her father was in the diplomatic corps of some South American country. However, I would have guessed that she was English. There were all sorts of ways to spend money at the event, all of which went to charity. I cannot remember what all I bought or participated in, but I do clearly remember buying a chance to guess the number of beans in a large jar. I did some mental computations and made my guess. My name was later announced as the winner. The prize was a beautifully done watercolor of the Madonna and Child, but it was unique in that the mother and child had Oriental features and wore Oriental-style clothing. I was delighted; it would be an excellent gift for one of my sisters.

During the evening my young lady friend spoke of visiting the Great Wall the next day. A group of her friends were organizing the trip. They were to go in the morning and return in the afternoon. She asked if I would like to go and I did not hesitate to accept. The thought of seeing the Great Wall was exciting, I had not thought a visit was possible to arrange without unusual effort. What a break!

We were to travel by train, so the next morning I joined the group at the station. The train we boarded consisted of an old steam locomotive pulling about five cars. Our seats were in the last car. They were very comfortable, but obviously a bit old. The train was much like those in America, except that the toilet was just a hole in the floor.

The Great Wall is hundreds of years old. Built to prevent raids and invasions from the north. It runs from the sea, westward, for about eight hundred miles. It is built right on the ridge of a mountain range. Because it is built on the ridge it blocks no streams, does not get flooded or eroded by streams, and is very difficult to reach.

We reached a station close to the Wall in about two hours. From there we had to walk uphill. My young lady friend was offered a donkey to ride, so off she went with me hanging on as best I could. We finally reached the Wall and ascended a stone staircase. The Wall was about two stories high and wide enough at the top for two lanes of automobile traffic. Of course, there were no automobiles there. About every two or three hundred yards, the Wall was structured to house troops so that there were always soldiers available to repulse an attack. Ramparts on both sides of the Wall offered protection for the defenders, as well as guards who were there to prevent sightseers from falling off. I was preoccupied with visualizing the activity of days of old, of the troops on guard, and even struggling to repel an attack when a boy sell-ing bottled Coca-Colas that he carried in a bucket brought me back to the present. I could not believe that Coca-Colas were available in such an out-of-the-way place, but I suppose they were promoted throughout the world.

We were able to spend about forty-five minutes on the Wall before we had to return to the train. Our trek back to the train was all downhill, which everyone enjoyed.

Once aboard, we settled down to eat the box lunches provided by the trip organizers. I was very pleased to have been able to visit the Great Wall. I still have a chunk of rock about the size of a baseball that I pulled from the Wall.

The day arrived for me to return to the ship. I had been fully occupied for my entire stay and felt I had been extremely fortunate to visit the Forbidden City and the Great Wall.

As I left the hotel to board the bus for the airport I saw my rickshaw boy. He presented me with about a pound of jasmine tea in a most unusual eight-sided glass jar. Jasmine blossoms were indeed mixed with the tea. He wished me well and I took the opportunity to give him a good tip. He had certainly been a big help in getting around.

The return trip was uneventful. I was happy to return safely to Tsingtao without falling into Communist hands.

In November, 1948, I was still enjoying my duty aboard the USS *Stickell*. I particularly enjoyed being in China. We were nearing the end of our deployment to the western Pacific and would soon be returning to our home port at San Diego. A number of the ships ordered to relieve us would be arriving shortly. The days were getting shorter and the weather was getting much cooler. When standing watch on the bridge I was now dressing to try to stay warm because the wind and the spray, not to mention the rain, could make you downright cold.

We were operating as a task force composed of an aircraft carrier, a couple of cruisers and about twelve destroyers. We were working our way to the eastern reaches of the East China Sea in an attempt to intercept and engage the task force coming out to relieve us. We had been depending on long-range, land-based aircraft to find them and give us their position so we would know where they would pass thorough the Ryukyu Islands to enter the East China Sea. However, the weather had been so bad for the past several days that the planes could either not operate or not spot them when they did. Our last known position for this task force was days old and they could be entering through any of a wide range of passes.

We were heading into the wind at a pretty good speed. It was an extremely dark night due to the heavy cloud cover and very uncomfortable because we were bashing into high waves. A couple of the destroyer skippers had already called the destroyer squadron commander and recommended that we slow a bit to prevent damage to the ships. So far, no orders to slow down had been given.

Our task force was running "darkened ship" (that is, no lights of any kind were showing) and I am sure the other task force was doing the same. With air and visual spotting impossible, our only means of picking them up was by shipboard radar. Under the best conditions, the maximum range of detection was about twenty miles. Radar operates on the line-of-sight principle. Because of the curvature of the Earth, the higher your radar mast and the higher the target above the water, the greater your detection range. Given the height of our radar and the height of our targets, we were limited to a range of about twenty miles. The problem was worsened by the false returns coming from the high waves. Our chances of interception were poor indeed. Because of this, I was spending my time in the CIC insuring we were doing everything possible to pick up our targets.

Our crashing and bashing into the sea was getting worse. We were now experiencing unusual shuddering and intermittent shaking of the ship. Our screws were probably rising above the surface as we pitched wildly up and down. My guess about the thrashing propellers was confirmed when I overheard the chief engineer on the squawk box, begging the captain to slow down because the engines were taking a terrible beating. We kept on going. Orders were orders, and several requests to slow coming from other ships had already been heard on the radio and rejected.

Then it happened. Our pitching and pounding noticeably decreased as we began to slow. I overheard a report to the bridge that our port shaft was out of commission and that the port engine needed to be shut down. Talk on the squawk box ceased. I was sure reports to the captain were now being made over the sound-powered phone. Shortly after that I heard the captain on the tactical radio circuit, reporting to the task force commander that our port engine was out of commission and we could not maintain formation speed. The answer was that we were detached and were to proceed to Tsingtao independently. This was a great disappointment to all aboard, but we held on to the hope that we could make repairs and rejoin the task force before it was all over.

A short time later, the executive officer announced over the loudspeaker system that our port reduction gears were badly damaged, could not possibly be repaired by ourselves, and that we were en route to Tsingtao. We knew that meant further participation in the exercise was out of the question. The knowledge that we were not only out of the game, but that we were also headed to the locker room left us in poor spirits.

We could not help but be interested in how the search was going, so we continued to watch the radar picture for as long as we were able to maintain contact with the task force. No other contacts appeared on the radar screen, just our task force — which was about to run off the scope. The radar operator flipped the switch, which permitted us to search at a much greater range. This brought the representation of our task force much closer to the center of the scope. We would continue watching as long as we could hold them on the screen. Much to our amazement we could now see another task force about sixty miles away! That was the task force we were searching for! Our task force was on a course that made it obvious our sister ships had not picked them up on radar yet. I called the bridge to report our amazing discovery and the captain told me I should report our discovery to our task force commander.

I reported the position of the raiding task force to our task force — their course, speed, composition, and shape of formation. It was astounding! I could not get over having such a clear representation with them sixty miles away! Unbelievable! In nothing flat, our task force turned to intercept the raiders and before long they finally made radar contact and were on their own.

Several days later our captain received a highly complimentary letter from our task force commander. He congratulated us for staying with the problem even though we were out of the action, and also for the unusually fine performance of our radar operators. A copy of an article enclosed with the letter explained that under certain weather conditions, when the air layers are of different density, radar beams can be reflected from the sky back down to the sea, thus greatly extending radar range. That undoubtedly is what happened to us. We just happened to be at the right place at the right time. This recognition of our contribution helped ease our disappointment over the breakdown.

It took an unusually long time to reach Tsingtao after our breakdown. The drag of our out-of-commission port propeller slowed us considerably. Because of this drag, we had to carry a good deal of starboard rudder to move in a straight line, which also slowed us considerably. Upon arrival we had been directed to moor next to the destroyer tender in the inner harbor. Whenever we moved into the inner harbor I would gaze at the deserted Japanese warships tied along a remote portion of the seawall as we passed by them. There were two destroyers and two destroyer escorts. A couple had some very obvious battle damage. World War II had been over for about three years and they were just sitting there, a vivid reminder of days past.

It did not take long for the tender's personnel to determine that repairing our reduction gear was beyond their capability. Some of the gear teeth had been broken off and many other teeth were badly damaged by the broken pieces passing along the gear train. The gearbox was about as big as a U-Haul trailer and weighed several tons. It would probably need to be removed from the ship, which meant cutting a good-sized hole in the hull and the removal of certain piping and other equipment. It was definitely a shipyard repair job. The damage had been caused by trying to make too much speed in the heavy seas caused by the storm. As the screws came out of the water during a downward plunge they would rapidly speed up and then receive a fierce, jarring jolt as they reentered the water. This wide variation in torque caused the gear teeth to break off and damage the following teeth. When the gears finally locked up, the engine seized.

The other three destroyers in our division had also received a good deal of damage, but not to their engines. Since we could no longer serve as an active member of our division, we were declared free game for cannibalizing to speed repairs to the other destroyers. In pretty short order, various pieces exposed to the weather on the main deck and above — such as ventilator covers, funnels, antennas, lifeline stations, and so forth — were being removed by the crews on the other ships to correct their problems. One destroyer had suffered damage to its forward 5-inch 38 twin-barrel gun turret. The force of the pounding sea had dished in the turret's heavy steel faceplate, through which the two gun barrels passed. The big steel plate was at least an inch thick and had reinforcing pieces, but it had caved in enough to bind the two barrels so that they could not move freely up and down. The quickest way to correct this problem was to switch out our forward turret for the damaged one on that destroyer. That, too, was a job that could be handled only by a shipyard. The nearest shipyard with that capability was in Yokosuka, Japan, so plans were immediately made to send the two of us there.

Workers from the tender had already begun to remove our port propeller and secure it on deck aft so that it would no longer drag through the water. A day or two later, after all the material needed to repair the other destroyers had been removed from our ship, we got under way for Yokosuka. The destroyer with which we were to exchange our forward gun turret stayed behind to finish up repairs being done by the tender. Because of our reduced speed with only one screw and the drag produced by having to carry a good deal of starboard rudder to steer a straight course, the other destroyer would be able to catch up with or even pass us. It was a lonesome, uneventful trip. Our spirits were dampened. It was quite a disappointing turn of events.

Several days later we sighted Japan. Seeing Japan, even from a distance, perked me up quite a bit. It was another country for me to see and I was determined to make it to Tokyo. A pilot boat met us as we approached the port of Yokosuka. It is always wise to engage a pilot at an unfamiliar port because they are well acquainted with the currents, shallow parts, sunken obstructions, and so forth. In fact, most ports require you to engage a pilot. We hailed the pilot boat and it came alongside for us to take aboard the pilot. He was escorted quickly to the bridge. He was neatly dressed, very erect, had a smart military bearing, and spoke good English.

The captain briefed him about our having only the starboard propeller, the fact that we had to use quite a bit of rudder to steer a straight course, and all the other points the pilot needed to know. That was it. The pilot gave the officer of the deck his orders and the officer of the deck carried them out.

The pilot was quite reserved. He chatted normally when spoken to, but he did not initiate any conversations. As usual, I was on the bridge, anxious as ever to see what was going on. I was especially interested in the Japanese pilot. I could not help but wonder what he had done during the war. Had he served in the military? Perhaps he had continued working as a pilot, which would have been an important post in the war effort. He looked as though he was too old to have been drafted. Apparently the officer of the deck was wondering the same thing, for he came out and asked the pilot what he had done during the war. The pilot proudly replied that he had been an admiral in the Imperial Japanese Navy! At one time, in his earlier years, he had commanded one of their destroyers!

I suppose I was a bit overwhelmed by it all. I wanted to sit down. I went to the wardroom and got a cup of coffee. Sitting there by myself, I meditated pretty deeply. I had never dreamed I would be in the presence of an admiral of the Imperial Japanese Navy. I thought of how we had grown to detest all "Japs," how they had attacked us without warning at Pearl Harbor, how they had sniped at us unmercifully in jungle warfare, how they had treated our prisoners, and so on. I knew the war was over and that we had to get on with life. My thoughts wandered to wondering what I would be doing now if we had lost the war. Well, we had not lost the war. I was doing exactly what I wanted to be doing. I knew we had to put all the bad memories behind us, lead a decent life, and pull this world back together again. I finished my coffee and went back to the bridge. I was back in the mood to see what was going on and learn all I could.

We moored in the shipyard uneventfully in our assigned berth and were met by a contingent of shipyard personnel. Some were there to see about the exchange of the gun turret and some were there to see about repairing the reduction gear. We learned that the other destroyer had arrived ahead of us.

United States personnel were there in Yokosuka to oversee and manage work on U.S. ships, but Japanese personnel performed all of the work. The need to have the reduction gear work performed in a shipyard back in the States was considered by this party. Replacement parts or even the entire reduction gear assembly were available only in the United States. Since we were already slated to return to the States, it would be more economical to wait and do the work there. The destroyer force commander accepted their recommendation, so the only work left to do there was transfer the gun turrets. It was estimated that we would be in the shipyard for about four or five days.

A few days later we sailed for home, which was several thousand miles away. The other three destroyers of our division were in great shape now. We, on the other hand, were a pitiful sight. Our ship bore the damage sustained by all our destroyers. We had one big propeller welded to our afterdeck, a dished-in forward gun turret, and quite a number of damaged hoods, screens, stations, and fittings. We were a sad sight indeed. Our normal speed was quite reduced with only one of two propellers, and we had to carry a good deal of rudder to steer a straight course. It was going to be a long, slow trek.

Initially we welcomed the reduced tempo of activity. It allowed us to catch up on sleep and enjoy some relaxation. However, within a few days we were all pushing to stay active. We got caught up on paperwork, cleaned out files, and worked our way down our "to do" lists to the point that we were searching for things to do. Our watches were boring. There were no other ships around because we had to stay clear of the normal shipping lanes. We encountered poor weather from time to time, but nothing really bad. The temptation to sit in the captain's chair grew steadily, but no one succumbed.

I had received orders detaching me upon arrival in the States. I was to proceed on leave and then to report to the U.S. Naval Submarine School. I was truly excited about this. I had developed a desire to be a submariner even before I went to the Naval Academy. I was drawn to the navy because I wanted to see the world and all the adventure it would entail. I was drawn to submarines because they operated independently rather than in task forces and because I thought it would be more interesting and exciting. During my first leave from the Naval Academy my mother asked me what I wanted to do when I graduated. I told her I wanted to be a submariner and she became distraught. I had never seen her so upset. She begged me to sail on ships, even fly airplanes, but to please not go into submarines. I assured her I would try to become a flyer because I did not want her to be so upset. My graduating yearbook even said I planned to enter aviation. As it was, when I graduated, an officer could not go into submarines or aviation until he had served at least a year on a surface ship and become a qualified officer of the deck. As it turned out, I had been ordered to serve on this destroyer, which I thoroughly enjoyed. In spite of all that, I realized I still wanted to become a submariner. I visited every submarine I found in port wherever I went. I was able to go to sea on several submarines for a daylong operation, with my captain's permission. When the notice came out that those in my class could apply for submarine school or flight training I sent in my request for submarine school. I was in China at the time and figured my mother would never know. A few days after receiving notice that I had been accepted for submarine school, a short article appeared in my hometown newspaper stating that I was headed for submarine school. I later learned in a letter from my sister that my mother had read it and eventually accepted it as a good thing for me to do. It was a pleasant surprise to learn that she had favorably accepted the news. Later on I think I finally figured out what changed her mind. During the June Week festivities just prior to my graduation from the Naval Academy, my family arrived to help me celebrate. Amongst other attractions and events that the navy had set up were five or six navy fighter planes and seaplanes available for inspection, a few warships, and a captured German submarine, the U-505 I believe it was. Anyway, it is now on permanent display in Chicago. I cannot remember why, but my mother was the only one in the family to go through that submarine with me. I think she was as fascinated with it as I was. We spent a good deal of time examining it from stem to stern. It was still as it was at the time it was captured except that a U.S. Navy crew manned it. I think that tour of the German U-boat helped her realize why I was so interested in becoming a submariner.

I cannot remember how long it took us to go from Japan to the Los Angeles area, but it seemed like forever. We arrived at our shipyard destination about sunset, but there was such heavy fog that we were not permitted to try to enter port. We were assigned an anchorage and then told to sit where we were, so close, yet so far away. It was a great disappointment not to get ashore. I not only wanted to get ashore, I had reservations for a flight home the next morning. The captain assured me I would be detached as soon as it was safe to send me ashore by boat.

A little after midnight the fog lifted sufficiently to permit boats to run. In accordance with the captain's orders to me, I went to his cabin and woke him, reporting that the fog had lifted sufficiently for boats to run. He signed my detachment orders and wished me the very best in my new career. He added further words of praise for my service aboard the *Stickell,* which pleased me greatly.

As I went over the side and down to the waiting boat, I felt a strong tug at my heart. I had often heard that a sailor could become very fond of his ship. I realized this ship had been a dear friend; it had provided pleasure, adventure, and protection to me for many days and many thousands of miles. It was not a dead hulk of steel like a deserted, mothballed ship. No, she was like a living thing, and I knew I would miss her. As the boat pulled away and headed for shore, I sat quietly, looking back until I could no longer see her in the darkness. It had all been a wonderful chapter in my life that I would never forget.

3

MY EARLY SUBMARINE DAYS

It was great to be home on leave. Nashville was back to its old self now that World War II had been over several years. However, I was not my old self. I did not belong there. I felt like I still belonged aboard the destroyer I had just left. The fact that I was about to become a submariner had not yet sunk in.

I learned that two of my closest friends were in New York City. I cannot remember why they were there, but I left Nashville a day or two ahead of schedule for a brief visit with them before going on to sub school up in New London, Connecticut. My timing was just right to join them for the big New Year's celebration in Times Square. What a mob! I was glad to be able to say I had attended this huge event, but I would not care to go through it again.

I made it to the submarine base with time to spare and reported for duty at the submarine school. I was surprised by the base's location. It is located well up the

Thames River, which flows into Long Island Sound. It occupies a narrow strip of land along the river with a railroad running through it from one end to the other. To reach it from the sea, a ship has to enter the river, sail against the current, pass under a tall highway bridge, and then through a draw in a very low railway bridge. The draw is normally closed only when a train needs to cross. The trains have the right of way. A surfaced submarine cannot pass if the drawbridge is down. I have been aboard a couple of submarines that flooded down enough for them sink sufficiently to clear the bridge by inches. This stunt was seriously frowned upon. The piers at the sub base extended out into the river perpendicular to the current. It was a real trick to make a landing there. You had to steam beyond your assigned berth and start twisting so that by the time you were broadside to the current you would have drifted back and be lined up so that you could shoot into your berth. The next trick was to back down hard and kill your speed before ramming the seawall. The piers, the seawall, and the submarines suffered a good deal of damage through the years.

Submarine skippers had the privilege of parking their cars along the seawall ahead of their assigned berths. One day, a skipper making a landing was unable to avoid crashing into the seawall at the end of his sub's berth. The submarine's bow ranged over the seawall and heavily damaged his parked car. He subsequently had to report to his insurance company that the submarine he was driving had hit his car!

Another time, a submarine smashed into a phone booth on the seawall ahead of a berth. The fellow inside the phone booth was not seriously injured. The fellow he was talking to on the phone asked, "What's all that noise?" The man replied that a submarine had just hit him.

Sometime later I learned why the base was where it was. Years before, the navy had used the strip of land as a coaling station. Trains brought coal into the base and the ships loaded it aboard. When the navy started adding submarines to the fleet it needed a base for them. It had seemed sensible at the time to haul them in on flatcars and give them a small section on the waterfront to call their own. As time went on, the need for a coaling station diminished and the submarines needed more piers, larger repair shops, torpedo shops, barracks, a hospital, administration buildings, and so forth. By then, the navy had invested so much in the base that it was too expensive to move it to a more desirable location.

This base was to be my home for the next six months. I was assigned a room in the Bachelor Officers' Quarters (BOQ). My roommate was a classmate with whom I was acquainted. Most of my sub school classmates were bachelors, so I got to know most of them rather quickly. The BOQ had a nice dining room. There was no assigned seating, so you got the chance to visit with almost all of them within a very short time.

Sub school students were not the only ones living in the BOQ. Among the residents were officers permanently assigned to the submarines based there, others who were assigned to jobs on the base, and a few who were there on temporary-duty assignments.

One morning soon after my arrival I had breakfast with a civilian who lived in the BOQ and spoke with a German accent. It turned out that he was an engineer brought there from Germany to teach us about German submarines. At the time we were operating a German submarine to learn what we could about how they designed and built their U-boats. The boat's snorkel system was of particular interest to us.

Our first few days of school were taken up with physical exams and training in submarine escape. The physical exams were normal with a few exceptions. A doctor who seemed to be trying to analyze our personality interviewed each of us individually. It made no sense to undergo six months of training if you were not going to be able to live in close quarters and fit in with the group. One of the tests was for night vision. It was also a good test for identifying anyone with claustrophobic tendencies. We were ushered into a room with just enough bench space along the wall to seat everyone jammed together. When we were all seated, they turned out the lights, leaving us in absolute darkness. They kept us there for nearly an hour (supposedly to let our eyes adapt to the darkness) and then showed faint pictures on a screen that was hardly visible at all. No one cracked, but anyone who could not stand close quarters would certainly have done so.

Submarine escape training was quite an experience. A huge water tank about twenty feet wide and 112 feet deep was used to teach submarine escape. Standing there about ten or twelve stories high, it was quite an imposing sight. An elevator operating in a shaft outside the tank carried you to the top or to locks at depths of twenty-five and fifty feet. The elevator was safe enough, but there was no heat and it had plenty of cracks for the wind to whistle through. It was January, and we just about froze to death every time we had to move from one level to another because we were all wearing swim trunks and were usually dripping wet. We had to go through retraining every few years and I always ended having to go in January or February. In the locker room on the ground floor we were introduced to the "Momsen Lung" escape apparatus. It consisted of an accordion-like rectangular rubber bag strapped around your shoulders and waist with a mouthpiece that permitted breathing in and out of the bag. The bag furnished positive buoyancy and was fitted with a relief valve that permitted air to be expelled as you ascended and the water pressure decreased. You breathed normally as you ascended. The mouthpiece kept your mouth open so that the air pressure in your lungs equalized with the pressure of the water surrounding you. If you did not breathe out, your lungs would explode as you went up.

After familiarizing us with the equipment, they took us to the top of the tank, which was enclosed and warm. We all got in the water along the edge and ducked down below the surface to become acquainted with wearing and using the device. Next we were taken down to the twenty-five-foot level for our first "escape." About eight of us entered the air lock. Water filled the pressure chamber up to the bottom of the access door. After we were all inside, the instructor who was with us closed and dogged the door. He then explained that he was going to open the flood valve, which would start filling the chamber, and that he would also open the air valve, which would build up enough pressure to hold the flooding water level just above the top of the escape door. When the water level was above the door and the pressure in the chamber had equalized with that in the tank, he would open the door and we would commence our escape. By the time he finished talking I noticed that the water level had begun to rise. Before the water level reached the top of the door, I had to start treading water and cheated a bit by hanging on the shoulders of others. Everyone else was able to stand flat-footed. Within a minute or so, the instructor was able to open the door to the tank. One by one we ducked out the door and started our ascent. Another instructor was outside the door keeping an eye on us and at least one more was hovering about midway up the line. There were speakers mounted inside the tank and the chief instructor at the top of the tank could give instructions as necessary. I was surprised at how clearly we could hear him talking to us in the water. Things went well, so we went down to the fifty-foot air lock and escaped from there. Again all went well.

We were scheduled to escape from the bottom of the tank the following day. When the time came, we entered a chamber that was different from the other two air locks. Instead of it being on the side of the tank, it was located at the bottom. It was about the size of a submarine conning tower and we escaped by ducking under the water and going straight up through a regular submarine hatch. This time there were about double the number of people loaded into the chamber. Of course the pressure had to be built up quite significantly to match the water pressure at the bottom of the ten-story tank. As the water level and pressure built up, our voices started sounding like Donald Duck's. We first noticed this as the instructor talked. We could not help but laugh. We all made it to the top in fine shape, but I had no desire to take this up as a sport.

Our training was spent in the classroom, in homework, in operating elaborate training devices, and at sea in submarines. I thought the course was very educational, interesting, and effective. I graduated with confidence that I was ready for submarine duty.

We did not start training at sea until we had learned enough to appreciate what we were seeing or doing on a submarine. We left port early and returned late the same day. We learned the basic requirements of how to operate various types of machinery and equipment. We took turns performing the key jobs involved in diving and surfacing and handling the submarine on the surface. Sea training was very valuable. It helped you become confident that you were truly learning the basics of submarine operations.

One day they took the whole class farther down the Thames River to tour the Electric Boat Company (EBCO). It had been building, repairing, and overhauling submarines for years. The first submarines were small enough to be transported on railroad flatcars or even aboard ships. The Electric Boat Company got its start when submarines were small enough to be called boats. Even though submarines became big enough to be called ships, submariners affectionately continued to call them boats. During World War II EBCO had expanded rapidly as it built and repaired submarines like mad. Now that the war was over, there were no building programs as the military had drastically cut back on expenditures. The company was struggling to do enough business to allow it to retain at least a skeleton crew of experienced workers and thus ensure it could handle submarine work if the demand developed again. We were surprised to see what they were doing in addition to their small involvement in sub repair and overhaul. Among other things, they were building water fountains. You may still see some of them in operation: The little knob you twist to get water has the abbreviation EBCO engraved on it. The company also built machines for stuffing tea in teabags. The most fascinating thing it was building was automatic pinsetters for bowling alleys. I had never heard of such a thing. The finished model had to endure a long testing period before it was pronounced ready for production. Shipyard workers were encouraged to bowl during their lunch breaks. During the rest of the day, one man conducted the testing. The balls were automatically fed back to the bowler, who sat in a chair. At the appropriate time he pulled a lever that released a ball from its special rack. The ball ran down a short chute and under a fast-rotating automobile tire, which shot it through a tube that the man in the chair could point. It was a pretty fast test to be conducted by only one man.

The Electric Boat Company and other shipyards got busy again as the Cold War intensified and really got going with the advent of nuclear power. It was swamped with work when the Polaris submarine building program began.

A couple of weeks before completing school, each of us submitted our preferences for submarine assignment. We were to list three available submarines as our first, second, and third choices. You chose which type submarine and base you wanted. Boats were based in New London, Norfolk, Key West, San Diego, and Pearl Harbor. Some boats were the type that had fought in the later part of World War II. There were also some that had been outfitted with a snorkel. Others had been streamlined and were called "Guppies."

I ended up being assigned to the USS *Sea Poacher* (SS-406) in Key West, Florida. It was presently being overhauled in Portsmouth, New Hampshire, so off to Portsmouth I went.

I had reported to my first ship, a destroyer, while it was being overhauled in a shipyard. When I went to my first submarine, I reported to it as it underwent overhaul at the Portsmouth shipyard. Just as I had with my destroyer, I was able to learn a lot about my submarine by seeing the machinery and equipment being reinstalled and then taking part in the testing. Something I did on my submarine that I had not done on my destroyer was to inspect the dive tanks. At least two people had to crawl up into each ballast and fuel-ballast tank to inspect them after cleaning and repainting. You donned a tank suit, which was a set of rather heavy canvas overalls, to protect yourself and your clothing. You then entered the tanks by crawling up into them through the flood ports or valves from the floor of the dry dock. You took along a droplight or a flashlight to do the inspection and to help you find your way from one part of the tank structure to another. You had to be careful because you could fall about twenty feet when you were at the highest point.

A heavy coat of grease protected the negative tank. There was some fear that a chunk of the finish applied to the other tanks might slake off and jam the flood valve. This tank was a real mess to inspect because you ended up with grease all over you. You had to do a lot of sitting in the grease and also scooting around on your backside to get around obstructions. After completing the inspection, you had to go peel off your clothing and do a lot of scrubbing before putting on clean clothes. That evening I took my dirty clothes home to my poor wife to launder. The next day, when she hung them on the clothesline, a neighbor who had come to visit spotted the terrible stain on the seat of my underpants and said she hoped I was feeling better.

As I got to know my shipmates, I was pleased to have joined such a fine group. They went out of their way to teach and train me, and I soon felt like a good member of the team.

My first submarine, the USS Sea Poacher *(SS-406).*

Some time after the *Sea Poacher* returned to Key West, we were rather surprised to learn that our operational schedule was being interrupted to permit us to provide our boat to a movie company for about five days to film scenes involving a submarine. We were all wondering what the movie was about, if we would be seen in it, and who had been cast in the starring roles. They were supposed to start using the submarine next day. Our wives got pretty excited about the possibility of seeing a movie made and particularly of seeing some movie stars.

The next morning, the camera crew came aboard early with quite a bit of equipment. We were anxious to help, but stayed clear and hopped in only when it was obvious they needed advice on where to go, how to get there, or how they might gain easier access to whatever they needed. Some officers and sailors attached to the base Public Relations Office had accompanied the camera crew to help keep things running smoothly. We all wanted the navy to put its best foot forward. The exec was busily engaged with the public relations group and some of the movie company staff. He turned, spotted me, and motioned for me to join up. He introduced me to a lieutenant commander standing there, said he had come over from a destroyer moored in port, and asked me to please give the commander a tour of our submarine. I did not like the idea of missing all the movie action, but the task would take only about half an hour. The officer was very pleasant and likable — and very interested in seeing a submarine. He asked quite a few questions, which pleased me because it substantiated his interest, but some of his questions surprised me. I could not imagine a lieutenant commander not knowing the answers. I took him from stem to stern, not missing a thing. At the end he thanked me, wished me well, and said he hoped to see me again soon. Later, I mentioned to the exec that I had completed giving the officer a thorough tour, but that I was a bit surprised at some of his questions. It seemed to me he did not know much about the navy. The exec smiled, then laughed and shook his head and asked if I knew who Gary Merrill was. Before I could reply he said, "He's married to Bette Davis and is playing the skipper of a destroyer in this movie." I was a little embarrassed. I had thought I had known him from somewhere, but I was trying to place him in the navy, not in the movie business.

The camera crew had their equipment in place to shoot a couple of scenes topside. I recognized Richard Widmark and Dana Andrews. A pretty large group of onlookers was assembling and I noticed a goodly number of our wives among them. It seemed like everyone wanted to see what was going on.

This was to be a scene in which the submarine had just surfaced and the officer of the deck and two lookouts were coming onto the bridge. Although the submarine was supposed to be in the open sea and it was supposed to be nighttime, it actually was moored to the seawall in broad daylight. A speedboat was racing around in the quiet water making good-sized waves, a fire hose was being used to flood the bridge and shears with heavy dripping water, and a dark filter had been placed over the camera lens. The camera had been placed so that only the bridge and the water just beyond it were visible. They spent about two days shooting such scenes topside in port, another two days shooting scenes inside the submarine, and one day at sea.

The actors were not permitted to do anything that was the slightest bit dangerous; instead, doubles were used. A couple of people kept careful notes on details so that the transitions from actor to double and double back to actor were the same in every way. Several times they had to interrupt the shooting to correct a sleeve rolled up or down, a tie not tied in the same manner, and similar minor details.

We enjoyed having all of those people aboard. I recognized several of the actors in bit parts from movies in the past and saw them even more in later films. The captain and his wife spent a good deal of time with Dana Andrews. They seemed to have quite a bit in common.

One morning, while serving as duty officer, I was standing topside waiting to welcome the captain aboard. I had assumed the watch at eight in the morning the day before and was due to be relieved shortly. I had, of course, spent the night aboard ship. The captain was in a good mood when he arrived. He said he had enjoyed being at my home the night before and was sorry I had not been there. Dana Andrews followed him aboard. He told me he had very much enjoyed meeting my wife. They both were immediately involved in urgent business and I was left to wonder what in the world had gone on. The whole day passed without me having the opportunity to find out what had happened. I did not learn the full story until I got home that evening.

My wife reported that our son, who was four or five months old at the time, had wakened her in the middle of the night demanding to be fed. While she was preparing the bottle she looked out the kitchen window and saw the captain, his wife, and Dana Andrews leave their car and approach the house. She said she tried to avoid being seen and at first had considered not answering the door, hoping they would go away. They were very persistent, however, so she finally went to the door and invited them inside. They said they were sorry when they learned I was not at home, but that fact did not change their plans. Every place in town was closed by that time and the captain had figured they could always get a drink at our house.

Dana Andrews was very taken with our baby. He insisted on feeding him the bottle. He talked a great deal about his wife and children and how much experience he had feeding babies. The little fellow was very content and downed the whole bottle. He smiled warmly and then threw up all over Dana's expensive camel's hair sport jacket. Things were shortly set straight, the sport jacket cleaned, and everyone was happy.

At that point, my wife said, our neighbor from across the way came out to pick up his newspaper. He had to get up very early because his submarine was supposed to get under way that morning. He was, of course, surprised when he looked up and saw Dana Andrews in our living room. His wife had been on him for several days to see to it that she got to meet the actor. He explained to her that since he was on another submarine their paths were not likely to cross, but she would not stop pressuring him. He picked up his newspaper, walked across to my house, and rang the doorbell. My wife welcomed him in and they shook hands all around. He explained to Dana that his wife was most desirous of meeting him. Dana said he would be delighted, so the two of them walked over to his house and went back to the bedroom, where my neighbor's wife was still sleeping. He shook her by the shoulder and said, "Honey, I want you to meet Dana Andrews." Aside from being flustered and shocked, I understand she was pretty upset with her husband for having chosen such a time to introduce her to the movie star.

One or two days before the movie company completed its work, the director discussed with the captain how they might show their appreciation to the officers and men for their splendid assistance and cooperation. The captain explained that the navy would not permit any monetary compensation, but the director could do something of a social nature. It would not be proper to single out specific people, but they could do something that included all of the officers and men who had helped. There was no facility available large enough to hold everyone, so it was decided that the movie people would host a barbeque at the base athletic field for all the men and their families and a cocktail party for the officers and wives at the Officers' Club.

From time to time, official functions were held in Key West for visiting dignitaries. Such functions generally occurred during the winter, and once you had attended two or three, you really did not care to attend anymore. Although we would have several weeks to plan, it was amazing how many excuses would crop up such as unavailability of baby sitters, illness, and so forth. In this case there was just one day's notice, but I do not know of anyone who failed to make it. Both functions were a huge success.

We rubbed elbows with all the actors. I had a chance to wish Gary Merrill my very best and offer my apologies for not recognizing him when we first met. My neighbor's wife had a chance to talk with Dana Andrews the way she had intended to do in the first place. It was not going to be easy to get back into the normal swing of things.

Being based in Key West, Florida, we were quite often scheduled to operate out of the U.S. naval base in Guantanamo Bay, Cuba. Our mission was always the same, provide target services to the Underway Training Service, tasked to train destroyers and aircraft in antisubmarine warfare. What we did depended on the status of training of the student ship or aircraft. In basic training we followed courses, speeds, and depths as directed. In advanced training we were on our own to evade or attack as we chose. We had been deployed for several weeks and the week we were just finishing had been rather boring since the ships involved had all been undergoing basic training.

Training had been declared completed for the week and we were en route to Santiago, Cuba, for a weekend of rest, recreation, and relaxation. Santiago was only a few hours west of Guantanamo Bay, so we expected to arrive well before sunset. Guantanamo was a very fine base, but we looked forward to something different. I had never been to Santiago and I looked forward to visiting there, particularly since quite a bit went on there in the Spanish-American War in 1898. The Spanish-American War came about after an explosive charge set by one or more unknowns sank the U.S. battleship *Maine* anchored in Havana, Cuba. The people of the United States were enraged and shortly were at war with Spain. America's war cry became, "Remember the *Maine!*"

Spain sent a fleet from Spain to Cuba and a squadron of U.S. warships commanded by Adm. William Sampson set out to intercept them. The two forces never met and the Spanish fleet sailed into Santiago. Admiral Sampson finally learned of their location and blockaded the port to prevent their exit.

In the Pacific, Adm. George Dewey sailed into Manila Bay in the Philippines and destroyed the Spanish fleet there. That was the end of the war in the Pacific. In Cuba, however, the Spanish army also had to be contended with. An army corps was landed in a couple of small ports between Santiago and Guantanamo Bay and headed for Santiago. The two forces met and the famous battle for San Juan Hill occurred. In desperation, the Spanish fleet in Santiago tried to escape. All of its ships were sunk or captured by Admiral Sampson's squadron in the waters outside the port. Meanwhile, the Spanish army surrendered to U.S. troops just outside Santiago. The war was over! All of the action that had occurred in and around Santiago made me anxious to sightsee and visualize what had happened.

Everyone aboard was looking forward to the visit for one reason or another. However, one member of the crew, an engine-man who was very well liked and respected, was sick and had been confined to his bunk since the day before. It was not unusual for someone from among the seventy people aboard to be sick. Being confined as we were, it was easy to pass a cold, the flu, or some other bug from one person to another. We were sorry he did not feel well and would miss the visit, but that was life.

As we commenced our run into the port of Santiago, I was impressed by the narrow passage between the high, rising banks and hills and the fact that it seemed to take about twenty minutes to reach the well-protected harbor. No wonder Admiral Sampson had not tried to sail in and attack the Spanish ships the way Admiral Dewey had in Manila. Both sides of the channel had been fortified and the ships would have had to enter one by one. Of course, the same restrictions applied to the Spanish ships as they tried to escape past Admiral Sampson's squadron.

It was a nice, quiet, protected port. Soon we were moored at our assigned berth along the seawall and shortly were changing into our going-ashore uniforms. My spirits had been dampened somewhat earlier when I entered our small wardroom and found the captain and the executive officer engaged in a serious discussion about our sick man. The gist of their discussion was that he might have polio. Although his symptoms were suggestive of, at worst, a case of the flu, both officers were aware of the number of military men in Panama who had come down with polio. Moreover, the Sea Poacher and most of its crew had transferred from Panama to Key West about a year before. The captain and the exec simply were not comfortable with the idea of not trying to get a physician to exam the sick sailor. We had a very fine hospital corpsman aboard, but he lacked the training of an experienced doctor.

As was routinely done upon entering a foreign port, the captain was on his way to call on the American consul. He told the exec he was going to ask the consul to recommend a local doctor and that he wanted the exec to remain aboard to await the doctor's arrival and explain their concerns to him. Soon, all the officers and most of the crew were aware of the deep concern for our sick shipmate. The excitement for going ashore calmed down and most of us hung around as we started thinking of the poor fellow's possible fate.

This was in the early 1950s. The wonderful Salk vaccine, which later stamped out this dreaded disease, had not yet been discovered. Polio was a crippling, if not fatal, illness. No one was sure how you got it, but there was concern that it was contagious. I later marveled that no one had expressed concern for himself, but rather simply for the sick man. The doctor arrived in a surprisingly short time and gave the man a thorough examination. He could find nothing indicating anything other than the flu, but he, too, seemed concerned and said he would look in every couple of hours. I do not know that he could have done anything more for the man if had shown signs of polio, but at least everyone knew that every effort had been made to take care of the man.

After finishing off a light evening meal, two or three of us decided to go ashore and have a couple of drinks. We walked to the main section of the little town and headed for what appeared to be the most popular café bar. Inside we found the captain and the consul. They had come there for supper and were enjoying an after-dinner drink. The consul was a pleasant gentleman, probably in his early sixties, and we enjoyed listening to his stories about the local goings-on and of how he and his wife got along with the local people.

The café bar consisted of a square room measuring about twenty-five by twenty-five feet with a square island bar in the center surrounded by bar stools. Tables and chairs filled the remaining area with plenty of space to move around. The floor and walls were tiled in white, giving it a rather sanitary look. A black-tile baseboard about four or five inches high ran completely around the room. The place was pretty well patronized, with only a few tables and bar stools left unoccupied. The atmosphere was rather cheerful and relaxed.

I sat facing a window and noticed that the men across from me were gleefully watching something going on behind me. I turned and saw a man lying flat on his face inside the open door to the men's room with his feet still in the café area. I saw nothing funny about this, but the others said I should just wait and keep watching the door to the restroom. By this time, the fallen man had recovered and the door was shut. A few minutes later, another fellow pushed the restroom door open and promptly fell through it and landed flat on his face. I suddenly found myself laughing. The problem was that the door opened not from the floor level, but several inches higher, at the top of the black baseboard running around the room.

Even some of those who were aware of the problem would forget and fall into the restroom. As if that were not bad enough, those coming out would forget about the step down and go through all sorts of gyrations — as though they were stepping off a cliff. This undoubtedly had to be the best show in town. We stayed there for a couple of hours. When I visited the men's room, I concentrated on what I was doing but doggone if I did not still trip and stumble through the door, but did not fall flat on my face.

When we returned to the submarine we found the doctor sitting in the wardroom talking with the exec. The engine-man's condition was unchanged. In spite of this, the two men were obviously still quite concerned. Their gloom was infectious. We found ourselves becoming more and more worried that the man was in real danger. I turned in for the evening, hoping things would be better in the morning.

The next day, Saturday, I found that nothing had changed. The sick man still showed no signs of having anything but the flu, but deep concern persisted. I no longer had the desire to go sightseeing. I stayed aboard doing paperwork and odd things that really did not require immediate attention. Many others did the same thing. This was not normal behavior for men visiting an interesting port for the first time. Late that afternoon, I went ashore with a couple of officers for dinner and a few drinks. We got back early and hit the rack.

Sunday morning I got up, put on some clothes, and slipped into the wardroom for coffee. I was shocked to learn that the poor fellow had died during the night. The doctor had been with him. Within minutes of noticing he was having difficulty breathing, he was dead. It was diagnosed as polio, which had paralyzed his ability to breathe.

The captain sent a message to the Guantanamo Bay base commander reporting the death and requesting to immediately return to base and off-load the body. Shortly after having my coffee we were directed to return Guantanamo. We quietly got under way. There was none of the usual kidding and laughter; ours was a very sad crew.

Late that afternoon we moored at our usual remote and lonely berth out in the boondocks. Waiting for us were the admiral who commanded the base, the captain who commanded the hospital, an ambulance, a large stake truck, and a couple of buses.

The first order of business was to off-load the body. It had been neatly covered and placed in a special, stretcherlike basket. This was a common piece aboard any navy ship. It was lightweight but strong, made of metal rods and metal screening shaped to fit a man lying on his back. The body was held snugly in the long, stretcherlike basket with buckled straps. Such a rig was essential to pass it straight up through an open deck hatch.

After the body departed in the ambulance, we assembled topside on the main deck to be addressed by the admiral. He explained that the best way they knew of to help insure that none of us came down with the same illness was to give us plenty of rest and good food to build up our resistance. We were instructed to load onto the truck only such items of clothing and toilet gear that we would need for two weeks, reduce the watch aboard ship to only one man at a time simply to insure that it did not sink, and to board the buses for the ride to the hospital, where we reside under the medical staff's watchful eyes. We were to be involved in no physical activity; we would only rest and eat.

I suppose everyone was as stunned as I was. It never crossed my mind that we would have to be confined for observation and to build up our resistance to infection. The exec's order to get moving got my mouth shut and the rest of me back into gear. It did not take long to get a few things together, toss them on the truck, and then climb aboard a bus. In pretty short order we were on our way to the more settled part of the base.

We made an unexpected turn at the commissary and Navy Exchange and once again headed for the boondocks in another location. We rounded a hill and then turned toward an entrance into the hill. We figured the bus driver must be lost. However, when he stopped at the entrance, the driver announced, "Here you are."

It turned out to be an underground hospital built during World Way II that, thank goodness, had never been used for anything other than a hurricane shelter. It was probably very extensive, but locked doors limited our access to only the space that we needed. There were two good-sized wards in which we would live, plus a couple of unfurnished operating rooms and recovery rooms adjoining the wards. The walls and ceilings were made of concrete and rounded in the shape of Quonset huts. There were no windows; florescent light fixtures provided the only illumination. Nor was there any air-conditioning. All it had was an air-circulation system and a few floor fans. It was just like living in a submarine. I suppose it was only proper to move us from a submarine to an underground hospital. We were sure isolated from everybody else.

The exec, assisted by the chief of the boat (the appointed senior chief petty officer), organized the assignment of spaces and bunks. Bedding was supplied at the main door and we all made our bunks and tried to get settled in for our isolated stay.

We had been supplied a phone with which to call the main hospital should we need medical help immediately or if we wanted to request some other form of assistance. No one was to have direct association with us. We were all by ourselves.

The hospital kitchen called to explain how we would be fed. There was a hallway inside the main entrance. It was about fifteen feet wide and twenty feet long, bounded by a cagelike structure with a door on either side opening into our two wards. Not long after the phone call, a truck arrived with our supper. Hospitals always seem to serve supper early. Two men set up some tables, then laid out the food, plates, trays, and so forth in buffet style. We stayed clear of the hallway until they left, then began serving ourselves. We took the food to tables in our assigned areas and had our first meal in isolation. When we finished, we took what was left back to the entranceway, scraped and stacked our plates, and deposited our silver and glassware in the containers provided. Some time later, after everyone was finished, the truck came back and carried everything back to the hospital.

A few of us sat around drinking coffee that we had made ourselves with equipment and cups furnished by the hospital. At least we could get coffee whenever we wanted it.

It was not long before I was ready for bed. It had been a busy, surprising, and sad day. I lay in bed reviewing the many things that happened. We were all sad about the loss of our shipmate. I imagine there were others besides me wondering who might be next. Putting us in quarantine forced us to think about that more than we might have if we had continued life as normal. But people our age — and particularly in our profession — rarely dwell too long on such matters because we know nothing is going to happen to us.

I slept through breakfast the next morning and thought I would starve before lunch. It was strange not having anything to do. I was rather pleased when the exec said that I was to be the liaison with the Red Cross to handle everyone's shopping needs. That gave me something to do. I kept track of who wanted what — toothpaste, razor blades, magazines, books, and so forth — and once a day, in the early afternoon, a Red Cross lady would come to a service window in a side door and I would give her the consolidated shopping list with adequate money to cover the purchases. Later she would return with the desired items and people's change. I would then distribute the merchandise and settle the bills.

During the first two or three days we experienced only three or four medical problems. In each case a call was made to the hospital and they promptly sent a pickup to carry the patient to the hospital for examination. All were determined to have minor colds — except for one fellow who had gotten up on the first morning, put on his pants, and was promptly stung by a scorpion that had crawled into them during the night. Needless to say, from that time on, all of us carefully checked our clothing before putting anything on. A few more scorpions were found and killed during our stay.

The phone we had for calling the hospital was not capable of handling long-distance calls, so no one was able to call home. However, we learned that our squadron staff in Key West had already contacted our families to explain what was going on and promised to inform them of any developments. The staff also explained how to address mail to us. In the meantime, a routine was established for picking up and delivering mail to us.

Copies of the base newspaper were passed to us to keep us somewhat informed of what was going on in the world. We had a couple of radios, but reception was not too good and most everything we tuned in was in Spanish, so we did not spend much time listening. No one had television at that time, so it was never missed.

We brought a movie projector up from the submarine during one of the watch changes and the base would send over a movie each afternoon for showing that night. After a few days we arranged for the hospital to bring us several cases of beer each night. We finally had gotten around to leading a pretty good life in spite of it all.

Once we got things sorted out we settled into a routine. I usually slept through breakfast and made up for it at lunch. After lunch I would perform my Red Cross chores. Following supper I would enjoy a beer while watching the movie and then join the other officers for our evening poker game. We played as though we had an inexhaustible money supply. However, like the crews on most ships, at the end of each evening we would tally our winnings or losses, as substantiated by the chips, and log them in a little black book. No cash was handled until the end of the cruise, or in this case, the end of our quarantine. We agreed at the beginning on how much the biggest loser would lose, usually about $20, and all other winnings and losses were figured proportionally. Following this scheme kept the game under control so that no one got hurt.

After about ten days we were told we would be released from quarantine the following morning. The Red Cross lady learned of this and slipped me a jug of martinis along with the merchandise she delivered that afternoon so that my fellow officers and I could do a bit of celebrating that evening.

We were all anxious to head for home, but first we needed to spend a day getting settled back aboard — checking to make sure everything was ready and workable, taking on fuel and water, and so forth. After that we needed a one-day sea trial not only to check everything out operationally, but also to permit us to get back in the swing of things. Then we could head home.

The captain called on the base and hospital commanders to thank them for all their help and support and to extend an invitation for twenty of their people to accompany us on our one-day sea trial (about eight hours under way).

We got under way at eight the next morning and headed for deep water, where we could safely dive. Our guests had arrived aboard well ahead of time and were full of enthusiasm. Five of the guests were nurses, including the hospital's senior nurse. The guests were divided into four groups, with all of the nurses in one group, and officers were assigned as "tour guides" for each group. I helped out later on, but at first was engaged in checking to ensure the boat was "rigged for dive." The guides took their groups to various parts of the boat to start their tours so the groups were well separated and would not interfere with each other. About the time we were ready to make our initial dive, the nurses ended up in the control room, which was the center of activity in diving the boat. I had completed my checks, reported that the boat was rigged for dive, and had settled in the wardroom — the compartment just forward of the control room — for a quiet cup of coffee.

After the diving alarm sounded, I heard the vents open and felt us start to go down. It was good to be getting back in the swing of things. When the down angle of the boat began to decrease I knew we were getting close to our ordered depth. I felt the jar and heard the sound of the negative tank being blown. That was followed by a couple of shrill screams and loud female voices asking what in the world had happened. I jumped up and ran to the control room, where I found the nurses and their tour guide, who was trying to calm them down. Slowly I learned what had happened. After arriving in the control room before the dive started, the tour guide had run through all the steps of the diving process, describing what to watch for and what it all meant. He could not resist the urge to tease them, so he said there was nothing to worry about, that it would all go smoothly. The only thing they needed to worry about would be if the diving officer ordered the negative tank be blown to the mark. He said that was a very bad sign because it meant the diving officer had lost control of the dive and would have to do his best to regain control. The truth was, we blew the negative tank to the mark on every dive. It was simply a way to get rid of the excess weight needed to help us dive more quickly. By blowing out that water we would reach neutral buoyancy and could level out at the ordered depth.

The nurses finally calmed down, but I am not sure they ever forgave him. They were good sports, though, and seemed to greatly enjoy the rest of the day.

After returning to port, as the guests departed, the senior nurse told the captain that he and all of the officers were invited to the nurses' quarters for a party that evening. She said it was an annual affair that they held to pay back all their social obligations.

The party was truly grand. Loads of people attended, and everyone was especially kind and attentive to us. It was almost as though a special going-away party was being held for us. It was a very festive way to end our quarantine.

The next morning we were on our way home. Good-bye quarantine, hello home!

The following incident occurred in 1951, possibly 1952, while I was still aboard the USS *Sea Poacher*. We were operating submerged at a couple of hundred feet about thirty miles south of Key West. It seemed we spent most of our time providing target services for the sonar school, also based at Key West. On this day we were providing those services for a helium-filled blimp carrying sonar operator students and also conducting an evaluation of a certain type of "dipping" sonar. We would come to periscope depth every half-hour, raise a radio whip antenna, and get directions from the blimp regarding our course, speed, and depth for the next half-hour.

The blimp was just like the ones you see flying over special events such as pro football games and golf matches today. It was about 150 feet long and had a single gondola underneath it that could probably carry ten to twelve people. Two radial-type engines driving propellers powered the airship. The sonar transducer it carried weighed fifty to a hundred pounds. They would lower it into the water, echo range for a brief period searching the immediate area, and then raise it, move to another position, and search again. At noon I assumed the "conn." My job as conning officer was to stand watch in the conning tower and run the submarine as directed by the captain. The conning tower is a small, pressure-proof compartment above the control room, where the diving officer and his team controlled the submarine's vertical movements. The conning tower contains the helm, which controls the rudder, and engine-order telegraphs for controlling the sub's speed. Both the approach and attack periscopes are controlled and used in this small space. Tactical radio circuits are also used from this compartment, which is situated on top of the long, cylindrical pressure hull. The conning tower not only provided the space that was needed to operate the periscopes, it combined with the main part of the submarine to accommodate them when they were lowered and to enable them to reach above the surface while the submarine was submerged.

It was time to check in with the blimp, so I ordered the diving officer to take us to periscope depth. As soon as we leveled off I made a quick search all around to make sure that we were not threatened by anything not detected on sonar. All was clear. I raised the whip antenna and called the blimp. "What would you like next?" I asked. "Come get me," he answered, "I've lost all power and I'm flying free like a balloon." I told him to hang on and we would get him.

I made a quick search with the periscope. By twisting the left handle I could look up at any angle, even almost overhead. He was nowhere in sight! I picked up the phone and called the captain, reporting the problem and the fact that the blimp was nowhere in sight. He ordered me to surface and start a radar search.

In no time at all, the captain was in the conning tower. He relieved me and told me to oversee the radar search. We started the search as soon as we surfaced and picked up the blimp about ten miles or so downwind from us. We headed for it at max speed. I reported to the blimp pilot that we had surfaced, had him on radar, and were closing on him as fast as possible. I asked about his condition and he explained that he could still control his altitude but that both engines had been ruined when he allowed the airship to get too close to the water. The propellers, which hung a bit lower than the gondola, had hit the water and torn up the engines.

We had recently completed a long conversion at the Charleston Naval Shipyard in South Carolina, which had changed the *Sea Poacher* from a typical World War II submarine to a sleek, streamlined "Guppy." The streamlining not only increased our speed through the water, it also made us highly qualified to work beneath blimps because we had no exposed masts, periscope shears, deck guns, and the like — any of which could easily rip open an airship's skin. Streamlining had not been intended for rescuing blimps, but it was a blessing in this case.

After we informed our squadron commander what we were doing, word undoubtedly spread quickly among all the other commanders at Key West, because very shortly a couple of destroyers appeared on the horizon and we could see several planes flying about. The captain called the destroyers and suggested that they stay clear and give us a chance to work underneath the blimp.

Once we were under the blimp we headed along the course the wind was blowing it and finally matched its speed. The blimp pilot reported he would attempt to drop down slowly until we could reach the handling lines dangling down from the airship. He also lowered the cable that normally suspended his dipping sonar. By releasing some of the helium, the pilot was able to get the blimp to descend slowly.

Having been relieved by the captain, I was free to go on deck to try to help capture the blimp. Just as the handling lines got within reach, the blimp's operator started dropping sandbags to stop the airship's downward descent. He dropped too many, however, and it started rising again. I think all of us figured it would be a simple job to control the blimp once we got hold of some its handling lines, but we were very mistaken. There were about fifteen men on deck and the blimp was trailing about four lines, each of which could be grabbed by a good number of men. As the blimp started rising again, however, it lifted some of the men off the deck. Some wisely let go, but several kept holding onto their lines. I yelled at them to let go, but I had to pound several on their backs before the last of them released their lines. I remembered a newsreel I had seen several years before showing sailors trying to moor a blimp ashore. Many of them were lifted into the air and several of those who did not let go finally fell to their death.

We quickly learned that we were not going to be able to capture the blimp by simply holding on to it. We were going to have to get a couple of our mooring lines and tie them to the blimp's handling lines, thus securing it to our submarine.

We managed to stay underneath the drifting blimp and soon it started down again. Just as the handling lines came within reach, the pilot started dropping sand again — with the same result. This time, however, the men who had managed to grab lines let go as soon as it was obvious they could not control the airship. We continued moving along directly below the blimp, ready for the operator to try another descent.

A few minutes later, the blimp started down again. Just as the lines were coming within reach, the pilot started dumping sand again. He stopped dropping sand, but this time the blimp kept coming down. Suddenly the blimp started dumping what we thought was water but quickly discovered was aviation gasoline! Men who were smoking cigarettes quickly put them out and we passed the word: "No smoking topside until further notice.

There's aviation gasoline all over the place!" The pilot finally stopped dumping gasoline and the blimp started rising again.

Within five or ten minutes the blimp started down again as the pilot released more helium. This time we expected him to dump gasoline when the lines came within reach, so it came as no surprise when he did. We grabbed a couple of lines with enough slack in them to try to tie them to a mooring line, but the airship drifted upward again before we could get the knots tied.

The blimp pilot informed us by radio that he was nearly out of gasoline and would have to start dumping loose equipment. He said it would be best for us to get a bit to one side so that whatever he dropped would not hit us. We eased off to one side as he suggested and down he came again. Sure enough, he ran out of gasoline and started dumping all sorts of stuff: tool boxes, manuals, shoes, equipment — anything that was not tied down. This time he was really having trouble stopping his descent. Just as the airship was about to touch the water, a couple of men dove out of the gondola into the sea. The blimp came to rest just barely touching the surface! We quickly moved in close enough to grab some handling lines and this time were able to tie a couple of the forward handling lines to our mooring line, which was well secured to the stern of our submarine.

Seeing that we finally had good hold of the blimp, several more men dove from the gondola and the blimp rose from the water. A nearby destroyer had dispatched a motor whaleboat when the first two men dove into the water and it was now close enough to start hauling the men aboard.

It was immediately apparent that one mooring line was not long enough to provide a comfortable altitude for the blimp. We added two more mooring lines and soon had the blimp up to a reasonable altitude for towing. We started off slowly to see how the airship responded and soon had safely increased to sufficient speed to get back to Key West well before sunset.

I was on the bridge with the captain and the officer of the deck and happened to notice a light blinking at us from the blimp's gondola. The quartermaster of the watch (we carried no signalmen) quickly came to the bridge with our signal light and started communicating. "Where are we going?" they wanted to know. We explained that we were headed to Key West. When we were as close as we could get to the naval air station, we would transfer their lines to a large crash boat that would get them close enough to shore to turn them over to their ground crew. Only the pilot and copilot were still aboard the blimp. They had dumped all their gasoline and their emergency generator could no longer run, so they had no power for their radio.

A couple of hours later we rendezvoused with the crash boat from the air station. We were as close to shore as we dared go; we sure did not want to

Here we are, doing our best to fashion a tow line for the blimp.

run aground. We spent some time discussing with the crash boat's crew just how we would go about passing our towline to them. It had to be done right the first time or we would lose the blimp again. Even with our preplanning, the crash boat almost lost the towline. However, the crew finally got it secured and off they headed into a small inlet running closer to the airfield. We headed home, happy that we had successfully brought back a disabled blimp with no one getting hurt.

After receiving our berth assignment along with permission to enter port, we set about preparing to land. Then it hit all of us: we had no mooring lines! We informed squadron operations of our plight and were told they would make arrangements. Soon we got word that no spare mooring lines were available, so we were instructed to pull alongside another submarine that was already moored. As we pulled alongside the other sub, several of its crewmen passed the excess portion of their lines to us and we fashioned an acceptable mooring for the night.

The next morning, the first lieutenant—the one who worried about mooring lines as well as many other things—signed out a pickup truck and headed for the air station with a couple of men to retrieve our mooring lines. It was Saturday and we would not be getting under way again until Monday. He returned several hours later, empty-handed. He had found our mooring

A SUBMARINE RESCUES A DISABLED BLIMP

Undersea craft makes naval history by towing lighter-than-air ship through stormy wind and water

Off the Florida coast a blimp engaged in a Navy test of electronic equipment hit a sudden downdraft and was slapped into the sea. When it bounced up again its propellers were bent and its engines flooded. Without their power to hold it down to a given altitude, the blimp became in effect a free balloon and rose 3,000 feet before the pilot could bring it down to the sea again by releasing helium. There it was either smashing its gondola into three-foot-high waves or being borne into the air by

gusts of wind. The crew moved the blimp's priceless equipment onto a rubber raft which had been launched from a nearby submarine, the U.S.S. *Seapoacher*. Sparks from the radio twice started fires in the gondola, full of gasoline fumes as a result of water pressure on the fuel tanks, but they were extinguished. Then a towline from the blimp was made fast to the submarine, the sub headed back for its base at Boca Chica, and the blimp rose in the air like a kite. For 3½ hours it was dragged along,

fighting a 50-mile gale which once slammed it back in the ocean so hard that the three men remaining aboard were hip-deep in water. The blimp had to spend all night outside the harbor entrance at Boca Chica because the channels through the coral reefs were too tricky to be navigated in darkness. But at dawn the haul was successfully completed, marking the first time in naval history that a blimp—one of whose chief functions in time of war is to destroy submarines—was itself rescued by a sub.

AFTER 3,000-FOOT DROP, BLIMP SETTLES TO SURFACE OF WATER BEHIND SUBMARINE "SEAPOACHER" WITH WHICH IT HAD BEEN COORDINATING MANEUVERS

The USS Sea Poacher *towing the blimp. As we gained speed, the blimp planed up and rode about sixty to eighty feet above the surface.*

lines, but they had been cut into two- to three-foot lengths and passed out to all the blimp and air station personnel as mementos of "the great blimp rescue by a submarine". He said he had explained to them that it would cost several thousand dollars from our quarterly operating fund to replace those lines and we could not afford it. Then he smiled and handed our captain papers authorizing us to purchase the line and charge it to the blimp squadron's operating fund.

The next week we were surprised to open a copy of *Life* magazine and find several pages devoted to the blimp rescue. Back then, *Life* was published weekly and was extremely popular. The most impressive picture was an aerial photo of us towing the blimp. It filled two full pages. There were several other shots, including one showing several members of the blimp's crew holding pieces of the mooring line.

Several years later, when I was company officer at the Naval Academy, I was telling this tale to a couple of officers when our boss, the battalion officer, came out of his office and announced that he had been the air station's duty officer when the crash boat brought the blimp back to the base. He was anxious to tell me the rest of the story. While passing the mooring line from the crash boat to the air station it had gotten away from them and started sailing slowly across the airfield. It was dark by then and the bright lights they had rigged to help them see what they were doing were blinding them instead. Once they had it secured they had to leave it at that and wait for daylight to recommence getting it properly moored. The pilot and copilot had to remain aboard overnight, high in the air. The ground crew managed to get food and water to them in a basket tied to a long line that they could pull up to the gondola. The next morning the blimp was properly moored and the pilot and copilot gained their freedom.

All of us aboard the *Sea Poacher* were pleased that we had participated in a most unusual and successful rescue operation.

I was just starting my assignment aboard my second submarine, the USS *Ray* (SSR-271). It was undergoing a major conversion in the Philadelphia Naval Shipyard to change it from a mothballed World War II submarine to a radar picket submarine.

During World War II in the Pacific, a lone destroyer would sometimes be deployed a hundred miles or so to a position between a navy task force and a base expected to launch air attacks against the task force. The destroyer's job was to detect such attacks visually or by radar and inform the task force. This early warning gave the task force extra time to prepare to defend itself. It was a great idea, but most of these surface pickets were destroyed after giving such warnings because they could neither escape nor adequately defend themselves.

The armed forces were drastically cut back at the end of World War II and all of the services were scrambling to justify what they thought were realistic levels or even their very existence. The submarine force seemed to base its strategy on the expansion of its capabilities. Many proposals were made and they did get approval for some, such as submarine tankers, submarine troopships, and submarine radar pickets. A submarine radar picket could do the picket job better than a surface vessel because it could then submerge to avoid detection and thus have a chance for survival. When the immediate threat had passed, it could then surface and continue operating as a picket.

Several submarines had already been modified to carry air-search radar, but the *Ray* was the first of four to be radically converted to produce the best product possible. It had already been dry-docked, cut completely in two at the bulkhead between the control room and the forward battery (just for-

The new look of the USS Ray (SSR-271), thirty feet longer and with a longer sail to accommodate a large air search radar and two more radio antennas, a vertical tank structure to house and support height finding radar, and a homing antenna a bit farther aft.

ward of the bridge structure), and pulled apart for the insertion of a thirty-foot section containing a large Combat Information Center (CIC) above the center deck, with supporting equipment and machinery below that deck. The CIC was to have two consoles for the display of air-search radar and height-finding radar, one console for surface-search radar, one console for the display of airborne radar, one watch officer's console, four illuminated plastic display panels, and any number of radio communications stations. It would take at least nine men to man the CIC during general quarters.

With the requirement to carry at least nine more personnel to man the submarine during general quarters, an additional nine bunks had to be added. A small section above the main deck at the forward end of the new thirty-foot section was used to provide additional bunks for seven enlisted men. The next compartment in which officers bunked was modified to accommodate two additional officers. To do this, a section that had housed four officers now bunked six. I ended up with one of those six bunks. The space between my bunk and the bunk above me had been compressed so much that I could not turn over; there simply was not enough space. If I wanted to sleep on my back instead of my stomach, I had to climb out of my bunk and then climb back in. I felt like a slice of bread in a toaster.

Members of the crew had been ordered to report as soon as they were needed for final installation and to check out various pieces of equipment and machinery. I had attended a four-month electronics maintenance course at the Treasure Island Naval Training Center in San Francisco, California, a year or so before, so I was ordered aboard fairly early to serve as the CIC officer and electronics maintenance officer. I was not too happy about leaving normal submarine operations, but I had to admit that all of this was pretty interesting and challenging. We worked closely with the shipyard to speed up completion of the conversion so we could get to sea. The project was already a couple of months behind schedule. The first ship of a type to be built or converted always proves to be the most difficult to complete because later ships can take advantage of the many problems that had to be worked out because of mistakes in design or construction. Once these problems were solved on the first ship, they generally were not repeated on the following ships.

Finally our conversion was declared complete and off we went to begin normal operations.

The equipment we had been outfitted with was exceptionally good. The air-search radar had been specially designed for submarine use and performed magnificently. Our ability to use the radar signals transmitted to us by high-flying airplanes was phenomenal. I recall one day when we were testing it for a maximum-range picture and the picture clearly showed the East Coast from Cape Cod all the way south beyond Washington, D.C. We could have operated as a first-class picket, but thank goodness those submarines were never required to do so. They no longer exist. Today's task forces have their own means of reaching far out to provide this necessary information.

It was midday and we were submerged about twenty or thirty miles east of Norfolk, Virginia, operating with a couple of destroyers as the target for their antisubmarine warfare training. Our hospital corpsman had just reported to the exec that we had a man aboard, an older man, who was very much in pain with some stomach disorder. The man could hardly walk. The corpsman had tried all the normal remedies, but nothing worked. He was afraid the man might be suffering from appendicitis and recommended that he be taken to a hospital as soon as possible.

We secured our release from the destroyers and surfaced. The captain sent a message to the squadron commander reporting the problem and requesting permission to return to Norfolk. We received his response in pretty short order. He wanted our exact position so that a helicopter could be dispatched to pick up the man and bring him back to the hospital. It seemed like a good plan. We could get our man to the hospital far more quickly that way and remain on station to participate in our next scheduled event that afternoon.

We strapped Joe into one those basketlike stretchers made of steel rods and metal wire. They make moving a man straight up a vertical ladder, through a hatch, and onto the main deck much easier.

This happened in 1952, back in the early days of helicopters. We saw them from time to time and had worked with them on rare occasions, but this was the first time we tried such an off-loading operation. We followed the instruction book and fashioned a lifting bridle to the stretcher. The bridle consisted of four pieces of very strong wire rope that ran from each of the stretcher's four corners to a steel ring that brought them together about three or four feet above the stretcher. When the helicopter arrived, its crew would lower a cable with a snap hook at the end. We would fasten it to the ring and the electric winch aboard the helicopter would then lift the stretcher.

The helicopter arrived a short time later, hovered about thirty feet overhead, and followed the procedure just described. After we hooked the snap hook into the steel ring, the helicopter commenced raising Joe from our deck. After raising him about ten feet off the deck, the helicopter pulled clear and continued raising him. They stopped hauling him up when the stretcher was still about ten feet below the helicopter. After a brief pause they headed for Norfolk with Joe still hanging underneath the helicopter. We thought it was a bit strange, but we figured they knew what they were doing. The important thing was that Joe was headed to the hospital. We watched until they were out of sight. Joe had still been hanging below the helicopter when it disappeared. We went on about our business, pleased that Joe was in good hands and would soon be receiving expert medical attention at the hospital.

A few days later we were back in port and Joe returned aboard. He was walking normally, so the doctors must have cured whatever was wrong him. He said he felt fine but that he never wanted to go through that again. "Why is that? What happened?" we asked. He explained that the electric winch had broken and they could not lift him up into the helicopter. They flew all the way to Norfolk with him hanging underneath. He was scared to death. When they were about five minutes from touchdown, the stretcher collapsed in the middle, jack-knifing him so that his feet and head were together. He said no matter how sick he got in the future he was not going to tell anybody.

We were running on the surface, headed south, about sixty miles east of Norfolk, Virginia. I was officer of the deck, and I was enjoying the good weather and relatively quiet sea. It was early afternoon and in about an hour and a half we were scheduled to rendezvous with one or two aircraft and run submerged target so they could sharpen their antisubmarine capability. No one was on the bridge with me except my two lookouts. We spotted a plane to the east, headed for us at fairly low altitude. We soon made it out to be a navy PBM, a twin-engine flying boat. I always thought it to be a beautiful plane. It was probably capable of carrying a fair amount of cargo or personnel and certainly enough fuel to give it plenty of range. I figured it had come out hoping to get started early, but it did not answer on the assigned exercise radio frequency. It flew right over us and continued heading for the mainland. I dismissed it from my mind and went back to paying attention to getting us where we were supposed to go.

The plane had just gone out of sight over the horizon when the starboard lookout yelled out, "Explosion! Starboard beam, over the horizon!" I turned and saw the last of a fireball followed by a cloud of black smoke. I ordered a course correction and called down to tell the captain what I was doing. He ordered flank speed to get us there as soon as possible. We figured it was probably the same plane that had just flown over us. The crash site was probably thirty miles or more from us considering his altitude and the fact he was out of sight at the time of the explosion.

We notified squadron operations what we were doing and knew that they would pass the information along to the appropriate air squadron.

I completed my watch about an hour later but remained on the bridge after being relieved. Shortly after that a couple of planes flew over us and then headed out directly ahead of us knowing we were headed for where we had seen the explosion. When they were almost out of sight we could see them circling and our radioman informed us they were giving directions to a couple of destroyers approaching the crash site from the opposite direction. As we neared the circling aircraft we finally spotted some debris. The destroyers were closing fast.

We slowed as we approached the debris. Soon we spotted a couple of bodies barely floating on the surface. It was obvious that they were dead. We slowed still more and continued creeping toward the crash site. The closer we got, the more bodies we spotted. Of course, we had no boats for recovering the bodies. We could have inflated some rubber life rafts, but recovering bodies with a life raft would be very awkward and we decided to let the destroyers use their boats, which they were already lowering into the water. We helped spot bodies until the destroyers had the recovery operation well in hand, then pulled clear to give them plenty of room.

I had seen six or seven bodies in the water. Later we learned that there had been twelve fatalities. We were all amazed that the bodies were floating. We surmised that they had been killed instantly by the explosion and thus had gotten no water in their lungs. Still, it seemed strange that their uniforms had not been torn. There was no sign of blood, wounds, or dismemberment — no apparent injuries. It was not what I had expected to see at all.

There were no survivors to tell what had happened and I never heard any more about this disaster. As the days passed it was hard not to think about those poor souls — their families, parents, relatives, and friends. To read about such a thing in the paper is one thing, but to see the results of such a mishap is something else. We regretted that we had been helpless to do anything to save them. It brought home to me that life is tenuous; that you need to enjoy it while you can because it can all be lost in a split second, when you least expect it.

After seven years at sea not only was I promoted to lieutenant, I was also ordered to shore duty at the U.S. Naval Academy to serve as a company officer.

ANNAPOLIS AND WEST POINT

I reported to the U.S. Naval Academy in June, 1954, to serve as a company officer for one of the twenty-four companies of midshipmen. I had graduated from the Naval Academy seven years earlier and now I was commencing my first year of shore duty. During those seven years I had served on one destroyer and two submarines. I had also attended submarine school and the electronics maintenance school at Treasure Island, California. I had lived in ten cities during this seven-year period because of the schools, overhauls at distant shipyards, and so forth. It was going to be great to stay put for two years in a row. I was very pleased with this new assignment. I considered myself very fortunate to have attended and graduated from the Naval Academy. I enjoyed it and it had meant a great deal to me. I was happy to return to try to help the midshipmen appreciate how fortunate they were and to help them grow into knowledgeable and dedicated officers. My first assignment was to work with the incoming plebes, as midshipmen in their first year were known, and get them ready to join their companies at the start of the academic year in September. It took a couple of months to indoctrinate and train them to the point where they would be able to join the others and participate as bona fide midshipmen. They had an awful lot to learn!

With the start of the academic year, I became the company officer for the 15th Company. Each company was organized so that a quarter of its members came from each of the four classes: first, second, third, and fourth (plebes). Each company had about 150 midshipmen. Six battalion officers (navy commanders or marine lieutenant colonels) supervised each group of four companies. The battalion officers reported to the executive officer (a senior navy captain) and the commandant (a rear admiral). All of their offices were located in Bancroft Hall, where the midshipmen were housed. My small office was in the same area where my company was billeted. Each company officer was responsible for the proper performance and conduct of the midshipmen in his company, but every one of us was expected to correct any irregularity committed by any midshipman at any time.

Every so often we served as assistant officer of the watch to the officer of the watch, who was usually one of the battalion officers. This was a twenty-four-hour watch. We spent the night in Bancroft Hall. During our tour of duty we inspected the various formations, the floors, and a certain section of rooms. We also kept an eye on all events involving midshipmen.

Supervision of midshipmen's activities occupied most of our time, but we devoted a good deal of time to individual midshipmen — answering their questions, advising them, and helping them learn how to abide by regulations. You could not help but pay attention to those who obviously needed assistance. It was surprising how well you got to know each one.

I truly enjoyed this assignment. It was also great to be able to see my family on a regular basis.

Time passed fast. Before I knew it, my tour as a company officer at Annapolis was a little over three months from completion. Although I had enjoyed this assignment very much, I was ready to return to submarine duty.

One day I ran across an admiral who had been my squadron commander a few years earlier. He had come to have dinner with his son, who was a plebe and a very fine young man. He asked me where I was headed next and I told him back to submarines, but that I had not yet received orders. He told me I should write a letter to the Bureau of Naval Personnel (BuPers) requesting that I be returned to submarine duty. I had never considered such a thing as being necessary. He explained that writing such a letter was unusual; submariners generally were sent back to submarines. However, he told me he had always made a practice of doing so just to make sure and recommended I do the same. I thanked him for his advice.

The next day I decided to do as he suggested. I really did not think such a letter was necessary, but he knew a lot more about the navy than I did. I submitted my letter to the Bureau through my chain of command and was somewhat surprised a couple of days later when the executive officer called me to his office and reported that the commandant of midshipmen did not want to forward my letter without first talking to me.

When I reported to the commandant he explained that he had other plans for me. He wanted me to go to West Point and serve as the exchange officer for a year. He said he had discussed the assignment with the Bureau and that they were in complete agreement. However, he did not want to send me unless he was sure I would exhibit the proper attitude and be enthusiastic in my duties. What a shock! I had never dreamed of such an assignment. What would it do to my submarine career? He went on to say that I needed to take some time to think about it and that I should go to Washington immediately and talk to my submarine detailer at BuPers. He wanted me to come back and see him the next day to give him my thoughts.

The hour or so drive to Washington gave me some time to think. I knew the commander who was the detailer and believed he would give me good, solid advice. As I walked into his office, he looked up and said, "Don't say a word, you're going to West Point." Hat in hand, I said, "Commander, what will it do to my submarine career?" He assured me that it would not hurt my career and would be a most interesting and rewarding tour of duty.

On the way back, and also that night, I did a lot more thinking. The family thought it would be a good and pleasant experience. I had to admit that it was a most unusual assignment and really quite an honor to be selected.

A brief explanation of the exchange officer's duties is appropriate here. After World War II, the Army Air Forces split away from the army and became an independent air force. The air force was to have its own academy, but it would take a few years to establish it — and then four more years to produce its first graduates. In the meantime, graduates from West Point and Annapolis could be commissioned in the air force to provide the necessary input of officers. While planning all this, it was considered a good idea to permit graduates from each of the three academies to be commissioned in another service provided the secretaries of the two services involved agreed. It was also considered desirable for each academy to have a couple of officers from the other two services on duty there to answer questions from cadets or midshipmen who were considering such a change. You therefore found two army and two air force officers at Annapolis and two navy and two air force officers at West Point.

During my last year as a company officer at the Naval Academy, Capt. Al Haig was the army exchange officer at Annapolis. The following year, when I was exchange officer at the Military Academy, Capt. George Patton was exchange officer at the Naval Academy.

I first met Captain Patton at West Point, where he was a company tactical officer, during my last year as a company officer at Annapolis when I escorted a group of midshipmen on a three-day visit to West Point. He had been assigned to show me around. We had just about completed a tour of their museum when I stopped in front of a glass case displaying the ivory-handled revolvers worn by Gen. George S. Patton Jr. I could not resist telling him what a great general I thought Patton had been. Then I noticed his nametag. I really had not caught his name when we were introduced. I stopped abruptly and said, "Were you kin to General Patton?" He said, "He was my Dad." At least he knew my admiration for General Patton was sincere. We started talking about the revolvers and he had an unusual tale. He said his father had never carried more than one revolver, but the press had made such a big thing about him having two of them that they had to go out and buy a matching revolver for display. They had a hard time finding a match. Some time later he told how, when he was a youngster, his father never missed an opportunity to visit a battlefield and explain to the children in great detail just how the battle had been fought. The general was very much an expert in military history.

Now, back to my story. After much thinking about being assigned as an exchange officer, I reported to the commandant the next morning. I told him my detail officer had said the assignment would not hurt my submarine career and would prove very rewarding. I added that, after much thought, I believed I would enjoy it, but whether I liked it or not, I would keep my mouth shut and always put my best foot forward. The commandant was pleased — and I was pleased that I had submitted my letter as advised. Now I knew where I was going.

≋

I was detached from the Naval Academy in early June, right after the graduation of the senior class. The army wanted me at West Point as early as possible for a bit of indoctrination prior to the arrival of the new plebe class. The quarters regularly assigned to the navy exchange officer, who was assigned to the Tactical Department, were unavailable for four to six weeks while undergoing a long-planned refurbishment. That meant we could not move directly from one place to the other, but instead had to have all our belongings, furniture, clothes, and such put in storage — with the exception of a trunk of my clothes and uniforms, which I would need in the interim, that I shipped directly to West Point. I drove the family to Nashville to stay with our families and flew from there to New York. From New York I took a bus to West Point.

As we neared West Point, I was taken by the beauty of the Hudson River and the surrounding countryside. It was an area of great strategic significance in the Revolutionary War. Everyone expected the British to sail their ships up the Hudson and take full control of the river from one end to the other. That would have been disastrous because it would have effectively split the colonies in half and made it impossible for them to move troops back and forth as necessary to bring maximum strength to bear wherever the battles were to be fought. As the Hudson River flows southward, it makes a sharp turn to the east and then shortly makes a sharp turn back to the south. The colonials devised an excellent defense against the English in the vicinity of this S-shaped curve. At the second sharp bend in the river they strung an enormous wrought-iron chain from one bank to the other. Wooden barges supported the heavy chain. At either end of the chain they set up sufficient cannon to destroy any ship that was foolhardy enough to try to force passage. The fort at this point on the west side of the river was named Fort West Point. Major General Benedict Arnold, who had fought so well up to this time, was given command of it. The plan he made with the English to send his troops hither and yon on pointless duties so as to weaken his ability to protect the chain was discovered before it could be accomplished, and he became our notorious traitor. Building the U.S. Military Academy at West Point was a wonderful decision. Not only is it a very beautiful place, it is also a most historic spot.

To my surprise, the regular route of the bus I had taken from New York City went right through the main gate and stopped right smack in front of the administration building. I went inside, found the right office, submitted my orders, and was told to report to the superintendent's office. The superintendent was a lieutenant general, three stars, who commanded all of West Point: the Tactical Department, the academic departments, all of the various support facilities, and, of course, all the officers, soldiers, and cadets. I had not expected to see him so soon and was concerned with my appearance, having just spent several hours on a bus. I was very concerned about making a good first impression and did all I could to get ship shape as I followed the general's aide to his office. The aide ushered me into the general's office through a heavy oak door that he released unexpectedly. The closing device was so strong that when the door swung back, it ripped my left shoulder board loose, leaving it hanging down from my shoulder. I quickly pushed the shoulder board back where it belonged without anyone noticing and spent the rest of my fifteen-minute call balancing it on my shoulder.

I was very favorably impressed by the general. He was most hospitable, but he made it very clear, in a most friendly manner, that he expected first-class performance at all times. I managed to make it out of his office with the shoulder board still balanced on my shoulder. I was then directed to the BOQ, which was within easy walking distance. I would live there until my quarters became available. The stone building was just beyond the Officers' Club, where I would take my meals. Both buildings were parallel to the wooded bank, which dropped quite a distance to the river. It was a beautiful setting. I was assigned a nice room on the first floor, overlooking the river. After unpacking my luggage, I repaired the loop that held my shoulder board in place, and took a quick nap. I made it to the dining room at the club just as they opened for business. I was starved.

The next morning, the beginning of my first full day at West Point, I received a call from one of the few army officers I had met on a previous visit. He said he would join me for breakfast and take me to my office. That would save me from searching around for everything on my own. This hospitable gesture was the first of many thoughtful favors done by my fellow officers throughout the year. I greatly appreciated their help in getting me settled, indoctrinated, and guided through our many required routines. I was very impressed with all the officers I worked with during my tour. Each of them displayed a sincere desire to do the best job possible. I made some very good and lasting friends that year.

We spent about a week before the incoming class reported attending lectures, practice presentations, discussions on the policies we were to follow, and helping the handpicked upperclassmen who would be in direct supervision of the plebes brush up on their techniques.

The day finally came for the candidates to report. The transformation process fascinated me. Hundreds of uniquely individual young men showed up on reception day, each with his own preference in clothes, each with his hair cut to suit his taste, various postures, various manners of walking, some talking loudly, some barely whispering — no two were the same. The next day they were all dressed the same, each had the same type haircut, their posture was already improving, they marched in unison, and everyone was beginning to speak in a good, clear voice. They had come a long way overnight, but they had a much longer way to go to become well-trained cadets.

The immediate goal of plebe summer training at both academies was the same: to produce a cadet or midshipman capable of integrating with the upper class at the commencement of the academic year, but summer training was also an excellent opportunity to train them in the basic requirements of their respective service. At the Naval Academy, midshipmen learned how to row and sail boats. At West Point, cadets learned how to move troops and live in the field.

The long marches and overnight camping completely took me by surprise. I had no idea such training was given to the plebes — and certainly no idea that I would be involved in such an effort. The first I heard of it was when I was told I needed to go to the quartermasters to draw combat boots and a helmet liner. When I asked, "What for?" I learned all about it. The plebes were to spend a week in the field. Each day they would march fifteen miles to a new encampment, and I, of course, would have to go with them! I had almost expired as a Boy Scout when I had to hike ten miles. I really did not look forward to this part of the training. The combat boots were brand-new and I had no chance to break them in, so I was rather proud of myself when I finished the first day of the hike. I had a couple of blisters, but the medics were experts at fixing you so you could keep going the next day.

By the third day I had developed a squeak in my right foot. It was not unbearable, but I knew something was wrong. I figured it would go away, but the next day I still had the squeak. At the end of the march that day I went to a doctor and described my symptoms. I said it felt as if I had lost all the lube oil in my Achilles' tendon. After checking me he said that my problem was exactly as I described it. He gave me a strip of soft foam rubber to wrap around my ankle to ease the pressure of my boot in that area and said time would heal my injury.

On about the fourth day out, as we were getting settled in our camp, George Patton came buzzing in driving a jeep. We asked how he was spending his days, and he told us about the "Slide for Life." He explained that the West Point graduates going to paratrooper school were not performing as well on the confidence course there as they would if they had experienced similar training at West Point. As a result, he had been directed to build an obstacle he called the Slide for Life, which the cadets would be required to master. He had just finished constructing it and wanted a few officers to come with him and try it out. Everyone seemed to have something else to do, so he turned to me and said, "I suppose you navy types are too chicken to try it out." That did it. "We are not chicken," I replied, intent on preserving the navy's reputation. "I'll try it out." He really sucked me into serving as a guinea pig.

He told me to put on some swim trunks and tennis shoes and then off we

What the well-dressed Navy officer wears to participate in a forty-five mile hike.

went. We eventually came to a lake that was a couple of hundred yards wide. We left the jeep and commenced climbing a steep, heavily wooded hill bordering the lake. We finally stopped at the base of a huge tree. He explained that he had just completed having a series of ladders attached to the trunk. We would climb up them almost to the top, where a platform had been built.

Up he went and I followed along, moving a bit slower than George because I wanted to hang on tight. It was a very tall tree. From the platform I had a wonderful bird's-eye view of the lake and a lot of the countryside. We were way above the surface of the lake. A steel cable ran from the tree, six or seven feet above the platform, clear across the lake. We must have been a hundred or so feet above the water. He rigged a snatch block with a short chain with a ring at one end on the cable and asked me to hold the ring while he rigged a second set. He pointed to a man holding a flag on the beach across the lake. He explained that we were going to ride the cable to the far side of the lake and drop into the water when the man dropped the flag. That was supposed to keep us from landing on the rocky beach. He told me to watch him and then off he went. He raced down cable and across the lake. When the flag waved, he let go and hit the lake with a big splash, then swam ashore. He turned and waved for me to follow him. Man! I wished I'd had something else to do like the rest of the guys. Off I went. In no time I felt like I was going ninety miles an hour. My cheeks were flapping like I had stuck my head out the window of a racing car. The flag dropped, and I dropped. When I hit the water, I thought the flesh had been torn off my bones. I am a poor swimmer, but I managed to get ashore. I then had to climb a roughly twelve-foot-high ladder and walk along first one and then another telephone pole rigged horizontally. Most of this was over the rocky shore below. When I reached the end I crossed over a plank to a similar rig, but about every ten feet there was a fence you had to climb without touching it with your hands. The rest of the course was similar to other such courses, and I was quite pleased to finish it successfully.

After a couple more days in the field we completed our marching and hiking back to the barracks. It was good to get to sleep in a bed again.

The rest of plebe summer went well. I looked forward to the return of the upper class so we could settle into the routine of the academic year with our full complement of cadets.

The academic year started smoothly. Everything was well planned and organized. I was assigned as the tactical officer (Tac — the same thing as a company officer at the Naval Academy) for Company G, 1st Regiment (G-1). Cadets were assigned to companies by height. This was to help sharpen the appearance of formations and parades. My company was composed of medium-sized cadets. The G-1 barracks were right next to the building housing the commandant of cadets and his staff, so we were under close observation at all times. I was anxious that we always present a sharp appearance. It was a rather old building. All the doorknobs, locks, faceplates, hinges, radiator valves, and many other fixtures were made of beautiful brass. The brass was not very well shined, however. This was particularly noticeable to me as I was used to the navy's tradition of making sure everything made of brass was well shined.

I was rather concerned about my relationship with the cadets. I knew that, if I were a cadet who had worked hard to attend and graduate from West Point, I would not be too pleased about having a navy officer as my Tac — particularly in my final year at the academy. I was therefore intent on being as professionally correct as possible and doing my best to assist them in developing pride in their company. I had no intention of trying to be their "buddy," but I did want to do all I could to guide, urge, and lead them to be successful in all aspects of their competitive performance to be the top company — something of which they could be very proud.

The first day was a real hustle and bustle as the upper classes returned from leave and field training and everyone received new room assignments prompted by the loss of the graduating class and the infusion of the plebes. The Tacs stayed clear and let them work at getting settled.

In midafternoon, the company commander reported to me. He introduced himself and asked if I had any instructions for him. He was a very impressive young man. It was immediately apparent that he had been well selected for the job. I explained that I considered it quite an honor to be associated with West Point, that I intended to do the best job I could, and made it plain that I wanted him to speak up if I overlooked something that needed to be done or if I obviously misunderstood something. In keeping with the idea of improving the appearance of the barracks and also of fulfilling my desire to challenge the cadets with something that they could enjoy throwing back at me, I mentioned that I was disappointed that all of that beautiful brass had not been shined and added that from then on I wanted everything made of brass to be well shined.

I gave them the rest of the week to get settled and spruced up for Saturday morning, when all of the Tacs had to conduct a formal room inspection. On Saturday, as I entered the barracks, I was immediately struck by how well the brass was shined and what an improvement it made in the overall appearance. In room after room I marveled at what a good job they had done. They had really shown me that they could shine brass as well as any midshipman.

Everyone except for the plebes was off at class. I finally reached the top floor and was near the end of my inspection when I entered a plebe room and was astounded by the sight of a big brass tuba sitting on the floor in the corner. Acres and acres of brass, all beautifully shined!

"Whose tuba?" I asked.

"Mine, Sir," replied one of the plebes in the room.

"What are you doing with a tuba?"

"I play it in the Rally Band, Sir."

"Great job of shining it. I want to see it that way again next Saturday."

"Yes, sir."

I headed down the steps and out of the barracks. I could not get over that tuba. Both of his roommates — and maybe others, too — had helped him shine all that brass. When I directed that all brass be shined, I had not been thinking of instruments such as that brass tuba. I had to tell my buddies about the tuba. They could not help but get a big laugh out of all this. Later, I asked what the "Rally Band" was. Someone explained that it was simply to make noise, not music, at football rallies. Various plebes were assigned instruments; it did not matter if they knew how to play them or not.

From then on, each Saturday all of my buddies wanted to know how the tuba looked. As for myself, I could hardly wait to get to the top floor to see it. On about the fourth Saturday I entered the room and saw no tuba.

"Where's the tuba?" I asked.

"I got permission to exchange instruments, Sir," the tuba-playing plebe replied.

"What are you playing now?"

"The piccolo, Sir."

The academic year was filled with room inspections, personnel inspections, parades, athletic events, special lectures, and more inspections.

Late in the fall, winning the army-navy football game held the cadets' attention. I started finding businesslike cards printed with "BEAT NAVY" behind radiators, on tops of lockers, behind books, and other out-of-the-way places. I did not want to write them up for having the cards, but I did write up a few for having "Dust on BEAT NAVY card." Then they had to go to the trouble of keeping them dusted, which helped slow the demonstration somewhat. Everybody wanted to make a bet with me on the game. If I had accepted all bets and navy had lost, I would have been wiped out, so I limited my bets to a reasonable number. As it turned out, the game ended in a tie that year!

I met several famous dignitaries during the year. One evening I was officer of the day and went to a lecture hall about half an hour ahead of the scheduled time to insure that all was ready. I was shocked to find Rev. Billy Graham sitting there all by himself. I had not realized he was speaking that night and explained that it would be about half an hour before anyone showed up. I enjoyed a pretty long chat with him, just the two of us. He was quite an impressive gentleman.

One day I met Gen. Anthony McAuliffe (retired), who had just finished taking a special group on a tour of my barracks. He was the general who said, "Nuts," to the Germans when they demanded he surrender the 101st Airborne Division at Bastogne during the Battle of the Bulge. He liked all the brightly shined brass.

Vice Admiral Milton Miles and his wife came to see me and tour the academy one day. He was commandant of the Third Naval District, headquartered in New York City and which included all of New York State. My wife and I took him and his wife to lunch at the Officers' Club. There was a large, primitive, carved wooden bowl on a pedestal in a corner of the reading room. On the wall above the bowl was a photograph of it surrounded by very dangerous-looking jungle savages. I always wondered how the bowl came to be there. Certainly no civilized person had ever been there to bring the bowl to West Point. The admiral stopped and examined the bowl and the picture very closely, then turned to his wife and asked if she remembered when they had been there. I was astounded. During lunch I was further surprised to learn he had spent a good deal of time in China before World War II helping the Chinese defend against the invading Japanese. His expertise was in communications and he had helped them significantly. The lessons he learned were very valuable to our own army and navy. A movie had been made of his escapades. I remember seeing it, but cannot remember the name. Tyrone Power played the lead part.

Although I did not meet him, I did get to see Gen. Douglas MacArthur when he visited to deliver a speech to the Corps of Cadets.

A few weeks before the end of my tour, I received orders to become the executive officer of the USS *Tirante* (SS-420), home ported in New London, Connecticut. I thoroughly enjoyed my tour at West Point. I had developed some lasting friendships, but it was time to get back to submarines.

5

BACK TO SEA DUTY

I reported to the USS *Tirante* (SS-420) in June, 1957. I felt very fortunate to have received orders to *Tirante*. It was a World War II–type submarine, converted to a streamlined "Guppy" with a snorkel system. Its primary mission was to shoot torpedoes. I had looked forward to becoming an executive officer and at last I finally was one. As exec, I was next in line to the captain. It was my job to see that everything ran smoothly and met his expectations. It kept me jumping, but I enjoyed it. The captain decided he also wanted me to serve as navigator. This significantly added to my workload, but I enjoyed it, too.

One day, to my surprise, I ran across a navy directive that outlined how to apply for nuclear power training, if you were so inclined. It had been promulgated while I was at West Point and I had never gotten to see it. In the early 1950s, a classified message was issued announcing that volunteers were needed for training to operate the power plant of the USS *Nautilus* (SSN-571), the first nuclear-powered submarine. I was too junior to apply at the time, but about six months later I found out that more junior personnel were needed and would be selected from among the officers nominated by the sub squadrons. I was lucky enough to be my squadron's nominee, but then my name was withdrawn because it was decided that I was needed where I was. From then on it was a "don't call us, we'll call you" system. Following the guidance in this newly discovered directive, I immediately submitted a letter requesting nuclear power training. However, I feared I was now too senior to be considered.

A month or so later I received temporary additional duty orders to report to Rear Adm. Hyman Rickover's office in Washington, D.C., to be interviewed for training and assignment as executive officer of a nuclear-powered submarine. Initially I was doing cartwheels because I was so excited. Then I started thinking of all the stories I had heard about interviews with Admiral Rickover and started worrying that I might not be selected. However, I got hold of myself and tried to think positive.

A couple of weeks later, on a Friday, I was on the train to Washington when I met up with a couple of other officers scheduled for interviews with Admiral Rickover the next day. We could not help but talk about the interview. One fellow named a goodly number of books he had recently read that he hoped would impress the admiral. I had not read a book in a year or two. Another talked about how the admiral disliked "nesters," officers who spent a good amount of their free time working on their homes. I had bought a new home the year before and spent just about all my spare time working around the house. Another talked about how the admiral was looking for officers with high grades from high school through college. I had done pretty well, but I was no straight-A student. By the time we got to Washington, I was ready to climb aboard the next train to New London. I was afraid this was all a waste of the admiral's time and mine as well.

A couple of weeks before, I had talked to a couple of guys who had been down for an interview and both had recommended that I stay at the YWCA because it was within easy walking distance of the main navy building. At first I thought they were joking, but they were dead serious: Stay at the YWCA — not the YMCA, but the YWCA! So I called and made reservations. After all, the location was good and the price was right. For once my expenses would not exceed my daily allowance while on temporary duty.

The room was clean and adequate. I got a good night's sleep. There were a goodly number of people at breakfast, but I was the only man in the place.

It was indeed a short walk to the main navy building. The admiral's offices were in a two-story, wooden building erected during World War II behind and parallel to the long main navy building. I reported at eight o'clock and was shown to a small waiting room where the officers to be interviewed were assembled. There was a table in the middle of the room, stacked with magazines, and six or seven wooden chairs were scattered about. There were about a half-dozen of us waiting to see the admiral. We sat and sat, thumbing through magazines and talking about first one thing and then another. Time dragged on. Nothing happened. At noontime we were told we might as well go get lunch. There was a cafeteria in the main navy building. After lunch we went back to our waiting room and continued our aimless activities. The first fellow to be interviewed was not called in until about five o'clock. My name was called about an hour later. I was the third to go in to see Rickover.

A captain who was the prospective commanding officer of one of the nuclear submarines being built escorted me into the admiral's office. The admiral looked up from a pile of papers, pointed to a wooden chair directly in front of his desk, and said, "Sit down." I did so and realized it was the chair I had heard so much about. The front legs had been sawed off enough to make it tilt uncomfortably forward. He immediately launched a barrage of questions. What was my class standing at the Naval Academy? Why hadn't I done better? What did I do in my spare time? What type of books did I read? Why had I not done better in high school? Did I think I was a good officer? How many years did I think were necessary to become qualified as an executive officer? Why had it taken me so long? He rambled on and on. I was beginning to think I was the most stupid, no-good officer on the face of the Earth, but I was determined not to let him beat me down. I began to think how ridiculous all this was. I started smiling when it occurred to me that I had never seen a grown man act like him.

"What are you smiling about?" He had caught me. How could I answer?

"Admiral, I'm in a helpless position. There is nothing I can do to correct what I have done in the past. What I need to worry about is doing better in the future."

Rickover pointed to the captain who had brought me in — he had remained seated in the back of the room — and said, "Take him out and try to put some sense in his head."

Out I went. The captain led me down the dark hall to an empty room where he told me to sit and relax. A few minutes later, another prospective commanding officer came in and introduced himself. No one wore a uniform. You did not know a person's rank until he told you. He explained that it was possible the admiral would call me back to complete the interview, or maybe not. If he did, then I should hang in there and answer his questions the best I could, short and to the point.

It seemed like hours, but it probably was only about forty-five minutes, before I was taken back to see Admiral Rickover again. It was more of the same, but I kept a straight face and was eventually dismissed with the words, "That's all, take him out."

Out I went. I was taken to wait in another room. About half an hour later I was given my orders, which had been endorsed as detached, and told that I would eventually be informed of the admiral's decision. I was afraid I already knew what it was. I caught the night train back to New London.

Weeks passed. I had stopped thinking about what the admiral had decided; I was too busy to think about it. To my absolute surprise, I received a call informing me that I had been accepted into the nuclear power training program and would receive orders shortly. It was hard to believe. I heard later that the fellow who had read all the books did not make it.

We were about to depart on a deployment that would last several months, so my replacement was hurriedly ordered to relieve me so I could remain in New London to commence training at the U.S. Navy Nuclear Power School in about one month. I received temporary orders to the staff of the commander, Submarine Force, Atlantic Fleet, there in New London. Everyone figured it would be a soft touch. I would probably report in each morning and then turn around and go home since there would not be anything to do. Not so. I reported in and was immediately given the assignment of conducting a thorough inventory of all the classified documents in the headquarters. This was a monstrous, detailed, and boring job. A big walk-in vault held the majority of the records and publications, many of which were signed out to staff members. Such an effort had not been undertaken for years. I barely finished before school started.

NUCLEAR POWER TRAINING

Nuclear Power School would be six months of grueling study to learn how a nuclear power plant is designed, built, and operated. After learning that I was to attend the school, I started brushing up, as well as I could, on math and physics. I had not used calculus in years and really had to do a lot of work on it. There were about thirty officers in the class. Five of us were eventually to be assigned as executive officers, and the rest were to be assigned as assistant engineers. We were split into two groups, each assigned to one of two classrooms in a building at the submarine school. A building specifically for nuclear power training was under construction right behind our building. It was right outside our window, so we could easily watch its progress. The noise of the construction was very distracting, especially the drilling of the dense rock bed for the foundation, which made it difficult to hear our teachers. From time to time we would hear someone shout, "Fire in the hole!" This is a traditional phrase shouted by construction workers to warn everyone that they are about to set off dynamite charges. Upon hearing those words we would all cringe, cover our ears, and hope for the best. It was a wonder our windows were never shattered by an explosion.

The school was tough from beginning to end. Some of the textbooks had not yet been printed. They were merely stacks of mimeographed sheets stapled together. I had never heard of the math we studied before. We went to school from eight to four, Monday through Friday. When I reached home each day, I went straight to my study room, shut the door, studied, came out for supper, went back in, and came out at eleven to go to bed. One night, as I lay in bed trying to unwind enough to go to sleep, I heard a tree frog outside my window that kept saying, "Rickover, Rickover." I heard that frog every night I lived there. I also studied almost constantly every weekend.

We all brought our lunch to school and ate at our desks. We could go out at noon break, but rarely did. Study, study, study.

A few weeks before the end of school, each of us was notified where we would go for prototype training. Before a nuclear power plant was built aboard a submarine, it was first built ashore so that design wrinkles could be worked out and the crew trained in its operation. The prototype for the *Nautilus* was built in Idaho in a very out of the way place. Those who were to serve on *Nautilus* were sent there to learn how to operate the plant before they were moved aboard the submarine. *Nautilus* was powered by a pressurized water reactor. The heat generated by nuclear power was moved from the reactor to the steam generators by pressurized water. Large electric pumps moved the water through the reactor to the generators and back to the reactor again, a closed circuit. The pumps were designed so that there was no water leakage through the pump-shaft seals. They were very ingenious and very expensive pumps.

A second type of nuclear reactor, a liquid sodium power plant, was also designed and built. The two reactors were then evaluated to determine which type was best for use in a nuclear-powered submarine fleet. Sodium is a metal. It becomes a liquid when heated and is moved through pipes by an electric field. Electric cables wrapped around the piping from the reactor to the steam generator created a field capable of moving heat from the reactor to the generator with no pumps involved and therefore no possible leaks. The prototype for this plant was built in upper New York State. The second nuclear-powered submarine carried the liquid sodium plant and was named *Seawolf*.

After operating both submarines for a period of time, it was decided to go with the pressurized water power plant. The liquid sodium plant was excellent, but if it had to be shut down for repairs in the reactor compartment, it took an unacceptable length of time for radiation to subside sufficiently for entry into the compartment.

Another prototype was built in Connecticut for a reduced-power pressurized water reactor plant.

I could have been ordered to any one of the three prototypes, but ended up being assigned to the one built in New York. The liquid sodium prototype no longer existed. Another pressurized water reactor plant had been constructed to replace it and was now being tested. The prototypes were all built in sparsely populated areas. That made perfectly good sense, but it also made it hard to find a place to live anywhere nearby. Several of the wives got together and went up for a weekend of house hunting so we would have someplace to move when the time came. My wife found a farmhouse within reasonable distance of the prototype, so we were ready to move when school ended. School could not end soon enough for any of us, but it finally did — right after Christmas. We had to move and be ready to start work at the prototype site by the first of the year.

Having to concentrate so much on my studies left no time for celebrating my promotion to lieutenant commander during that period. However, we did have a brief celebration just prior to moving.

On New Year's Eve a moving company packed our belongings and loaded them aboard a truck for our move from New London to Ballston Spa, New York. We spent the night at a motel along the road and the next morning continued our trip in a snowstorm that had already covered the roads pretty well. In the early afternoon we arrived at the farmhouse that was to be our home for the next six months. A thick blanket of snow covered the countryside. It was sometime in April before the snow melted enough for me to see whether or not we had a paved driveway. The farmhouse was very close to the road at the top of a hill. It was a two-story house, obviously very old, and had a peculiar shape. I learned later that it was merely a portion of what had been a hotel many years before, serving the travelers on this road, which had been a toll road before the advent of motorcars. Farther down the driveway, about fifty yards beyond the house, stood a large hay barn that was about twenty years old.

The couple that owned the house had moved out just to rent it to us. They were now living temporarily with relatives. It did not take long to learn that just about everyone in the area was trying to scrimp and save enough money to move to Florida to get away from the cold and miserable climate. About the only person who ever smiled was the fellow who sold heating oil. His business was great.

The day after we moved in I reported to the prototype site to start my six months of practical training. It was about a twenty-minute drive. There was no sign of life for several miles before reaching a gate in the tall chain-link fence that bordered the big tract of land where the prototype had been built. There were about twenty or so of us reporting for duty. A goodly number of people were stationed there on a permanent basis. About half were civilians — scientists, engineers, and equipment specialists — and the other half were navy officers and crewmen who operated the plant, helped with our instruction, and performed certain maintenance functions. Most of our instructors were civilians, both scientists and specialists.

For the first few weeks all we did was attend class, learning the details of this specific power plant, learning about each particular pump, each control circuit, each purifier, chemistry requirements — every piece and detail of the plant.

We were then divided into three groups. We served in shifts that rotated each week so that we took turns being there from 8 A.M. to 4 P.M., 4 P.M. to midnight, and midnight to 8 A.M. You would just about get used to going to sleep at a certain time before you had to change to another shift. It was enough to drive a person batty.

We soon were spending the majority of our time in the plant, learning how to operate the various pieces of equipment and so forth. We stood watch with qualified personnel to learn how to operate the equipment they handled. Finally we started working at the main control panels and at last learned how to operate the full power plant. In order to be certified, we had to appear before a board of experienced personnel and satisfy them that we were fully qualified. I was one of the earliest to go before the board, but it was decided that I needed more work. I was disappointed, but I did not want to leave there until I was judged to be properly qualified.

Several weeks before completing my prototype training, I received orders to report to the superintendent of shipbuilding at Ingalls Naval Shipyard in Pascagoula, Mississippi, for eventual duty as executive officer of the USS *Snook* (SSN-592), which was still under construction. I was delighted. Not only was the *Snook* to be a tremendously capable attack submarine, but I knew that Comdr. L. D. Kelley Jr., a long-time friend of mine dating back to high school days, was slated to be the commanding officer. He was the very first submarine officer to be selected for duty by Admiral Rickover. He had been the engineer officer for USS *Nautilus* and was currently working in Admiral Rickover's office.

"Dorris," as he was known in Nashville, "Les" as he was known in the navy, was a top-notch student and football player in high school. He was pushed into going to Vanderbilt University by the school's assistant coach,

Bear Bryant, for the one-year of college he had before gaining his appoint-ment to the Naval Academy.

This time we were not given an opportunity to house hunt, so we headed south with high hopes of finding a nice place to live as soon as we arrived. As we departed our farmhouse, I had to admit that, now that it was June, everything looked beautiful. No more snow, flowers blooming, crops grow-ing, blue skies and sunshine. Farewell to Ballston Spa.

We arrived in Pascagoula having enjoyed our trip but with no place to live. A couple who had lived near us in the New London area took us into their home for several weeks before a house became available to rent. My friend was going to be the commanding officer of a diesel-powered subma-rine being built there, the first submarine to be built by Ingalls Shipbuilding Company. He had grown up in Pascagoula and had many relatives there, in-cluding his enjoyable mother and father. The house we eventually moved into was right next door to his parents. Our house was in easy walking dis-tance of the shipyard and was right on a fair-sized lake that joined the Pascagoula River, which almost immediately flowed into the Gulf of Mexico. Fishing in the area was unbelievable. The lake, river, and gulf were all within a stone's throw. I spent much of my off-duty time fishing.

I reported to the navy superintendent of shipbuilding and was given a small office to call my own. I drafted the ship's orders, emergency bills, a rough of the "Rig for Dive" bill, and collected all of the copies of the ship's blueprints that I could scrounge from the shipyard.

After about four or five months, *Sculpin* (SSN-590), the first SSN to be constructed by this yard and scheduled about six months ahead of *Snook,* was ready to be launched. This was the point in building where the ship is moved from the dry dock into the water to complete its construction. Tradi-tionally, the launching is a gala event. The shipyard issues invitations to those deserving to participate not only in the launching ceremony but par-ticularly to attend a grand reception following the launching ceremony. Those with invitations are seated in bleachers, while everyone else who has clearance to come on the base can watch from any point possible.

The shipyard made a special effort to invite those who had served aboard the old *Sculpin* (SS-191). Ships names are quite often used over and over again as ships are lost or decommissioned.

There is an interesting story about the old *Sculpin.* In the early 1930s, a submarine named *Squalus* (SS-192) made a test dive after completing an overhaul in the Portsmouth Naval Shipyard in Portsmouth, New Hampshire. The main induction valve failed to shut and tons of water rushed in, sinking it to the ocean floor. When time passed and nothing was heard from the *Squalus* and it could not be contacted by radio, a search was organized. The

Sculpin participated in this search and was the ship that finally located the *Squalus*. Noises from the submarine were detected and an all-out effort was made to rescue survivors. I remembered reading all about it in the newspapers. About half the crew was lost. The other half had been able to seal off some compartments by shutting watertight doors.

During World War II, the *Sculpin* had been racing on the surface to, I believe, gain a better position from which to attack Japanese shipping, when she ran hard aground and was unable to get free. The Japanese captured her crew.

The *Squalus* was eventually raised, overhauled, and placed back in service. It was renamed *Sailfish*. Sometime after the *Sculpin*'s crew was captured, *Sailfish* attacked and sank a Japanese transport. The *Sculpin*'s crew was aboard the transport, being moved from one prisoner-of-war camp to another. I understand many members of the *Sculpin*'s crew survived. The surviving members of the *Sculpin*'s crew had become so separated during the rescue that they had very little idea who had been lost and who had survived.

Back to the launching ceremony. It was nearly noon. The sky was heavily overcast, making it a rather gloomy day. The president of the shipyard was introduced to give a few comments before introducing the guest speaker. He related how the shipyard had attempted to invite as many of the old *Sculpin* crew as possible and really had no idea how many were present. The clouds overhead started parting. He asked that former crewmen please stand so they could be recognized. All at once we were bathed in bright sunlight. Here and there men rose to their feet. Each of them looked around to see who else was present. There were about seven or eight of them. Then they started yelling, "Hey, Joe," "Sam, Hey, Sam," and on and on. Each of them was jumping and yelling. Then they started trying to get to one another. It was some time before they tried to start the ceremony once again. All of us thought how wonderful it was that after so many years the crewmen of the old *Sculpin* were able to see their buddies alive and well. The sun breaking through right at that moment added a touch the best Hollywood producer could not have managed.

After about five months I received orders to report to the USS *Sargo* (SSN-583) in Pearl Harbor to serve as executive officer. I was ready to go. It would probably be another six months before the *Snook*'s crew would begin reporting. My friend who was to be the captain was also ordered to another assignment.

We had made a number of wonderful friends in Pascagoula, but the navy never lets you stay too long in any one place.

7

DUTY ABOARD *SARGO*

We drove to New Orleans, checked into a hotel, and then I turned my car over to the navy for shipment to Hawaii. No one knew when the car would actually depart New Orleans. It would have to go through the Panama Canal, so it would be many weeks before we saw it again.

We enjoyed our night in New Orleans, and the next day flew on the latest and finest commercial airline in service: a four-engine, propeller-driven Lockheed Constellation. Upon arrival in San Francisco we were met by a navy driver who took us downtown to the Marine Hotel, which catered to service members and their families.

The next day we boarded a navy transport and were assigned a cabin large enough for all four of us. I had never sailed on a navy ship as a passenger and really looked forward to a lot of rest and relaxation on our five-day cruise to Hawaii. We stood at the rail and enjoyed the scenery until we passed under the Golden Gate Bridge. What a great relaxing time this would be.

A messenger located me and said that the executive officer would like to see me. The exec explained that, as the senior military passenger aboard, it would be my responsibility to inspect the troop spaces. That took a bit of shine off my plans for complete rest and relaxation. A couple of times each day I had to put on my uniform and inspect the spaces.

The morning we arrived in Hawaii we again manned the rail and enjoyed the beautiful scenery of Waikiki Beach and Honolulu. As we closed into our berth, I spotted the fellow I was to relieve. He was a good friend and was there to greet us and take us to our hotel. I was then happily surprised to see a colonel I had worked for at West Point waving at us from the dock, also welcoming us to Hawaii. I wondered how he had known we were arriving.

We were taken to a good hotel on Waikiki Beach, not a grand hotel, not the Royal Hawaiian, but one that my per diem would cover.

My friend also had arranged for me to pick up a car from the navy recreation office for temporary use. That afternoon we loaded in the car and went sightseeing. I had visited Honolulu twice when I was aboard my destroyer, the *Stickell,* so I knew my way around. I first wanted to show my family the Royal Hawaiian Hotel. I could not find it. I knew where it was supposed to be, but I could not find it. I could not figure out what was wrong. It had sat way back from the street, close to the beach, and had a beautiful, immense lawn with palm trees. I finally spotted a portion of it. A row of shops had been built on that magnificent lawn and now hid that beautiful hotel. A lot had changed since I had last been in Hawaii.

My friend, the fellow I was to relive, had told me that he really would not be free to start our turnover until Monday and that I should enjoy the beach until then. That sounded great to me. It meant we were free from Thursday through Sunday.

On Saturday morning I was just getting settled on the beach when I heard an announcement on a nearby radio. "A tidal wave is predicted to hit Hawaii about nine o'clock this evening." That really got my attention. The beach is no place to be when a tidal wave hits. We needed to get up in the hills.

We had already contacted another friend who had been our neighbor in Annapolis. Her husband commanded a submarine that had deployed to the western Pacific and would be gone for a couple more months. He had been an assistant football coach when I was a company officer at the Naval Academy. Their two sons were the same age as our two sons and were real buddies. He had been a tackle on the football team during our midshipmen days. He was really big, huge compared to me. We called his wife and asked if we might visit until after the tidal wave hit. She begged us to come, so we did. They had a delightful home. We stayed and had dinner on their patio.

We kept a radio tuned for news of the tidal wave. Nine o'clock came and went. The estimated time of its arrival kept being delayed. By eleven o'clock that evening there was still no tidal wave. Our hostess produced one of her nightgowns and a pair of pajamas for each of our boys. Jokingly I said, "Don't I get a pair of Bo's pajamas?" The boys yelled their delight and begged her to produce a pair of his pajamas for me. She did. I figured my putting them on would be quite a show the boys would surely enjoy. I had to roll up the legs practically to the crotch to keep them from dragging on the floor. The top completely engulfed me. I was a ridiculous sight. I went to find the boys so they could see how I looked. They rolled on the floor yelling and laughing. I was glad I could give them such wild enjoyment.

Sometime after midnight, the tidal wave hit Hilo on the Big Island and wiped out their waterfront. I understand they decided not to rebuild much of it because tidal waves had hit the city several times in the past.

A couple of months later Bo's submarine returned home. They had a royal welcome for all hands. The band was playing loudly, and the pier was crowded with wives, children, girlfriends, and friends. After the submarine was moored, Bo was coming across the brow as the band finished playing a piece. At that point his son Billy yelled out, "Hey Dad, you should have seen Mr. Summitt in your pajamas!" The band immediately struck up another tune, but everyone had heard Billy. What an amazing bit of news for everyone.

Bo's wife tried to shout a brief explanation, but the band drowned her out. My name became well known and my reputation suffered mixed adjustments — some good, some bad. Thank goodness Bo thought it was hilarious.

On Monday morning I reported aboard the *Sargo* and commenced the process of relieving my friend. We had some easy local operations that week, which enabled us to get through everything that needed to be turned over. At the end of the week I formally relieved him and started my new job.

I was really pleased to be aboard the *Sargo*. She had an excellent crew, and I admired the captain very much. I figured I would learn a lot from him. We continued local operations for a couple of weeks and then commenced a two-week upkeep period in preparation for sailing to the western Pacific for several months.

Late in the afternoon on the day before my departure I was enjoying a shower in preparation for dressing in civilian clothes to get ready to go out with my family for a special farewell dinner. I was going to miss them. My wife's shouts interrupted my relaxing shower. She excitedly reported that she had just heard a radio announcement that the *Sargo* was on fire. There were no details, just that brief announcement. I hurriedly dressed in my civilian clothes, which were already laid out, said I would get back when I could, and raced next door to ask my air force neighbor to take me to the base as our car had not yet arrived from Mississippi. He was having supper, but rushed out to his car and off we went. At the first open space on the road we could see a huge column of smoke rising from the base. It was obvious that this was no normal shipboard fire; something devastating must have happened.

As we neared the base we saw streams of cars and people on foot leaving the base as fast as they could. The base was being evacuated! No doubt everyone was thinking about the possibility of the nuclear reactor's involvement in this disaster. However, I could not imagine it being associated with the power plant. What worried me was something that few people knew: we were loaded with torpedoes with live warheads, not the dummy warheads used during training exercises.

It was no problem getting through the entrance gate, but once inside, the roads were so jammed with people leaving that I thanked my neighbor, jumped out of the car, and started making my way to the *Sargo*'s berth on foot.

We were moored alongside the seawall of the submarine base. As I finally rounded the corner of the last building blocking my view of the *Sargo,* I was sickened to see the sub's bow high in the air and its stern completely sunk. There was no longer any smoke or flame. All I could imagine was that something dreadful had happened in the submarine's stern. It was a terrible sight. I stopped and stared.

I quickly pulled myself together and headed for the small mob gathered near the submarine. Several fire engines were near the ship with hoses running here and there. I spotted the captain and headed toward him. He was also in civilian clothes. In fact, just about everyone was in civilian clothes, including our division commander; squadron commander; various staff officers from the headquarters of the commander, Submarine Forces, Pacific Fleet (COMSUBPAC), and the commander in chief of the Pacific Fleet (CINCPACFLT); and shipyard personnel. It was quite a high-powered gathering.

By talking to first one officer and then another, I pieced together what had happened. The big navy tank truck specially configured to load oxygen had been parked alongside the seawall next to the hatch leading down into the stern room where the manifold for our oxygen-tank banks was located. A specially manufactured reinforced rubber hose was fed from the equipment on the truck across to the submarine and down the hatch into the stern room, where it was connected to the air manifold. The equipment on the truck turned the liquid oxygen into gaseous oxygen and pumped it to the submarine. Our man aboard the sub then opened and shut valves on the manifold, filling one huge flask after another. It took several hours to fill our flasks to a pressure of three thousand pounds per square inch. Just as the charge was about completed, our deck watch, who happened to be where he could plainly see the truck and the hose feeding into the stern-room hatch, saw a pinhole leak pop open in the hose. It immediately caught fire. The hose became a lighted fuse, with the flame quickly disappearing down the hatch. A huge flame erupted from the open hatch and quickly developed into a blowtorch reaching about thirty feet straight up. We later learned that the intense heat in the stern room melted hydraulic lines, high-pressure air lines, and the lines to all the oxygen flasks.

The deck watch sounded the alarm, called the fire station, and called the captain at home. I was a bit miffed that he had not called me, but then remembered I still did not have a phone at my home. The captain had burned up the highway getting there. The firemen were trying to pump water through the hatch, but the roaring torch prevented them from pushing the hoses down the hatch.

Upon arrival, the captain quickly sized up the situation and ordered the after vents opened so that the stern would sink, flood the compartment with seawater, and put out the fire. I arrived on the scene shortly after that.

We knew that our man in the stern room handling the oxygen charge was lost, but there was no sure way of immediately knowing if anyone else had been with him. All other members of the duty section had been accounted for, but we were going to have to muster the rest of the crew to assure ourselves that no one else had been lost. We were aided by the fact that most of the men who were off duty had come in as soon as they learned of the fire. The chief of the boat asked us to order everyone coming back to check in with him so that he could account for them.

I went aboard to look around to see if there was anything that needed doing that was not already being done. The sub's steep angle made it difficult to get around. Going down the ladder to the control room was normally very easy, but the steep angle made me feel awkward and clumsy. I tried to go forward, but could not open the wardroom door. It was jammed. The furniture had probably piled up on the other side of it. I finally gave up and headed aft. I had to hang on to first this and then that to keep from sliding down the deck uncontrollably. When I finally made it to the engine room, which was next to the stern room, I was relieved to find that everything was well and being carefully monitored. What did concern me were the bulkhead and various fittings separating us from the burned and now flooded stern room. The bulkhead was retaining its watertight integrity in spite of slight buckling here and there due to the intense heat on the other side.

Someone informed me that there had been some leakage in the watertight door leading to the stern room because the heat had distorted the rubber gasket, but it had been caulked successfully. A shipyard worker was putting the finishing touches on some wooden wedges that kept the door tightly shut.

I made my way back off the submarine and found that it was now dark, but floodlights had been rigged so we could see all that we needed to see.

A commander on the squadron staff found me and asked that I give him the plaque that was to be presented to Prince What's-his-name the next day. I had completely forgotten that we were to take a prince from some Southeast Asian country to sea for several hours before departing for the western Pacific. The plaque, suitably engraved, was to be presented by the captain as a memento of the prince's visit and cruise aboard ship. Another submarine had now been picked to carry the prince, and the engraved plaque would have to be redone with that submarine's name. My immediate thought was that this was a hell of a time to worry about such a thing, but it had to be done. I went back aboard ship knowing I would have trouble getting the plaque, which was in a drawer in my stateroom. The normal way to my stateroom was through the wardroom door, which I had previously found to be firmly shut by what I had imagined to be the wardroom furniture. The door was still firmly blocked. I finally made it through the door of the ship's office, which was just outside the wardroom. It, too, was blocked by all sorts of stuff piled against it, but I was able to open it far enough to squeeze through. There was a sliding panel between the office and my stateroom that measured about twelve by eighteen inches. After much struggling, I wiggled through the opening and got the plaque. On my way out I cleared the tangled mass of metal chairs blocking the wardroom door. Once ashore, I delivered the plaque to the waiting commander and off he went. I could not help but think, "The show must go on!"

I found myself staring at a good-sized trailer that had been dropped nearby. It was a Red Cross trailer with its hatches open to permit the ladies inside to serve coffee, cold drinks, and sandwiches. My initial thought was one of disgust. The recovery operation was being turned into a sideshow.

However, it did not take me long to realize that the ladies were providing us with a valuable benefit. I was anxious to get at least a drink of water, but I did not want to leave the scene to wander around in search of a drinking fountain or hose with potable water. None of us had eaten supper, and we had been on scene for several hours. A cup of coffee really hit the spot.

A huge floating crane from the shipyard was being positioned to lift our stern back to its normal level so that the seawater could be pumped out of the compartment. The fire had melted the lines to the ballast tanks, so they could not be blown. Divers were in the water placing lifting straps beneath the hull. Once the stern was raised, the fire trucks would start pumping the water out through the open hatch. It would take hours to do this.

By about three or four in the morning, the stern room had been pumped out enough for us to examine it. Two explosive experts in wetsuits went inside to examine the torpedoes They came out after about five minutes and reported that material in the compartment was still smoldering and that the torpedoes were still hotter than they should be. They recommended flooding the compartment again. Fire hoses were fed through the hatch, and the flooding commenced.

At about seven o'clock, the sailor we had been unable to locate came running to the ship. He was loudly and warmly welcomed. He had not heard about the fire until he saw the headlines on a newspaper being read by a passenger on the bus he had taken to return to the base. We were all relieved to see him.

Unexpected problems kept surfacing. Ten or twelve crewmen bunked in the stern room. It was their home. All of their belongings stowed there were lost, their uniforms, special personal belongings, pictures, keepsakes — everything. They had been paid the day before, but now all of them were broke. In very short order the navy, the Navy Relief Society, and the Red Cross pitched in to get them back on their feet.

About noon, suction hoses were again dropped into the stern compartment to pump it out. Several hours later the explosives experts declared it was safe to leave the compartment dry. Because it was so difficult to get around inside due to the tangled mass of piping, wiring, twisted deck plates, and such, no one was allowed to enter the compartment who did not absolutely have to be there. We did not begin the cleanup effort until a team from the hospital had located and removed the body of the man we had lost.

Plans were already under way to tow the *Sargo* to the Pearl Harbor Naval Shipyard so that it could be properly inspected in a dry dock. There was great concern that the intense heat had so warped the stern that proper propeller shaft alignment could not be gained without first restructuring it.

By late afternoon, the majority of us had been there for almost twenty-four hours. We were all very tired and greatly appreciated the Red Cross refreshment trailer. It had been our sole source for coffee and snacks to keep us going. Most of us were still in our civvies with no caps or hats. I was really starting to feel sunburned.

We called it quits at about four o'clock and left the submarine in the care of the duty section. I hitched a ride home and explained to my family what we had been doing.

Sargo was towed to the shipyard the next day and we began the staggering job of reworking the stern room. Several sections of buckled hull plating would have to be replaced. Luckily, the prop shafts could be realigned without major effort, but replacing all of the melted pipes and wiring and rebuilding the compartment would be a tremendous task. The shipyard performed magnificently. A very optimistic completion date was beaten by a goodly number of days. I cannot remember just how long it took — it was several months — but we managed to finish in far less time than most of us expected. We could not praise the shipyard workers enough.

It was good to get back to sea again! Some of our more experienced men left us while *Sargo* was being repaired to serve as the nucleus for crews being formed to man the new Polaris submarines, which were being built at a rapid pace. The fleet of forty-one Polaris subs was being built without decommissioning any of the submarines already in the fleet. Manning the Polaris subs thus placed a heavy burden on the submarine force. Each Polaris submarine was to have two complete crews of about 124 officers and men assigned. Multiply that by forty-one and you can begin to see the magnitude of the task. Each operating submarine was training its personnel as rapidly as possible so that well-qualified men could advance to fill the vacancies opening up in the ranks above them. Training and qualifying were given a high priority, but our operating priorities were not reduced. Everyone was busily engaged making it all work.

There were only a handful of nuclear-powered submarines at the time, so the strain of producing qualified nuclear-power-trained submariners was particularly severe. On we went, training like mad and operating like mad. The newfound operational capabilities of a nuclear-powered submarine were in great demand. All our operations were rather high priority and required the best performance possible.

I gained a lot of experience very rapidly. I was fortunate to have an excellent commanding officer, Comdr. Nick Nicholson, who had served with the original crew of the *Nautilus*. I always learned a lot from my commanding officers, both right and wrong. Commander Nicholson taught me only how to do things right.

During World War II a small contingent of members of Congress were briefed on how submarine operations in the Pacific were going. Shortly thereafter, one of those congressmen, intent on praising the success of the Submarine Force, spoke on the House floor and mentioned that a great deal of success was due to the Japanese setting their depth charges too shallow. In no time at all, the Japanese started setting their depth charges to explode at an increased depth. Our submarine losses jumped significantly. The Submarine Force quickly became known as the "Silent Service" because from that time on submariners refused to tell outsiders anything they had not been instructed to say.

The Submarine Force commander regularly promulgated a quarterly schedule listing each submarine's operational assignment for the coming quarter. This was a carefully thought-out document to insure the highest priority requirements were met as well as the regularly required overhauls and upkeep periods. Since the precise date for the completion of our shipyard repairs was not known, our schedule had to be pieced together from the time we finally left the shipyard and the beginning of the next quarter.

One morning as I came aboard I noticed some repair workers welding on top of our sail. No one seemed to know what was going on. I asked the captain and he replied that he would explain once we went to sea.

Word was promulgated that we were to get underway the next day for an extended cruise lasting several weeks. I forget what "cover story" for our cruise was published.

After clearing port the next day, we headed west, submerged and continued on our way. Several hours later we surfaced well out of sight of land and well off the normal traffic lanes. There was no one around.

When directed by the captain, the engineer oversaw the removal of various odd-looking pieces made of angle iron, each about two inches in width, of various lengths and shapes, from where they had lain unseen behind various pieces of machinery. They were hauled to the bridge and assembled to make a most unusual structure that was bolted to the pads I had seen being welded on top of the sail. The structure was immediately called a "cowcatcher" but it was not exactly like the cowcatchers on the front of locomotives. The vertical pieces, which bolted to the sail, extended about five feet upward. They held three arms reaching out about six feet on each side. On the three arms were bolted about eight pieces spaced equally from one extremity to the other. Those pieces were about four feet long and reached up and down, bent forward at top and bottom. The structure undoubtedly was designed to catch something as we moved forward through the water. However, I had no idea what it might be.

Some time later, the captain met with some of the officers in the wardroom and revealed our mission. The Russians had launched their first man into orbit. He was supposed to return to earth sometime in the next few days. Whenever we finally got to the point of bringing a manned module back to earth we planned to land it in the ocean. We assumed that the Russians would also do that. Our orders were to go to a certain point, wait for the space capsule to splash down, and attempt to grab the parachute, its shrouds, or even the capsule, and quietly drag it off to where we could eventually turn it over to one of our ships.

There was a moment of silence. We sat there with slack jaws and wide eyes before unleashing a flood of comments and expletives. "What about the astronaut?" someone asked. My guess was that we would have one very irate Russian on our hands and no one who could understand what he had to say. The captain appointed me to deal with the astronaut. I might have to strap on a .45-caliber pistol before I tried to explain what I wanted him to do.

Several days later we arrived at our destination. We went up for a look and by George, there was a Russian ship! It was not a warship, but a fair-sized ocean-going vessel requiring a crew of at least fifteen. It was fairly calm, and the vessel was dead in the water.

We searched the surrounding area and saw no one else. Both of us stayed in the area. It seemed as though the Russians were also expecting something to happen at this spot.

On about our third day on station we received word that the orbiting astronaut had landed somewhere in Russia. They had decided to land their spacecraft on solid soil rather than recover them in the ocean.

We headed home and in the next day or two we surfaced well clear of prying eyes, disassembled our cowcatcher, tossed it over the side, and in the days to come never mentioned anything to anyone about our adventure. The "Silent Service" was well ingrained in all.

We still had several weeks before the next quarter, so we used the time to try to perfect our ability to trail another submarine, which was certainly possible with our nuclear power capability. It was simply a matter of improving our ability to work with sonar, which was the means of detecting another submarine and then maintaining contact over an extended period of time. We sure needed more sensitive sonar. When taking the part of the submarine being trailed, we worked at improving our tricks for breaking contact with whoever was on to us.

All in all, I really enjoyed being on the *Sargo*. Our operations continued at a rapid pace. There was never a dull moment. I was really getting a lot of good experience and learning a lot. I do not think a day ever passed during all my submarine duty that I did not learn something new. There was an awful lot to being a good, experienced submariner.

After seven or eight months aboard *Sargo,* I received orders to command the *Seadragon* (SSN-584). I was ecstatic. However, when detached from the *Sargo,* I first had to report to Admiral Rickover's office for three months of training to qualify as the commanding officer of a nuclear-powered submarine. The navy would not move my family to Washington for that brief period. At least we could keep our home in Hawaii and not have to move again.

I was sorry to leave the *Sargo* so soon, but I looked forward to taking command of the *Seadragon* with great enthusiasm.

8

PROSPECTIVE COMMANDING OFFICER TRAINING AT NAVAL REACTORS

I left Hawaii in late January, 1961. President John F. Kennedy had been inaugurated only a few days before. I departed on a bright, beautiful warm day and arrived in Washington, D.C., a day or two after an unusually heavy snowstorm. The streets had been cleared, but snow was everywhere else. My taxi pulled up to an old four-story brick building about a mile north of the main navy building that housed Admiral Rickover's offices, where I would be studying. The building was a poor excuse for a hotel that existed to house officers on temporary duty. There was no dining room, but a lunchroom offered hamburgers, chili, and a narrow selection of sandwiches. There was also a bar that was pretty popular with those who wanted to stop by before going to their rooms. The only way to get from the cab to the building was by climbing through a snow bank created when the streets were plowed. I sank into snow well over my shoe tops and carried a good bit of it along with me in my shoes. The only rooms available were singles. A friend from my Georgia Tech and Naval Academy days and I had planned to room together but would have to wait until a double became available.

We established a routine for catching a bus that took us directly to the front door of the main navy building. In the evenings we would walk back to the hotel. We ate dinner at a nearby cafeteria.

Admiral Rickover's group, known as Naval Reactors (NR), was as small as it could be. No one ever had to look for something to do, it was a very challenged and hardworking group. Three or four temporary two-story buildings had been built during World War II behind the main navy building overlooking the Reflecting Pool, which runs between the Lincoln Memorial and the Washington Monument. The buildings were intended for use only during the war, but here it was some twenty years later and they were still needed. Naval Reactors occupied the second floor of the building closest to the Washington Monument. Our section of the building had never been repainted, refurbished, or spruced up in any way. Dark-red linoleum laid some twenty years before was still in use. When truly needed, repairmen would patch holes in it with yellow linoleum in the shape of coffins. The admiral insisted on this. There were no curtains. Once, when a secretary tried to get the admiral to approve the purchase of curtains for her window, he responded by having sheets of paper glued to the panes with "CURTAIN" written on each sheet. There was no such thing as matching furniture. However, the offices and cubicles were cleaned each night, just like other offices. I think the admiral wanted to show any visitors he might have that money budgeted for the nuclear power program was not used to make offices look pretty. It was like working in a warehouse.

There were about six of us there for Prospective Commanding Officer (PCO) Training. We were each given a desk, chair, and filing cabinet anywhere they could find a space for us. I ended up in a room next to the admiral's office. The door opened to a decent-sized office with two fully enclosed cubicles, each with a window. One of these cubbyholes was mine. An elderly, very brilliant physicist whom the admiral valued highly occupied the other one. It was difficult to understand anything the old physicist said. This problem, plus the fact that his thinking was so far ahead of anyone else's, caused the admiral to have difficulty communicating with him. To solve this, the admiral directed that another physicist always be present when they needed to talk. The interpreter, who could understand what the old scientist said, would then explain in layman's terms what it was he was trying to get across. This second physicist normally talked in a very loud voice that carried for miles. When talking on the phone, he seemed to increase his volume even more. He talked so loudly that, even with all the doors closed, he greatly disturbed Admiral Rickover next door. The admiral had a wooden box measuring about two feet square and lined with sound-absorbing material constructed. He then ordered the scientist to stick his head in the box with the telephone receiver whenever he used the phone. Even with the box and the door between our cubicles closed, I would have to give up studying whenever he was on the phone. I simply could not concentrate. If the call went on for some time, I would go down the hall and find something else to do.

Every now and then a few candidates would be brought in for interviews. No officer was ever selected for nuclear power training without the admiral's personal approval. We PCOs were used during the interviews. One of us would escort a candidate into Rickover's office and sit in the back of the room. You had to stay on your toes, because the admiral might bounce a question to you or ask you to comment on what the candidate had just said. When the interview was over, you got the candidate out of the office and took him where he was to go next. Generally, a candidate left when his interview was over, but sometimes the admiral would want to see a man again. In this case, he was normally turned over to another PCO, who would take the fellow somewhere private, help him return to normality, and discuss how he might best handle himself in his next session with the admiral.

Admiral Rickover was a small, thin person. He was especially tough on candidates who appeared overweight. On several occasions he got candidates to promise they would lose so many pounds in a certain period of time, and then would hold them to it. In every case, if they really wanted to be accepted, they would lose the weight. One day, we PCOs were admonished for carrying more weight than we should. He got us to agree to lose five pounds within a certain period of time and then wrote to our wives, advising them of our agreement. My roommate and I figured out a plan to limit our meals so that we consumed only so many calories a day. Eating all our meals in a cafeteria helped us to select foods that would fit our plan. Each morning we went by the sick bay and used their medical scales. We kept a graph of our progress. It took about a week or ten days to notice any loss, but we were able to lose our five pounds a little ahead of schedule. We decided to continue our scheme and see just how much we could lose. After losing ten pounds, I decided to stop. However, to my surprise, I had trouble eating more than I had while I was dieting. My weight kept going down, so I finally had to force myself to eat fatty foods. Only then did I stop my steady decrease.

Sometime toward the end of my dieting, I developed a problem that caused me to go to sick bay. There they decided to send me to Bethesda

Naval Hospital for a thorough checkup. Bethesda, which is considered to be the navy's best hospital, also takes care of the president and other high-ranking government officials. The hospital is a very pretty and unusual building. A high tower makes it very conspicuous.

A clerk efficiently processed my admission papers, handed me another stack of papers, and told me to catch the elevator in the lobby. I headed for the lobby reading the instructions on the top sheet of paper and was rather perplexed to see that I was to go to the thirteenth floor. I do not consider myself superstitious, but I have always avoided anything to do with the number thirteen. However, orders were orders. As I stepped off the elevator on the thirteenth floor, I met a very attractive nurse who told me she had been expecting me and that I was to follow her. We walked to the end of the hall, and she ushered me into a room. As I entered, I looked up and saw that it was room number 1313. That got to me. It was a large private room at the corner of the tower with big windows on two walls. I asked if she had a room without so many windows, but she said this was the only room available and that I would have to take it even if it was room 1313. She handed me a pair of pajamas and a robe, asked that I change into them, and said she would be back. As the nurse left, a little lady dressed in the candy-striped uniform of a volunteer, wheeled in a cart of books. As I set about selecting a couple of books, I remarked that the hospital should have skipped the thirteenth floor like most hotels and apartments. "Oh no," she answered. "We need every room we can get!" I thought I might be talking to Gracie Allen.

After spending two days in Bethesda I was released with the pronouncement that there was nothing wrong with me.

My roommate rarely spent the weekend in Washington. His mother and father lived in New York and his in-laws were at Annapolis. To keep from going stir crazy, I spent practically every weekend visiting the Smithsonian Institute, several other museums, art galleries, and the zoo. I saw more of Washington than most of its permanent residents.

We received no certificate of completion at the end of the three-month course, but the admiral did present each of us with a wooden paperweight with a brass plate reading, "O, God, Thy sea is so great and my boat is so small." This quotation is from some ancient Greek narrative. On the back was another brass plate. This one reads, "To LCdr. Charles D. Summitt, USN from Vice Admiral H. G. Rickover, USN." I do not think he handed out many of these, and it remains one of my most prized possessions.

Now that the weather in Washington was becoming beautiful, I was heading back to Hawaii. So far as I was concerned, everything was now beautiful.

The date set for our change of command would give me three or four days to tour the *Seadragon,* review an inventory of the weapons aboard, the food storage, a listing of all classified publications, and the inventory of all supply stores and repair parts. I needed to acquaint myself with the ship's emergency bills, policy statements, and ship's orders. These few days were an excellent time to meet the officers and members of the crew and chat with them as time permitted. The *Seadragon* was built from the same plans as the *Sargo,* so I was familiar with the ship and how it operated.

Immediately before the formal change of command ceremony, I signed a number of documents giving me custody of everything and acknowledging my responsibility for it.

We were moored alongside the seawall at the Pearl Harbor submarine base. A podium was set up in the middle of the forward deck facing ashore. Forward of this stood the admiral in command of the Submarine Force, Pacific Fleet, my squadron commander, and my division commander. The ship's officers were formed on the other side. Ashore were seated the wives, children, and guests. The crew stood in formation on the left, and the band was to the right. The officers and crew were in their dress white uniforms with medals.

The exec introduced the admiral, who praised the *Seadragon*'s past performance, explained the ship's value to the Pacific Fleet, and wished us all success in the future.

The exec next introduced the current captain, who praised the work of the officers and men and wished me well in the future.

The exec then introduced me. I read my orders and then turned to the captain, saluted, and said, "I relieve you, Sir." I then spoke briefly about how pleased I was with getting the command, how pleased I was with what I had observed of the officers and men, and promised to do my best to continue *Seadragon*'s sterling performance.

The exec announced that the ceremony was completed and the band started playing once again. We retired to the officers' club for a reception to celebrate the grand occasion.

I took the remainder of the day for rest and relaxation and to savor the fact that I finally had my first command, which I had looked forward to for so long.

SEADRAGON OPERATIONS

I had taken command on Saturday, we spent Sunday in port, and now it was Monday and time to get to work. We were scheduled to move to the ammunition depot to turn in a few torpedoes and take aboard some more. We scheduled our underway time for around 9:30 so as to give those who were going to sea a chance to clear port. The depot was on the far side of the harbor, beyond Ford Island. It usually took only about forty-five minutes to get under way, transit the harbor, and moor at the depot.

Moving the submarine, even for this short distance, gave me cause to reflect just what being in command meant. Before taking command, if I got in trouble handling a ship, such as misjudging the set and drift, the strength and direction of the wind, not using enough power or using too much power, or whatever, the captain was always there to step in and set things straight. Now that I was captain, there was no one else to turn to for help. I was it. I believed I was capable of handling everything, but I knew I had better be right. The buck definitely stopped with me.

Several times during this short run I was tempted to make suggestions, but I held back, waiting to see if the officer of the deck recognized the need to correct what he was doing. As long as we were not in real trouble, he would learn better if I left him alone.

We operated locally for about a month. This allowed us to remain overnight in port several times a week and thus spend some time with our families. Operations were such that there were quite a few periods during which I could poke about the boat and get still more familiar with it. This also gave the crew and me opportunities to get to know each other better.

In short order, I sensed a slight division within the crew. Those associated with the power plant were acting, and also being treated, as a somewhat separate group. I quickly made it known that *Seadragon* was one submarine and had only one crew. The atmosphere changed in no time at all. I could no longer sense the division I had noted earlier, which pleased me greatly. After a couple of weeks I felt very comfortable with *Seadragon*.

That month of operating around Hawaii was all I got to prepare for our deployment. We were then to sail to the western Pacific (West Pac) for a period of several months. Before departing, I was briefed by the COMSUBPAC staff as to what we would be doing during this deployment.

Guam was to be our first stop. There was a small navy base there and a good ship repair facility. A Polaris submarine squadron was eventually going to be based there. Meanwhile, we were counting on the repair facility there to do general repair work on the few nuclear-powered submarines then operating in the Pacific. We were to be the first nuclear-powered sub to enter that port. Even though *Seadragon* was in excellent condition, we were directed to submit sufficient work requests to enable each shop to be involved in working aboard our submarine in order to familiarize them with the boat.

From Guam we were to sail to Subic Bay in the Philippines, where there was another navy base with a good repair facility. We were not the first nuclear-powered sub to visit there, but we needed to further accustom them with handling a nuclear submarine.

From there we were to become an active member of the Seventh Fleet to help them to learn more of a nuclear submarine's capabilities and how to cope with one of them in action.

Upon completion of the briefing, the operations officer asked me to stop by his office, which I did. He explained that at the end of World War II, each country that had laid minefields was required to sweep them clean and report to all the others when they had been cleared. The Russians had one

The USS Seadragon *running on the surface. Notice that the bow is plowing along under the water. This is due to its speed and streamlined design that enable it to run faster when submerged.*

minefield they had never reported as cleared, and they had ignored all requests for clarification. Although it was assumed that the task had been accomplished, we wanted to confirm it. The operations officer gave me the minefield's location and dimensions and asked me to confirm that it had been cleared since we would be out in that general area. I found what he had said hard to believe, but further conversation proved I had heard right!

On my way back to the submarine I decided to tell no one about this tasking until a day or two before we arrived there. We could detect mines if they were buoyed, but detecting magnetic mines lying on the bottom was very unlikely. This was no "Oh, by the way" item. I am sure a good deal of thought had gone into this request and that getting confirmation was very important.

We were very favorably impressed with the repair facilities at both Guam and Subic Bay. The workers there had a very positive attitude about learn-

The Seadragon *demonstrating her maneuverability so that task group personnel can appreciate her capabilities.*

ing and complying with the special requirements of working aboard a nuclear-powered submarine.

We also enjoyed joining up with a task force of the Seventh Fleet. They were impressed with the increased threat of a nuclear sub, especially its speed and inexhaustible energy supply.

After several weeks of work with the fleet they cut us loose to proceed to the Philippines for our scheduled two-week upkeep stop at Subic Bay. We were warmly received in Subic Bay by those we had gotten to know during our previous visit there. It was good to get ashore and relax a bit. During the last few days we were there, a team of four or five electronic intelligence gathering experts quietly moved aboard with some special equipment. They remained aboard ship and generally stayed out of the way.

The day before our departure, a gentleman dressed in civilian clothes came aboard asking for me. He indicated that we needed to meet privately in my small stateroom. After closing the door, he identified himself as an official of one of our hush-hush national intelligence agencies. He instructed me — verbally, there were no written instructions — of what we should do if one of our U-2 spy aircraft went down in the ocean. This was not long after the capture of Francis Gary Powers, whose U-2 was shot down while flying over the Soviet Union on a photoreconnaissance mission. That was all he had to say. He immediately departed.

After seeing him off, I returned to my stateroom to think. What he had said did not jibe with the instructions I had been given by the COMSUBPAC intelligence officer. I could not discuss with anyone else what I had been instructed to do. I cannot remember the specifics, but I was in a dilemma. I finally decided to worry about it when it happened. Thank goodness it never did.

The time to sail finally arrived, but I had to delay our departure for about two hours while we awaited the arrival of a Minolta camera we had ordered at the beginning of our upkeep period. It was an inexpensive, easy-to-operate camera, but it worked better than more expensive, complex models for taking pictures through the periscope. I had learned aboard the *Sargo* that it could be readily adapted to the periscope eyepiece by using the cardboard tube from a roll of toilet paper. The navy had a periscope camera, but it was large and bulky — well adapted for taking a series of pictures of a beach over a long stretch when you needed that kind of photography, but the Minolta could be used in a couple of seconds when you wanted a very brief periscope exposure.

Once under way, we could comfortably talk about where we were going. We were headed for the Sea of Japan. We would be patrolling about two hundred miles of coastline. It would be like patrolling between Norfolk, Virginia, and Philadelphia, Pennsylvania — a lot of coastline. We were roughly two thousand miles away, so we had several days to get acquainted with members of the team of specialists, who had been more or less staying out of sight.

Finally, we transited the Korea Strait into the Sea of Japan, where we would operate for about four weeks. Once we arrived in our designated patrol area we went into patrolling mode. We came to periscope depth and after a careful periscope search I ordered that the necessary antennas be raised. I was very uncomfortable. We wanted to remain undetected, yet to do our job we had to have the antennas raised, which was to me like raising my arms and waving at somebody to attract their attention. Although I never got over this uncomfortable feeling, I have to admit that the team was gathering a great deal of information as to Russia's electronic capabilities and communications. Several of the intelligence team members spoke fluent

Russian. They primarily gathered information to be taken back and analyzed, but sometimes they were able to recommend that we go to a particular location where there might be better data.

We kept moving to different locations from time to time, up and down the assigned coastline. Warships were scarce and of no real interest; we already had plenty of information on all of them, but we still checked them out. One day we picked up a ship headed our way, making a great deal of noise. It finally came into sight. It appeared to be a cruiser and I wanted to get a good look at it. Just as I was raising the scope for a closer look, someone announced, "Fire in the battery compartment!" I told the exec to take care of it and keep me informed. The ship was indeed an old cruiser, which interested me. I wanted to check its armament and found no signs of recent modification. A short time later, the exec reported that all was well in the battery compartment. It had been a very minor problem, thank goodness.

About midway through our patrol, I decided we might as well check the minefield in our assigned area. I called the officers together and explained what was desired. I was pleased that all of them were of the opinion that there undoubtedly was a good reason we had been asked to do it and that only a submarine could conduct such a survey undetected. The minefield's boundaries were plotted on a chart and the exec and a couple of others worked up the tracks we would have to follow as we covered the whole area. I told myself that the unusual thickness of our hull might protect us should we cause a mine to detonate.

We were able to cover the entire minefield in about five hours. Everyone breathed a welcome sigh of relief when we finished. There had been no explosions; no mines had been detected.

We gathered information twenty-four hours a day, so I let the exec handle things from about ten o'clock at night to about six in the morning. He would call me on any matter that I needed to know immediately. He slept during the day. We had to get our rest.

Several weeks into our patrol we encountered a very heavy storm. Control at periscope depth was extremely difficult. I did not want to broach within plain sight of a nearby ship, so I decided to call a holiday. We went deep for twenty-four hours and everyone relaxed.

About two-thirds of the way into our patrol we received a message saying that Soviet premier Nikita Khrushchev had complained about submarines operating off the coast of Russia. We were warned to be careful. It seemed possible to me that some really good land-based radar may have detected us here and there as we moved up and down the coast and they figured there were several submarines out there. Ours was the first nuclear-powered submarine to operate in the region. It was nothing for us to run up and down the coast submerged the whole time, which the battery-powered boats could not do.

One day, after transiting to a new area, we detected nothing around us so I came to periscope depth. Up went the scope and the first thing I saw was a Russian submarine on the surface, dead in the water, with some of its crewmen on deck. I stared unbelievingly at three officers on the bridge, not a hundred yards away, and shouted, "Down scope!" I took us deeper and eased away to a point where it would be harder for them to see the periscope. When we came back up, they were gone. They must have dived and slipped away. Although it was possible, I do not think they saw us.

Early one night we started hearing a most unusual underwater sound. It reminded me of the noise a European ambulance makes: *Wooo Eee, Wooo Eee.* It was loud. At first I thought it was some type of active sonar. Then I thought it might be an underwater communication device. The sound was so loud that the direction of its source could not be established. We did not know if it was coming from a ship, another submarine, a buoy, or what. It was not constant but erratic. After several hours it stopped. The following night we heard it again. We had stayed in the same general area just to see if it sounded again. Once more it lasted for only several hours. We were unable to pick it up after that, day or night. We never did discover the sound's origin or figure out what purpose it served. We recorded it, of course, but we never heard what the shore-based experts had to say. Very strange.

In the final hours of our patrol we came upon a new destroyer. It was important that we get close enough to photograph not only the ship, but also the very small bow numbers. Our ships have large numbers painted on their bows for easy identification, but not the Russians. Theirs are small so they cannot be read until you are very close.

We got in pretty close — closer than I wanted to be, but we had to get close — and sure enough he started turning toward us. I knew we had been spotted. "Down scope!" I shouted. I ordered the helm to turn away and increased our depth as we sped away — quietly. We had opened the range a good distance in short order when *KA-BLAM!* By George, he had dropped a depth charge!

Some people just do not like having their picture taken. We kept on going. We needed to rejoin the task force anyway.

Finally the day came to head back to Hawaii. We transited submerged at a pretty good clip. We normally ran fairly deep. One day we felt a bit of rolling, which was unusual. Later on we learned that we had passed under a fairly strong typhoon. I was sure glad I was not still on a destroyer.

We arrived in Pearl Harbor to a big welcome from our families and friends. It was great to be back home again.

We were to be in port for about three days. On Saturday I received word from the division commander that I was to be present in such and such a room on Monday at nine o'clock for a meeting. That was a bit odd. Up to that point I had always seen him in his office. I wondered why I was being asked to report to such a large room to meet with him.

I arrived at the designated room a bit early and was soon joined by the captains of the other two nuclear-powered attack submarines in the Pacific. None of us had any idea what was up. Other officers started arriving: members of the squadron, division, and COMSUBPAC staffs — even the CINCPACFLT staff. What could this meeting be about? Finally our division and squadron commanders arrived. They were accompanied by Dr. Waldo Lyon, head of the U.S. Navy Sound Laboratory in San Diego. He was an expert on submarine sonar, and also an expert on operating under the Arctic ice cap. Something big was being planned!

Doctor Lyon was introduced. Most of us knew him well. He was very well liked and admired. Then it was explained that we needed to learn if our homing torpedoes would properly function beneath the Arctic ice cap or if echoes from the underside of the ice would be so distracting that the torpedoes would become confused and miss their target. Two submarines would be required: one to act as target and one to do the shooting, taking turns. The idea was to use a nuclear submarine from the Atlantic Fleet and one from the Pacific Fleet. The USS *Skate* of the Atlantic Fleet had already been designated. The main task this morning would be to select the submarine that would go from the Pacific Fleet. I was on the edge of my chair, and the other two skippers appeared to be also. Man, I hoped *Seadragon* would be chosen.

The deliberations commenced. One of the submarines was due for overhaul during the planned time of the operation, which would take place from late July into September. That left two of us. Then comparisons of other factors were made, such as the remaining life of the reactors, future commitments, and so forth. I was almost overcome with joy and excitement when *Seadragon* got the nod!

After the meeting broke up, Dr. Lyon congratulated me and explained that there was a fair amount of equipment that had to be installed in order to fulfill all of the planned requirements. We would get into that later.

I headed back to the *Seadragon*. Man, was I excited! I was ready to jump up and down and yell for joy. As I walked along in my short-sleeve uniform, enjoying the tropical breeze rustling the palm trees above my head, the cold reality of it began to sink in. The North Pole was a long way away. Could I get us there? Operating under the ice would require a lot of unusual ship handling that would be new to us. We had an awful lot of training and learning to do. By the time I climbed aboard the *Seadragon* my excitement had subsided as my mind gradually filled with many things that had to be accomplished.

I called the officers together in the wardroom and announced the exciting news. They reacted the same way that I had. Excitement and jubilation reigned, but not for long. The realization of all we had to do to get ready for such an operation had a sobering effect.

I explained that the operation was fully classified. Once we were back from under the ice, the navy would announce that we had been under the ice cap and divulge some of the things that we had done. In the meantime, we would be furnished a cover story we were to use when answering questions about where we were going, for what purpose, and for how long. Even our families were not to know. Our schedule from that moment until the time we departed would remain as promulgated. The training we had planned would have to be done during any spare time we could find in our busy schedule, day or night. The reason for being so secretive was so the Soviet navy would not be lurking about.

We started discussing the many things we had to do to get prepared. In addition to the ship-handling skills we needed to practice was the installation of various pieces of equipment that we would learn about later.

Discussion then turned to the desire to reposition some of our existing equipment. The *Seadragon* had been constructed in the Portsmouth Naval Shipyard in New Hampshire. When it was learned that she would go to the Pacific Fleet upon completion, there was great interest in sailing her there by way of the Arctic rather than through the Panama Canal. When the decision to transit via the Arctic was finally made, there was a rush to install additional equipment needed to operate under the ice. The equipment had been installed in the best places that could be found, but having it scattered all around the boat made it difficult to coordinate its operation. We needed to figure out how we could reasonably move things around to attain the best arrangement possible.

There were so many things we had to do to get ready. It quickly became obvious that we needed a detailed plan we could review together, make any necessary modifications, and then follow enthusiastically to make sure all was accomplished. The chief engineer, Lt. Comdr. Al Burkhalter, took on the task of drawing up a detailed plan. A couple of days later he presented his proposal for critiquing. He called the plan "Operation Moonlight," which I thought was very appropriate. It was an excellent piece of work that addressed such things as ship-handling exercises, equipment rearrangement, equipment installation, unusual supplies required, additional foul-weather clothing needed — even the requirement for a Santa Claus suit so we could have our picture taken with Santa at the North Pole. All my officers were outstanding, but I counted Al as one of the best.

I was a big believer in planning as well as possible for any undertaking. Planning well helped insure success. Accomplishing the most difficult tasks successfully without a hitch was a great reward well worth the effort.

We had a good, sound plan. Now we had to carry it out.

I suppose most of the officers and men were as concerned as I was about all that we had to do in preparation for our journey to the Arctic. It would be several months before we departed, but we were to be constrained to carry out our normal operations schedule right to the time of departing. That was a pretty big job in itself without taking into consideration all of the additional equipment we had to install. Moreover, it required a good deal of innovation to ensure the equipment was placed where it could best be operated in the cramped spaces of our submarine. At about the same time, we learned that only specialists could operate some of the equipment. We already knew that we were going to be taking a doctor with us because we would have no chance to off-load anyone to go to a hospital. We also expected to have Walt Wittman, an expert on the Arctic from the Navy Hydrographic Office, with us. Now we were going to have to find still more room for three or four more people to operate the specialized equipment we were installing.

We had already planned to rearrange several pieces of the ice-related equipment so that we would be better coordinated, but we did not dare start doing so until we knew exactly what equipment we had to install. We wanted to do all of this work only once. That meant doing it right the first time so we would not have to keep rearranging things as more and more was added. We did not want any surprises.

To our pleasant surprise, we received more cooperation and spirit of urgency than we could ever have expected. Experts who were knowledgeable of the equipment to be installed showed up and helped us figure it all out. Al Burkhalter's Operation Moonlight plan guided our activities. We also came up with a general scheme for checking out equipment after installation and conducting training in how to use it.

The new equipment that had to be installed for our Arctic operation included an inertial navigation system; an upward-beamed Fathometer; a large bank of recorders for collecting information on water temperature, salinity, and other data; special communications equipment; and a plankton sampler.

The inertial navigation system came from the head of a missile and needed a special factory technician to be along to work with the navigator and insure its continued proper operation.

The upward-beamed Fathometer was an integral piece of our "ice equipment" and would also be used to collect and store information on the shape and dimensions of the underside of the ice cap. Five transducers were installed in our deck topside, equally spaced from stem to stern. We would select one of the heads to feed the recorder continuously during our time under the ice. Whenever we were about to surface, we would check each of the five heads to see just what was above us in that area, ice or water. If it turned out to be ice, we would be able to determine its thickness.

With our grand plan for rearrangement, installation, checkout, and training, we set to work as best we could while still fulfilling our other operational requirements.

Most of the training we desired to do required the use of equipment not yet installed or equipment in the process of being rearranged. However, we did concentrate, whenever possible, on learning how to surface and dive absolutely vertically. The normal way of diving and surfacing is with the submarine moving ahead at reasonable speed so that you plane up to the surface or plane down from the surface. Changing the submarine's angle up or down is all that is involved, except for blowing or flooding the main ballast tanks.

In the summertime, the openings in the ice do not freeze very fast, so you can find an opening large enough to accept a submarine and then position the sub right under the opening and surface straight up. Diving has to be done straight down, and you do not start moving until you are well below any nearby ice ridges, which sometimes go down about a hundred feet and sometimes far deeper. In some areas we would be operating in rather shallow water, so we had to be able to submerge vertically until we reached a depth deep enough to clear nearby ice ridges but not so deep that we hit the bottom. It takes a fine touch to be able to place the submarine exactly in an opening and then go straight up — but not so rapidly that you damage the submarine if you hit the ice. We watched a vertical accelerometer as we went up, controlling our upward movement by the speed of our pumps so that we did not exceed a certain rate. It took a while to become proficient in moving straight up and down, but within a couple of weeks we became quite good at it.

The *Seadragon's* submarine class was built to operate in the ice. The propellers were made of steel to try to lessen the damage if they hit ice. The sail — the structure that rises above the main deck to provide a bridge and streamlined housing for the periscopes, radar and radio antenna masts, and snorkel mast — was made of steel several inches thick to prevent its being crushed if we had to surface through ice that was several feet thick.

We did not generally operate in shallow water, but we had to pass through the Chukchi Sea, just beyond the Bering Strait, to reach the true Arctic Ocean. This sea was normally about twenty fathoms (120 feet) deep. From the top of the sail to the keel of the submarine was about 50 feet. Even though we would be passing through that sea in the summertime, it was possible that we would still encounter ice with ridges reading at least 20 or 30 feet deep, which meant we would have very little space between the ice and the bottom. We thus had to learn how to twist and turn while remaining fully horizontal. Whenever you put the rudder over to change the direction of movement, a submarine will tend to "squat," sending the stern down and the bow up. We had to learn how to twist and turn while preventing the sub from squatting by using the stern planes to keep her level. After several training periods in which we practiced manipulating the stern planes to maintain a horizontal-attitude, I ordered the *Seadragon* to shallow water and we gained confidence in our ability to manage flat turns well.

We used every opportunity right up to the time we departed for the Arctic to practice vertical diving and surfacing and making flat turns.

One piece of ice equipment, the "iceberg detector," did not have to be included in the rearrangement effort because it was already mounted in the most desirable spot. It was fashioned from a mine detector used by submarines in World War II. It had a fixed (not movable) transducer mounted just short of the top of the sail pointing forward from which it transmitted a narrow fixed beam of sound pulses. The beam was pointed slightly above the horizontal. The scope presented a radarlike picture of whatever it saw within the range you selected. We had other equipment that detected ice and presented the information in different ways. The iceberg detector was used primarily to tell you if you were going to successfully pass beneath ice that had been detected dead ahead. It allowed you to determine how many feet you would pass beneath the ridges. Say, for example, that you did not intend to pass beneath ice detected ahead by any less than ten feet. If the detector indicated you were not going to clear the ice by at least ten feet, then you could go deeper (if you had enough water below you) or turn (if you had the room) or stop and try backing out. You sure did not want to hit the ice, though, and you sure did not want to get wedged between the ice and the bottom.

To properly use this equipment, the submarine has to be trimmed until it is exactly horizontal (using a zero bubble). The scope allows you to see the ice as it enters the narrow beam. You know the presentation will disappear from the beam when it closes to a particular range for the clearance to be ten feet. If it disappears before that range, then you will clear it by more than ten feet. If it persists closer than that range, then the clearance is going to be less than ten feet. If it persists all the way in, then you obviously are going to hit it

The navigator had to learn how to use the inertial navigating system. It took a great deal of time and patience on the part of the manufacturer's representative to see that it was installed properly and to assist the navigator as necessary.

Navigating in the Arctic presented some unusual considerations. The magnetic North Pole is located in northern Canada, but it would be to the south of us in the Arctic. However, we never seriously used the magnetic compass even in normal operations. During the summer months the sun would never set, so we would have no stars by which to navigate. At the true North Pole, every direction you look is south. There is no east or west. I could not help but wonder which southerly heading I would take to go back home after reaching the pole. Just kidding, of course, we had several ways to determine our position and which direction to go.

We completed rearranging our equipment and installing all the new equipment several weeks before our departure. Now it was time to train as though we were under the ice and wanted to surface.

First, let me describe the ice. If there was never any wind, and if there were no ocean currents, the Arctic Ocean would be covered by a layer of ice about twelve feet thick. However, there are currents. There also are winds, breezes, and storms. Currents and even light winds can produce great forces over a large area of the Arctic ice, causing it to pull away from one area and jam into another. Jamming into other ice produces a line of ice ridges, the places where the edges are pushed up and down. The ice is broken into hundreds of large pieces along this line. On the other side of this moving area, moving ice breaks away from the stable ice producing a crack as it moves apart. Imagine putting both hands on a sheet of Kleenex tissue lying on a tabletop. You move one hand away from the other, and you produce a rip from one end to the other. Generally, this is a fairly straight tear. Now, if you move one piece toward or away from you, letting the two pieces touch, you see that, since the break was not absolutely straight, you will end up with a series of openings along the rip. This is what the ice does, leaving ponds of open water all along the line. Years ago, these openings were named *polynyas* by the Russians. When you wanted to surface, you looked for a *polynya*.

The procedure we would follow to surface in the Arctic was rather simple, but you had to do it just right. When I desired to surface, I would instruct the officer of the deck to watch for an opening of at least 300 feet. He would instruct the quartermaster to watch the upward-beamed Fathometer trace and let him know when we passed beneath such an opening. One of the five upward-beamed Fathometer transducers was always in operation, tracing the thickness of the ice above. When the trace went to zero feet thickness, you knew it was open water. If the trace continued long enough to go 300 feet, then we knew we had an optimum place to surface. When the quartermaster found a 300-foot opening, he reported it to the officer of the deck, who then passed the word for members of the surfacing party to take their stations. This trained team of men operated the essential equipment, plotting sheets, and ship controls. The officer of the deck would hold his course and speed for about a hundred yards, change course sixty degrees to the right, and then turn to the left until he reached the reverse of his original course. This maneuver was known as a "Williamson turn." As soon as I could get there, I would take over the conn.

I knew from the plot of our track when we were about to run under the opening, but I still needed to know the width and shape of the opening so that I could maneuver the submarine to the optimum position within the *polynya* for surfacing. Another piece of sonar equipment, the "*polynya* delineator," provided us with that data. The head for this sonar device was small and mounted on a very short mast, about two feet tall, which could be remotely swung up out of its housing in the main deck near the bow. As it trained around, it would present the range of the ice it was pointing to and in that way we could determine the shape of the opening. I could then twist the submarine about as necessary to provide maximum clearance all around us. As soon as I was satisfied that we were properly and safely positioned, we would commence surfacing by pumping water from our trim tanks. If I was confident there were no large pieces of ice above us, I would raise the periscope and visually check to ensure that we were well positioned before starting up. The sun was always up, so there was plenty of light to see well, and the water was crystal clear.

With a good deal of effort we completed Operation Moonlight and by the date of our departure for the Arctic felt confident that we were ready and equal to the challenge.

It had been decided in the early planning stages of this Arctic operation that the two submarine commanders involved would be afforded the opportunity to fly over the ice cap along the routes they would follow for several hundred miles under the ice so that they would have an appreciation for what they would be facing. It was also believed that the two of us getting to know each other would enhance the operation's chances of success. This brief exploration had been scheduled to occur a couple of weeks before we were to sail.

As it turned out, Comdr. Joe Skoog, the skipper of the *Skate,* and I were already acquainted. Still, I welcomed the opportunity to get to know him better, particularly since he was senior to me and I would be following his orders while we were working together. The timing was just right: *Seadragon* was already scheduled for two weeks of upkeep about a month before we were scheduled to sail, and I would be free to leave the ship while it was in port.

I flew from Hawaii to New London, Connecticut, on the appointed date and joined Joe on a Friday afternoon aboard the *Skate,* which was also in for upkeep. We were to commence our journey on Monday, and he insisted I spend the weekend with him at his home. We spent the rest of the afternoon discussing the operation and then headed to his home.

Joe had been at sea for several weeks, so there were many things he had to do around the house before we hit the road on Monday. Of course, I offered to help him, and we spent most of the weekend working on the house. Toward the end of the weekend I was insisting that he come visit me sometime.

On Monday we were driven to the naval air station at Quonset Point, Rhode Island. Shortly after arriving we caught a flight to the air station in Halifax, Nova Scotia. We checked into the BOQ there and relaxed for the rest of the day, awaiting our scheduled meeting the next morning with the commander of the navy unit that would fly us over the Arctic.

Joe and I had agreed that we would not wear our "dolphins"— our submarine insignia, which is older than the wings pilots wear — so as not to be conspicuous and arouse interest in what we were doing there. Soon after arriving at the BOQ, however, as we rode the elevator to our rooms, a porter turned to me and said, "What is a submariner doing here?"

I was really taken back. "What makes you think I'm a submariner?"

"Your tie clasp has a submarine on it."

"Oh, that," I replied. "A friend and I swapped tie clasps. He's a submariner." Needless to say, I quit wearing the tie clasp.

The next morning at breakfast I bumped into a young navy officer who had been a midshipman in my company when I was a company officer at the Naval Academy. He knew quite well that I was a submariner, of course, and it was obvious that he saw I was not wearing my dolphins, but he never mentioned it. He probably thought I had been thrown out of submarines for some reason and felt sorry about it. I forget how I explained my presence in Halifax.

We kept our appointment with the commander of the air unit, who was well informed concerning our upcoming operation. We were to be flown in a four-engine navy plane similar to the Constellation flown by commercial airlines. It was painted black with a large, bright international-orange band on part of the wings and fuselage. This coloring would be very noticeable to searchers if we were forced down on the ice. A big radar array was housed beneath the belly of the plane to support its primary function, which was to fly patrols for the air-warning system intended to detect Russian attempts to penetrate our airspace from the Arctic.

He introduced us to our pilot, a commander who was very experienced and reliable. We were to commence our flight the next day and needed to go to their supply building to be outfitted with cold-weather clothing for the trip. On the way to supply we drove past the airplane in which we would be flying. The pilot excused himself, saying he was going to join his crew of about seven or eight, which had gathered by the plane for a group picture. He explained that they wanted it as a memento of the trip, but that Joe and I could not be in it for security reasons.

We drew our foul-weather clothing, which we later learned was truly needed, made it back to the BOQ, and relaxed for the rest of the day. Although we were disappointed not to be leaving that day because some needed repairs to the plane had not been completed, we were in full agreement with delaying our departure until they were finished. Besides, it gave us a chance to eat one more delicious lobster dinner.

We took off at about midmorning the next day and headed in a northerly direction. We were free to wander from one end of the plane to the other. There were adequate windows to easily look out on each side, and we were permitted to enter the cockpit area to look well ahead. We flew at a rather low altitude so that we could get a better view of things. I had always thought of Nova Scotia being pretty far north, but it took quite some time to get to the Labrador Sea, where we started spotting an iceberg here and there. We had flown a distance about equal to that from Miami to Baltimore. The icebergs looked so lovely and peaceful — although they could prove deadly if you collided with one. Close watch is maintained on those floating far enough south that they approach normal shipping lanes. Their positions are periodically broadcast to alert ships in the area. Some are no larger than

The stalwart crew, with their four-engine aircraft, who took Joe Skoog and me on our flight over the Arctic in 1962.

an automobile, but they can be massive. An iceberg is a chunk of a glacier. Greenland foals the majority of icebergs as its glaciers grow in size and push down the mountainsides into the sea. As the glacial ice thaws, big pieces constantly break free and slide into the sea with a mighty splash. Submarine sonar can hear the noise of those splashes at surprising distances. I did not expect to encounter any icebergs on my route, but Joe was certainly going to have to be vigilant and make sure he steered clear of them as he sailed to the Arctic.

We finally reached the Arctic ice covering Baffin Bay, between Canada and Greenland. It was awesome. We were about as far from Nova Scotia as Nova Scotia is from Miami. We dropped down to between five hundred and a thousand feet so we could examine the ice more closely. Even ridges no more than a few feet high could be seen clearly. *Polynas* of any size were rare.

After a couple of hours over the ice we turned and headed back for the air base at Thule on the western edge of Greenland. I was behind the pilot as we made our approach to the airfield. He suggested I cross my fingers because the landing had to be just right on the first pass. It would be impossible to make a second run because there was no way to climb up and over the glacier that lay dead ahead. This was the only way in or out. I expressed my confidence in his ability and then crossed my fingers on both hands. He brought us in beautifully.

As we disembarked, I found I had to concentrate on walking. I was a bit stiff from the inactivity on the plane. We had been flying since midmorning and it was nearing my bedtime. Thule was a rather bleak place. The buildings were very plain and simple. None of the piping was buried. Instead, pipes were suspended in the air on tall posts. They appeared to be heavily insulated. It was cold. Thank goodness for that heavy foul-weather clothing we had been furnished.

We were led to a single-story building where we would spend the night. There were no windows, and no lights showed, except at the doorway. The door fascinated me. It was built like the door to a large walk-in freezer. It was made of wood at least six or eight inches thick. The door and its frame had several rows of gaskets that had been stepped three or four times like on the door to a big bank vault. When it opened, we passed from a bitter cold and silent environment to a pleasantly warm and noisy atmosphere. Near at hand was the crowded club bar, exuberant with party life. Beyond was a pleasant and popular dining room. We were shown to our sleeping quarters. The room Joe and I got was painted black. It was very small and held two double bunks. A single bare light bulb hung from the center of the ceiling. There was no appropriate place for our small amount of luggage or the clothes we began shedding. However, we each had a bed in which to sleep. We dropped our stuff and returned to the bar and dining room. First things first.

We were ready to go at it again fairly early the next morning. Our plane roared back down the same runway we had landed on, this time headed in the opposite direction. This leg of our journey would take us to Alaska, a distance about the same as from New York to San Francisco. Instead of flying a beeline, the pilot wandered farther north so we could see more of the true Arctic. We were truly in a world of ice and snow. There was nothing else to see in any direction. It looked so cold, so lonely. Like being on the moon. The Arctic Ocean presented a much more impressive and awesome sight than the bays we had flown over the day before. The ridges were much, much bigger. Good-sized *polynyas* could frequently be seen. A couple of times we spotted polar bears. We were again flying low. As they heard us, they would stare and then, when the sound of the engines could plainly be heard, they would turn and lope rather hurriedly to the nearest *polynya* and dive in. They were huge.

After several hours we reached Alaska. We expected it to be much warmer than where we had stayed in Greenland. Surprisingly, from Alaska to the North Pole is about the same distance as from Miami to Nova Scotia. I was becoming very impressed with how far the North Pole is from civilization and just how immense the Arctic is.

We landed safely at Eielson Air Force Base outside Fairbanks. We had been flying for about twelve hours and I was ready to get my feet on the ground. We had flown many hours in the past two days. The pilot announced that we would remain there the next day for some much needed rest. I agreed wholeheartedly.

Our quarters in the BOQ were quite comfortable. I got back to my room around 9:30 following a few drinks and a very good dinner. I was ready for a good night's sleep. It looked like it was late in the afternoon outside, which gives you a strange feeling when you expect it to be nighttime. My room had several windows. It was quite a bit different from the completely enclosed black room we had shared the night before. I closed the blinds, but they failed to shut out the light.

I climbed into bed in short order, ready for some much desired sleep. Nothing happened. I just lay there. This was not right. I was usually able to go to sleep at the drop of a hat. I kept tossing and turning, longing for the black, dark room we had been given in Greenland. Eventually I dozed off, but woke up after a short time. It was still bright outside. I did this time after time. At about four in the morning it appeared to be dusk, but a little later on it was daylight again. I got up around six, dressed, and went to get some breakfast. What a night. It is strange how you unconsciously react to day and night. At least aboard the submarine we can control day and night with light switches.

I spent the day poking around, reading and taking catnaps. I shopped at the base exchange to get a couple of presents for my two boys. I always tried to bring them something after a trip. To my delight, I found a cap that was just what I wanted for wearing topside at sea. It fit good, had a good bill, and would stay on in a strong wind. I still have it.

The second night I was so sleepy I finally got a halfway decent rest in spite of the daylight. The next morning, we were off again. This time we followed the route I would be taking as *Seadragon* proceeded to the heart of the Arctic. It was more of the same: ice, ice, ice, ridges, *polynyas,* and polar bears — what a wilderness. We were flying very low, about five hundred feet. That is very low. I was up on the flight deck talking to the captain when the engineer announced that the inboard port engine was losing oil pressure and requested permission to shut it down. The captain gave the order and started climbing, making a wide turn to reverse course. He let me know we could handle it on three engines, but that we ought to discontinue our trip and head back to the base in Alaska. It sounded good to me.

Several hours later we successfully touched down at the base near Fairbanks. The skipper told me we had just set a record for distance flown on three engines. The longest route flown at the time was from the West Coast to Hawaii and its midpoint, which determines whether you turn back or fly on with an emergency, was much less than the distance we traveled that day on three engines. I am glad we were able to break the record.

At dinner, Joe and I discussed the trip so far. We were both impressed with what we would be facing on our planned submerged Arctic operation. We now had a clear understanding of what lay ahead. The next day we were due to fly back to Nova Scotia, provided they got the engine repaired by then. From there I would have to make my way back to the West Coast and then to Hawaii. We had completed our flights over the ice, so why go all that way simply to fly back to the West Coast when it was obvious I needed to head back to Hawaii immediately?

The next morning, I caught a commercial flight from Fairbanks to Seattle. After a short delay there, I was on my way to Hawaii. By the time we landed in Honolulu, I had had my fill of flying for a while. It was good to get back home; I was anxious to turn to and make sure we were fully prepared and trained for our adventure under that awesome and massive ice cap at the top of the world.

10

OFF TO THE ARCTIC

The anxiously awaited day for the commencement of our most unusual adventure finally came. It was a beautiful Hawaiian day. The thought came to me that, even if we had announced we were going to the North Pole, no one would have believed us. It was hard even for me to accept.

We had scheduled our underway time for midmorning to let the morning traffic in the harbor die down, to let us calmly accomplish all that needed to be made ready for getting under way, and particularly not to rush our families, who always came down to see us off when we were departing for a long period of time. I have forgotten exactly what we told them we were going to be doing on this cruise, but it was something like, 'We are off to the West Pacific, where we will be continuously submerged to test some new equipment.' They wished us well and pleaded for a quick return.

The sea and wind were relatively calm. We cleared

the harbor and headed in a westerly direction, which was the normal course we set when departing on long deployments. As soon as we reached deep water, we dived, got a good trim, then headed deep and turned northward. We were on our way.

I always enjoyed settling into the calm routine of a long transit. We had worked hard to prepare for this operation, and we had reached the point of feeling comfortable that we had done all we could do to be ready for our undertaking. All those not on watch seemed to be settled into a "Rope Yarn Sunday" routine. "Rope Yarn Sunday" refers to a routine in sailing ship days, when crewmen not on watch on Sunday could forego shipboard work and attend to their personal upkeep needs. Rope that was no longer fit for its intended purpose was saved and the men could cut off a section, unravel it, and use the strands to sew up their torn clothing. They would gather in small groups to do their sewing and tell sea stories. These periods became known as "Rope Yarn Sunday," regardless of what day of the week they occurred.

We had five "guests" aboard for this expedition. Lieutenant Art Rehme, a submarine doctor, had been ordered to sail with us. Having a doctor aboard was most unusual, but considered very necessary in this case, because it would be nearly impossible to get help if we needed it. Walt Wittman of the Navy Hydrographic Office in Washington D.C., a wonderful shipmate with boundless information and knowledge of the Arctic, was aboard to clarify any questions we might have about the Arctic and make suggestions any time he thought necessary. Once we went under the ice, however, he was to give no assistance or suggestions unless I deemed it an emergency. The idea was to force us to carry out our mission strictly on our own. We also carried two technicians from the Hydrographic Office. They were aboard to operate and maintain the equipment installed for gathering scientific information. Finally, we had a representative from the Sperry Gyroscope Company whose job was to ensure that our "missile" inertial navigation system performed properly.

I toured the ship and was pleased to see that everything was well and properly stored and that everything was clean and shiny. Not only was the crew extremely competent, they took pride in keeping everything shipshape. I was indeed fortunate to have command of such a remarkable ship manned by such a marvelous crew. (For the sailing list, see appendix.)

I ended up in the wardroom to enjoy a quiet cup of coffee, feeling very pleased that everything was going so well, when the engineer came in and informed me that the port main condenser had a leak that needed to be repaired. To repair it meant shutting it down, opening it up, and working for quite a few hours. The water at the depth we were running at was very cold and the condenser was bounded on one side by the hull, with no insulation.

It was going to be so cold working in that space that the two-man work party would have to be changed about once an hour. Each work party would consist of one experienced man with a helper, no experience necessary.

I gave the order to commence the repairs and asked the doctor to keep an eye on the workers so they did not get overexposed and become sick.

No alcohol is carried on U.S. Navy ships except what is necessary for medicinal purposes, and the captain has to approve any such use. We carried brandy for that purpose. It was very strictly controlled. Some time later, the doctor came to me and recommended we give each of the workers a jigger of brandy when they finished their work period to help protect them from their unusual exposure to the cold. I agreed. I did not want anyone to get sick.

After several hours I went back to the engine room to see how the work was going. A line of six or eight men more or less blocked the passageway outside the condenser.

"What's going on?" I demanded. "What is this line for?"

The nearest man explained that they were waiting their turn to work on the condenser. At first I was pleased to see that there were so many volunteers for this unpleasant task. Then it hit me: they had heard about the ration of brandy each worker would get. I could not help but chuckle. I was tempted to stand in line myself.

We accepted a slight reduction in speed to accomplish this work, but it was not enough to cause us to violate the movement report we had filed. Whenever a U.S. Navy vessel moves outside of normal operating areas, it must submit a report to the Movement Report Center giving the time of departure, courses, speed of advance, and estimated arrival time at the next operating point. The Movement Report Center then informs all commands having a need to know of this movement to avoid interference. An imaginary box moves along planned route at the reported speed of advance. The box is several miles wide on each side, its front is about twenty miles ahead of the steadily moving point, and the back of the box is about forty miles behind it. The vessel is free to move anywhere within this box, but it must submit a change to the movement report if it is unable to stay within the box. I made it a habit to stay close to the forward edge of the box so I had more freedom of movement without having to report a change.

The condenser repairs took a couple of days, and then we were back to normal again. We passed through the Aleutian Islands on schedule and altered course to head for the Bering Strait. Once we passed through the strait we assumed the planned heading that would take us under the polar icecap.

Shortly I got a report that something was wrong with our radio whip antenna. There was no way to correct the problem without surfacing. We could only guess what the problem was before examining it on the surface. I definitely wanted everything to be in perfect shape before going under the ice, but we were not too far from Russia at that point, and I did not want to take any more chances than I had to of being spotted by a Russian ship or aircraft. I decided to wait until we reached the edge of the ice. The farther we could go before getting to the ice, the less chance there was of being spotted.

Several hours later, the officer of the deck reported picking up signs of ice here and there. Our equipment showed the pieces to be sporadic, so I ordered that we continue submerged. Within an hour the pieces of ice were becoming more dense and larger. I figured it was time we to surface and get our repair work done before going any farther. There was no clearly defined opening similar to a *polynya,* so I spent quite some time probing to convince myself there were no pieces of ice overhead. We came up slowly to avoid as much damage as possible if we encountered any big pieces above us. Fortunately, we made it up without incident. Inspection of the antenna showed that a bit of welding was necessary. The work was completed within several hours and we were ready to proceed.

In sailing from Hawaii to the Aleutian Islands we had been able to run deep and at pretty good speed, except that we had been forced to reduce speed somewhat during the work on the condenser. We came up a bit shallower and reduced our speed somewhat as we passed through the Aleutians and transited the Bering Sea. Then, as we neared the Bering Strait, we ran still shallower and somewhat slower. I went to periscope depth as we transited the Bering Strait to see if I could see land on either side, but my eye height was so low that I could see nothing. Our Fathometer readings showed us to be following our intended track. By now we were in rather shallow water. Earlier I explained that the Chukchi Sea, which we had entered after passing through the Bering Strait, is generally about twenty fathoms, or 120 feet, deep. This did not leave too much water above or below us.

Once we completed the repairs on our whip antenna, my thoughts focused on squeezing our way under the ice in the very shallow Chukchi Sea to the deep Arctic Ocean. We had many miles to go in that very restricted passage. The ice had not receded as far as predicted, so we had to go much farther in this shallow sea than we had planned.

In very short order we were well under the solid icecap. By this time I had reduced our speed to only three knots (roughly three miles per hour), which gave us just enough forward movement to permit turning left or right and gaining passage through all this, but was slow enough to prevent serious damage if we hit the ice.

We were easing along about ten feet off the bottom and clearing the ice

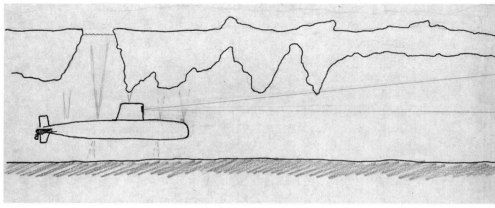

My sketch illustrating Seadragon's *tight passage under the Chuckchi Sea.*

ridges by about ten feet above us. The iceberg detector was working marvelously. Steering a straight course was impossible, however. We were constantly turning right or left to clear a ridge. The navigator coaxed the officer of the deck to move to the right or left only when necessary to avoid getting off our intended track.

I would never have done this just for the heck of it. There was a tendency to want to turn around and head back out. I believed we could make it, but I do not think I would have bet a lot of money on it. We had to get to the Arctic. We did not come this far to give up. On we went. There was no mention by anyone that we needed to call it off.

Soon after coming aboard the *Seadragon* I had obtained a folding lawn chair from Sears. It was the kind that had an aluminum frame with wood slats for the seat and back. I kept it folded up in an out-of-the-way space in the control room, ready for those occasions that required my presence there with the officer of the deck. I simply wanted to be present to quickly respond to questions or step in and take over if necessary. From the start of our transit under the ice, I had taken my seat in this chair, staying out of the way, but within feet of the officer of the deck. Operation Moonlight had prepared us well, and I had great confidence in my officers of the deck. I simply wanted to be readily available if needed. From time to time I would get up to take a look at a plot of our movement, look at the presentation of the iceberg detector, or to check something the officer of the deck wanted to show me. I had coffee and food brought to me when I wanted it and snoozed as I pleased. I had no desire to be anywhere else.

We had many tense moments, but we never ran aground or touched an ice ridge. Making the Chukchi Sea passage took several days. It was 137 miles from beginning to end. Imagine driving a car a 137 miles at three miles an hour, all the while never steering a straight course. You can imagine our relief when we finally reached the deep Arctic Ocean. There was a huge sigh of relief throughout the ship as the Fathometer showed the bottom dropping far below us. As soon as possible we went several hundred feet deeper to get clear of any really deep ice ridges. We were now in water that was two thousand fathoms (twelve thousand feet) deep.

Later, after we had completed our operations under the ice and Walt Wittman was free to discuss his thoughts freely, I asked him what he thought had been the most interesting part of the trip. Without hesitation he said: "Squeezing under the ice in the Chukchi Sea was my greatest thrill. I did not think we were going to make it!" I'm sure glad he had not been free to give me his expert opinion at the time!

During the time I spent in my folding lawn chair in the control room, I looked forward to climbing into my bunk for a long sleep. As soon as we reached the Arctic Ocean and settled down to running deep along our planned track, I headed for my bunk. I was able to get a decent night's sleep, disturbed only a couple of times by the officer of the deck phoning me to make necessary reports. After about six hours of good sleep, I awoke and was ready to find out how everything was going.

There were several events we had to observe each day. One was to receive whatever messages, if any, were being sent to us. A submarine broadcast occurred each hour. Messages intended for us appeared on six or more successive broadcasts. We thus had to ensure that we copied at least one broadcast every six hours. Each message to a particular submarine bore a serial number. As long as you had all of the messages in sequence, you could rest assured that you had not missed any messages intended for your boat. If you did, you were in trouble. We received these broadcasts on a floating wire antenna. The wire was about a half-inch in diameter and floated on the surface. It was permanently attached to the aft end of the top of the sail. It extended to just short of the propellers so it would not become entangled. If you were submerged dead in the water, it would reach straight up. If you were going fast submerged, it would trail directly aft, horizontally. If you were going at a moderate speed fairly close to the surface, then the after portion trailed along on the surface. During our transit of the shallow Chukchi Sea, it dragged along under the ice and worked just fine. Now that we were in deep water, we had to come up to a shallow depth and slow down so that the wire would float up against the ice in time to receive a broadcast.

We usually needed to "shoot" the ship's trash and garbage and blow our sanitary tanks once a day. We planned these two events to occur when we went shallow for a broadcast because it was best to accomplish them against the least possible outside water pressure. The ship's sewage drained into sanitary tanks. When they became fairly full, we needed to empty them. This was done by shutting the valves on all the drain lines, building up air pressure in the tanks until it reached sea pressure, opening the sea valve, and blowing the tanks dry.

The ship's trash and garbage cans were lined with porous plastic bags. The plastic mesh was similar to the wire screen used in windows. We had a trash disposal unit similar in appearance to a torpedo tube, only pointed straight down. The bags of trash and garbage were weighted with weights we carried specifically for this purpose to ensure that they did not float to the surface. The disposal was filled with the bags, the door shut and locked, the outer door opened, and the contents pumped into the sea. The outer door was then shut, the water pumped out, and the inner door opened, ready to receive more trash and garbage.

At nighttime at sea, ships are "rigged for red." Those men requiring, or possibly requiring, night vision must work strictly in the dark or in areas illuminated only with red light. Aboard submarines, the normal lighting in compartments where someone is apt to immediately require night vision is turned off and the red lights turned on. For the sake of comfort, this is also done, for the most part, in those compartments where people are sleeping. This light change is what helps people on a submarine know night from day. Now that we were in the world of constant daylight, it was not really required that we run rigged for red. However, having learned my recent lesson of trying to get to sleep in Alaska, I required that the custom be continued.

Joe Skoog and I had addressed the time difference between our two submarines because we were going to be working together and it would be awkward if we did not follow the same working and eating schedule. As an example, he would be getting up just about the time I was going to bed unless we shifted our clocks around. There is a five-hour time difference between New London and Pearl Harbor (six hours when Daylight Savings Time is in effect). We agreed on how many hours we each would lose or gain to bring us to the same local time. Wes Harvey, my executive officer, had worked out our plan so that we changed our clocks one hour on certain days so that we reached the agreed upon local time over a period of several days rather than all at once.

Our operation order required us to come to the surface from time to time to test and evaluate certain new pieces of communication and navigation equipment and also to retrieve samples of the plankton picked up by our scientific equipment. The time had come for us to make our first surfacing attempt from under the true icecap. We were all anxious to give it a go.

Instructions were given to watch for the first *polynya* measuring at least three hundred feet across. After about half an hour the officer of the deck passed the word summoning the surfacing party to its stations. He had already started his Williamson turn by the time I relieved him. Shortly after turning around and heading back down our track, the *polynya* delineator began describing the shape of the opening. We were several hundred feet deep, well below any of the ice ridges. As soon as we were dead in the water in what appeared to be the center of the opening, I twisted in place a bit to align the ship with the shape of the *polynya* and then ordered the diving officer to take us up slowly. I raised the periscope to have a look and was amazed at how clear the water was. I could see clearly all around. We were positioned perfectly. I lowered the periscope. The last thing I wanted to do was damage it. As we reached the surface, I ordered the main ballast tanks blown so that we would become fully surfaced. I climbed the ladder to the bridge along with a couple of lookouts. A few other crewmen followed. What a sight! It was awesome: a beautiful sunny day with miles and miles of ice in every direction. This beat traveling on a dogsled. Ice ridges and mounds were everywhere. There were few flat areas of any size and it was so very quiet. I made a point of always wearing sunglasses while on the surface in the Arctic. The sun's glare was exceptionally bright.

I had a pair of Ray-Ban sunglasses that I had bought eighteen years before when I was a midshipman. At the time this is being written they are fifty-five years old. I had thought about writing the manufacturer when the plastic earpieces disintegrated. That was thirty-five years ago. I had to replace them. The new ones are holding up much better.

We stayed on the surface for about two hours, giving everyone aboard a chance to look at the awesome scene. I explained to the officer of the deck that we had to keep a very close watch so that the *polynya* did not close in on us. We needed to submerge at the first sign that it was closing up to avoid any possibility of becoming trapped. I believed it was quite possible for the ice to close together and prevent us from diving. I sure did not want to become a permanent fixture in the Arctic. As it turned out, we surfaced thirty-one times in the ice and only once did I deem it necessary to submerge because of ice movement.

We made our dive very easily and soon were on our way. I was extremely pleased with our performance. It was as though we had been operating in the ice for years. Our training had certainly paid off. I was extremely impressed and proud of everyone.

I was particularly pleased with the diving officer, Lt. Bob Pirie, who took over that watch every time we dived and surfaced in the ice. Depth was controlled by pumping water in or out of our trim tanks. The planes and angle of the boat were of no help in going up or down because we moved very slowly, if at all. His ability to time the movement of water in or out of the trim tanks, as well as how much to move, could not have been better. When we surfaced, he had to carefully watch the rate of rise, measured by a vertical accelerometer, and ensure we did not exceed a certain rate. We would not suffer damage if we hit the ice while coming up at no more than that rate. Once we reached the surface and were clear, we would blow the main ballast tanks in order to quickly surface completely.

Over the next few days we surfaced a couple of more times. I sat and reflected on our performance in each instance to determine if we needed to improve in any area. The only thing that disturbed me was the reporting of different measurements from the various pieces of equipment as I called out for the readings. One piece measured in yards, one in feet, one in meters, and one in fathoms. I was about to go nuts trying to relate one to another. I had to convert one measurement to another, and the mental arithmetic was a real bother. I was worried that I might make a mistake in a conversion that would prove costly.

The equipment we used for operating in the ice had been pieced together helter-skelter. It was not designed as an integrated system. We were fortunate to have what we had, and I could not do without perfect performance from each piece, regardless of what system of measurement it employed. Within a couple of days I had designed a chart that permitted me to put my finger on any particular measurement and read what it was in any other system. As an example, if I was given a measurement in meters and wanted to know what it was in feet, I simply read it right off my chart. It proved invaluable to several others and me. I named it the "Idiot Board" and included it in my operation report. My superiors recommended it for use by others. It was my most significant contribution to Arctic operations.

We continued heading north along our planned track, gathering scientific information automatically with the equipment installed by the Hydrographic Office. Soundings of the depth of the Arctic were being regularly recorded. We were intentionally following a track not followed by others so that more soundings could be obtained than ever before. Only a sparse amount of information existed on the various depths under the Arctic ice. Soundings had been taken around the edges of the ice cap even back in sailing ship days, but they were few and far between. Little had been learned of the Arctic Ocean's currents.

Then, four or five years before our operation, a monstrous slab of ice measuring about two hundred feet thick and ten miles across slid into the

Arctic from the eastern section of northern Canada. This was an unusual occurrence. A camp for scientists was established on it by flying in the necessary materials, equipment, supplies, and, of course, the scientists — about a dozen people in all. The planes used for this were outfitted with skis for landing gear. Over a period of several years the ice station completed a full trip around the Arctic and ran aground near where it had first started drifting. The forces of wind and current acting on this roving ice island eventually started breaking it up. It was urgent that the personnel be removed as soon as possible. Ski landings by aircraft are not possible year round, however, and it would be several months before planes could safely land.

A most daring means of extracting them thus had to be employed. A cargo plane airdropped a crate with the necessary equipment and instructions on how to use it. The crate contained two poles and a specially designed harness and long length of strong rope for each person in the scientific party. Following the directions supplied with the equipment, they erected the poles about fifteen or twenty yards apart and stretched one of the lengths of rope tautly between the tops of the poles. The ends of the rope were then brought back to where a man stood midway between the poles and attached to the harness he wore.

When all was ready, the plane flew overhead as low and slow as possible, trailing a hook that snagged the rope stretched between the poles and snatched the man from the ice. I imagine it was quite a thrill, being snatched from a standing position on the ice, instantly accelerating to more than a hundred miles an hour, flying through the air.

The process was repeated until everyone in the party had been safely rescued from the ice. There was only one incident to report. One of the men did not become immediately airborne, but was instead dragged facedown for about thirty yards over the ice. He was pretty badly bruised but no doubt felt proud of his record for facedown land speed in the Arctic.

About two years before we made our journey under the ice, the remnants of this huge iceberg broke free and commenced drifting in the Arctic once more. The largest piece was still about two hundred feet thick and about five miles wide. Another ice station was established on that monstrous piece.

The next event in our operation plan called for *Seadragon* to rendezvous with this ice station. It was now located north of the Bering Strait and about halfway to the pole. They wanted to meet with us to explain an evaluation they wanted us to help them conduct that would require only about one day of our time. I was rather interested in their plan and quite excited about visiting the ice station.

To help us find them, they had agreed to detonate charges in the seawater at precise times. As those times approached we would listen intently, starting a stopwatch precisely at the designated times. If we heard the explosion, we would know from which direction it had come. Knowing the exact amount of time the sound had taken to reach us, we could then compute the station's distance from us. This would enable us to precisely plot its position. Without this information, it would be like leaving Nashville, Tennessee, by automobile, intent on finding a particular gas station somewhere in Nebraska.

As the time approached for them to detonate their first charge we huddled around our searching sonar with the stopwatch poised and ready. When the time came, a crewman started the stopwatch. A short time later we heard the explosion. It was easy to get a good bearing and in no time we had computed the distance. As I recall, it was 230 miles. I really had not expected to hear the first couple of shots. Some hours later we waited for the second planned shot. We picked it up, too, and the plot confirmed that we had a precise fix on the ice station.

The next day, as we approached the huge piece of ice, our eyes were glued on the upward-beamed Fathometer trace, which we expected at any minute to start tracing a straight line showing the depth of the ice to be about two hundred feet. There it was. Not a jumbled mass of ice, but one solid piece, two hundred feet deep. We called the ice station on our underwater telephone to inform them that we had arrived and to learn if they could recommend a nearby place to surface. They answered immediately and, after a brief interval, came back with their recommended surfacing point. They said it lay in a particular direction from the underwater phone transducer they had lowered into the water to enable them to talk to us. We thanked them and in no time at all passed directly under their very small transducer, which printed out on our upward-beamed Fathometer trace. We turned in the recommended direction and very shortly found an excellent *polynya*. It is amazing what you can do with the right equipment. The *polynya* was right at the edge of the huge piece of ice and fairly close to their camp.

The surfacing went smoothly. We had plenty of room. Once on the bridge, I maneuvered to place us as close as I dared alongside the big ice island. It was common that at a shallow depth below the surface the ice would abruptly shelve out a few feet and could not easily be seen. These protrusions are called "rams." In spite of my concern, I still bounced off one of these rams, but it caused no real damage to the ship. We had to stay too far away from the surface of the ice for us to reach with our brow (gangway). We inflated a seven-man rubber life raft and one of the men rowed to and from "shore" carrying a couple of our visitors at a time. There were six or seven men in their boarding party. I went down on deck to welcome them aboard, singling out, as I approached them, the one who appeared, from the impressive furs he was wearing, to be in charge of the party. He turned out to be the Eskimo cook. The senior man was dressed much less impressively.

Before we made our rendezvous, I told the exec that I thought it would be good to get out a clean white tablecloth and be prepared to serve them a first-class meal in the wardroom. I was sure they would appreciate such a treat since they undoubtedly were living in a rather primitive style. We had no idea what local time they observed. It was midmorning our time.

I invited them into our wardroom, suggesting that they prepare to enjoy a real treat. They graciously declined, saying that they had just finished their evening meal. It soon became evident that they were enjoying a very comfortable lifestyle.

I had the white tablecloth and the place settings removed and we gathered around our table to sip coffee and learn what it was that they wished us to do for them. What they desired us to do was quite simple yet something they very much needed.

The senior man was sitting next to me. I could not help but notice and admire the big revolver he had strapped to his waist. In fact, each of them was armed.

"What in the world are you fellows about to do?" I inquired. "Hunt polar bears?"

He smiled and explained that they were not "hunting" polar bears, they were simply prepared to defend themselves in the event a polar bear attacked. He then explained that polar bears are extremely aggressive and that it was not unusual for them to attack people on the ice. They had not had any bad experiences thus far, and they did not intend to, if it could be helped.

After about an hour and a half, they were rowed back to shore and shortly thereafter we submerged and headed along our planned track, carrying out the evolutions they had requested. We were now commencing our lone, circuitous track leading eventually to our rendezvous with the USS *Skate* somewhere off the northern coast of Russia.

Our track from the ice station to the point where we were to join up with the *Skate* took us in a westerly direction, more or less paralleling the north coast of Russia, and roughly midway between Russia and the North Pole. We had about fifteen hundred miles to go. Our rendezvous point was in the Laptev Sea, which is on the far side of the North Pole from Canada. There were no recorded soundings along this track. We were pioneer travelers in a previously unvisited world, explorers in an unknown territory.

Looking ahead on the charts, I noticed that there were a few soundings along that part of our track running closest to the Russian coast. Ships had taken them through the years when the edge of the ice receded quite a bit. I was struck by the fact that at one point the readings abruptly jumped from about twelve thousand feet to only a couple of hundred feet. These soundings were not always accurate, and I was afraid they could be far less than a couple of hundred feet. I did not mind going into shallow water, but I wanted to do so where the bottom came up more gradually — not all at once. It did not require much imagination to picture us running smack into the side of a steep cliff. With that sobering thought in mind, I took advantage of ancient soundings and plotted a route where the bottom supposedly came up more gradually and eventually took us to the same shallow area. From there we could come back on the originally planned track in the opposite direction, taking us from shallow to deep water. We did just that. It was astonishing how quickly the bottom dropped to twelve thousand feet. What a sight that would be if we ever drained the Arctic Ocean!

We were getting used to operating under the ice and surfacing from time to time to fulfill our commitments. It did not take long before making vertical surfacings became routine. Our training in preparation for this operation certainly paid off.

Our constant printed trace of the depth of ice above us was of interest to everyone. Every member of the crew would stop by a couple of times a day to check on what exceptionally deep ice ridges we had passed beneath. There was much excitement about the unusually deep ridges. Sometimes the ridges reached several hundred feet. Once we cleared the shallow area we did not pay much attention to Fathometer readings because the bottom was so far below us. The equipment the Hydrographic Office had put aboard was maintaining constant readings of the depth as we went along.

One day, Walt Wittman came to me, very excited. He reported that we had just passed over a large mountain ridge in the ocean floor similar to the Lomonosov Ridge. It appeared to run parallel with that ridge, but they were a good distance apart. The Lomonosov Ridge had been discovered some years before by one of the Arctic exploration missions. It was a submerged mountain range. Now we had found a similar mountain range. Too bad we could not drain the Arctic to see all these sights. When I completed my report of our operation soon after arriving back in Hawaii, I included this finding and recommended that it be named "Wittman Ridge." A few days later I called Walt and told him I had recommended that the ridge bear his name. He responded that he had recommended in his report that it be named "Summitt Ridge." To this day I have not heard anything about that ridge, so

I do not know if it ever got named. Walt's recommendation reminded me of the popular song "Summit Ridge Drive" back in the late thirties. I had a couple of girls believing I had actually composed the song.

Soon we would arrive at the rendezvous point. I had planned to arrive there a bit early. I always liked to work a bit ahead of schedule so that if any unexpected delays occurred we would still have a good chance of being on time.

11

SEADRAGON AND SKATE
CONDUCT JOINT OPERATIONS

Our rendezvous with the *Skate* was planned to occur at a specific latitude and longitude. For safety's sake, just in case our navigation did not match exactly, a good-sized area was described about that point. We were to enter it below a certain depth and the *Skate* would enter it well above us. Once we knew each other's exact location, we would be free to operate at any depth as long as we coordinated our movements.

I was anxious to get there and prepare to intercept Joe Skoog when he arrived.

We took care of copying our broadcast and performing our usually daily chores right before entering the restricted area. We had to be prepared to stay deep for possibly a pretty long time.

We listened attentively, but the appointed time for our rendezvous came and went. I had expected Joe to be there a bit ahead of schedule, too, but I did not worry. However, after several hours went by, I became a bit concerned. Maybe our navigation was a bit off, I thought. Maybe his navigation was a bit off. Maybe something had happened to him. I started thinking what the best plan would be to search for him, but I knew I should not go rushing off looking for him — that I needed to give him more time. I was beginning to really get worried when the sonar operator sang out, "I got him!" He gave a bearing that matched the direction I had expected the *Skate* to come from, and estimated their range at what was still a petty good distance.

I was much relieved. I wanted to call Joe on the underwater telephone, but thought it best to wait until our range closed some more so we would have clear communications right off the bat.

After a while, judging from the noise level, we guessed that the range had closed sufficiently for talking. I called but got no response. I called again; still no response. I waited a little longer and tried again. No response. Maybe there was a temperature gradient between us. That would bounce the phone's sound waves down so that he could not hear us. I knew where we were and that we were well clear, so I came up to his depth and this time got an answer. I then headed back down to our depth. We were able to maintain communications, so we performed a range check on the phone. The *Skate* was a lot farther away than we had expected. It was very strange.

Once Joe had us located clearly, he announced a course change that would take us to the North Pole. He instructed me to take station about five hundred yards on his starboard beam and come to his depth. We had about five hundred miles to go to get to the pole. It was nice to have company. In conversation with him on the underwater phone, it came to light that I had not received word on the change of time for the rendezvous. I do not know how it occurred, but I am glad we were early rather than late.

The underwater telephone was a marvelous piece of equipment. The device looked just like a regular telephone, but only one person could speak at a time. Sound travels through the water much, much slower than electricity through a wire, so you have to become accustomed to the delay between your message and the reply. This delay enabled us to use the phone to determine the range between the two submarines. The person initiating the range check would say, "Standby for a range check: five, four, three, two, one, mark." At the moment he said "mark," he would start his stopwatch. The person receiving the message would start on his own, mimicking the rhythm of the countdown, and say "mark" in his phone at the exact same time he received it. When the man with the stopwatch received the acknowledging mark, he would stop the watch and announce how many seconds had elapsed. I cannot remember the exact formula for converting the

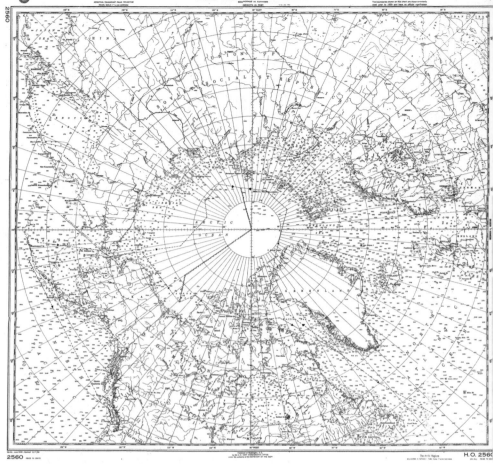

Navigation chart showing the planned tracks of the USS Seadragon *(from the Pacific) and USS* Skate *(from the Atlantic) for the entire operation.*

time to distance, but I believe it involved dividing the number of seconds by two, with the result being the range in thousands of yards.

I was really surprised at how exact our rendezvous occurred. The *Skate* had come upon the scene headed right for the *Seadragon*. We had both been traveling submerged for several weeks. No star sightings. No positioning using identifiable landmarks. No precise sounding information. He had come from the Atlantic, and I from the Pacific, yet we both went to the exact same spot. It was quite a remarkable navigation feat.

We were making our way to the North Pole quite relaxed and well coordinated, but we were filled with excitement and could hardly wait to get there.

The day started with me trying to make myself realize that in a couple of hours we would be at the North Pole. You dream of such things as this and wait and wait for them to happen, then, when it is finally about to happen, you cannot believe it.

Our navigators exchanged positions, and there was full agreement on our exact location. When we were a couple of miles from the pole, we started watching for a large enough *polynya* to hold both of us. However, we reached the pole without either of us having any luck. About a mile beyond, we both found *polynyas* we thought would be acceptable. Joe designated his *polynya* as the one we would use and told me to stay clear until he was up and settled. He would then call for us to join him.

The *Skate* surfaced in short order and Joe called me shortly after that to report he was clear. He wanted us to surface, but not until his camera party got into position and was ready to get a movie of us coming up. I thought that was a great idea.

He called again about fifteen or twenty minutes later and told me to come on in and surface. I knew where he was from the bearing of his underwater telephone, but we did not have a good fix on his *polynya*. I headed for him and shortly started getting an idea of the lay of the land, or rather the shape of the *polynya*.

He asked me to shoot a couple of "smokes" when we got to the *polynya* so he would know where we were. "Smokes" were smoke floats launched from signal tubes located at our bow and stern. I ordered them loaded, but held off shooting them until we got there. When we were under the *polynya* but had not yet raised our periscope, I ordered them shot. We continued toward the center of the *polynya* and shot the smokes, but I was not about to surface until I got a good look all around.

Suddenly someone on the underwater telephone started shouting, "Don't come up, don't come up, the smokes have straddled us!" I could appreciate the fellow's excitement, but I was not about to come up until I knew exactly where they were. I was shooting the smokes to verify that we were in the same *polynya*.

I raised the scope to check the *polynya* and see exactly where the *Skate* was. We were still moving slowly toward the center of the *polynya* when I spotted the other sub. We were passing beneath her. I had looked up at ships before, even submerged submarines, but I was mesmerized by what I saw

Nuclear-powered submarines USS SKATE (SSN-578) and USS SEADRAGON (SSN-584) seen surfaced at North Pole after historic rendezvous under Polar ice pack.

After rendezvous procedures began, SKATE and SEADRAGON carried out submarine versus submarine operations en route, assisted by the icebreaker USS BURTON ISLAND (AGB-1) and Alaska-based Navy aircraft.

After reaching a point where underwater communications were established - first by sonar contact, then by the common or "garden variety" underwater telephones that are standard submarine equipment - the two ships proceeded together to the North Pole and surfaced together through a hole in the ice two days after beginning rendezvous procedures.

Landing parties then exchanged greetings signed by VADM Elton W. Grenfell, USN, Commander Submarine Force, U. S. Atlantic Fleet, and RADM Roy S. Benson, USN, Commander Submarine Force, U. S. Pacific Fleet (since relieved by RADM Bernard A. Clarey, USN). Members of the two crews visited each other and took "a walk around the world" at the geographic North Pole.

The President of the United States announced the submarines' Polar rendezvous at a press conference, calling it "an exceptional technical feat. "

CDR Joseph L. Skoog, Jr., USN, is in command of SKATE and was in tactical command of the combined operation during the period that the submarines were together. CDR Charles D. Summitt, USN, is in command of SEADRAGON.

through the periscope. The surface was absolutely still, not a ripple. The lighting was such that as I looked straight up into the sky there was no hint of the underside of the surface above. The *Skate* could just as easily have been a blimp flying overhead. I could see the men on deck so clearly that I could have easily identified them if I had known their names. It was an unbelievable sight. As the thought crossed my mind that I should let someone else see this amazing sight, we moved beyond the optimum angle of sunlight and the view was once more back to normal. The surface again became apparent and all I could see was the *Skate*'s hull. I would give a lot to have a photograph of that incredible sight.

We maneuvered into the best position for surfacing and soon got the word to surface. Joe's camera party shot beautiful footage of us surfacing, and I do have a cherished copy of that.

As soon as we surfaced, Joe moved the *Skate* to the edge of the ice so that we could moor bow to bow.

With the *Skate* moored in position, I maneuvered the *Seadragon* to the edge of the ice. The chief of the boat had launched a couple of inflatable life rafts that were used to ferry several crewmen onto the ice. They carried sledgehammers and steel stakes, which they drove into the ice to receive our mooring lines.

I stayed on the bridge for a while after we completed mooring, just to look

Here I am at the North Pole with Joe Skoog, captain of the USS Skate *(SSN-578), in 1962.* Seadragon *is in the background.*

NAV___S 1111 (REV. 11-54)
NAV___ARL HARBOR

SHIP'S POSITION

U. S. S. *SEADRAGON*

TO: COMMANDING OFFICER

AT (*Time of day*)		DATE	
1200		*2 Aug 1962*	

LATITUDE	LONGITUDE	DETERMINED AT
SURFACED AT	*NORTH*	*POLE*

BY (*Indicate by check in box*)

☐ CELESTIAL	☐ D. R.	☐ LORAN	☐ RADAR	☐ VISUAL

SET	DRIFT	DISTANCE MADE GOOD SINCE (*time*) (*miles*)

DISTANCE TO	MILES	ETA

TRUE HDG.	ERROR		VARIATION
°	° GYRO	° GYRO	°

MAGNETIC COMPASS HEADING (*Check one*)

☐ STD	☐ STEER-ING	☐ REMOTE IND	☐ OTHER	°

DEVIATION	1104 TABLE DEVIATION	DG: (*Indicate by check in box*)
°		☐ ON ☐ OFF

REMARKS

RESPECTFULLY SUBMITTED (*navigator*)

_____ *, LT, USN*

CC:

"Ship's Position" report, submitted by the navigator to the captain at noon each day.

around and let the knowledge soak in that we were actually at the North Pole. It was a beautiful day with a few friendly, white, fluffy clouds scattered about the sky. A few of the men went out on the ice to see what it was like, being sure to stay within sight of us. It was not as cold as I had expected it to be. A light breeze blew now and then, and the temperature hovered around freezing. There were puddles of water here and there on the ice, showing that the sun was able to melt it somewhat. To my amazement, I spotted signs of life — not polar bears, thank goodness, but small birds zipping around. They were smaller than sparrows. I have no idea what they ate.

It was late morning and I was anxious to talk to Joe about how things had gone thus far. He had invited me to join him for lunch, so I trudged on over to the *Skate*. It felt sort of strange walking the few hundred feet it took to get to a submarine that several weeks ago we had traveled several thousands of miles and across a continent to meet.

I had an enjoyable visit. We swapped tales for about an hour before eating. Following lunch, we celebrated our arrival at the pole with a special cake — baked and decorated by one of his cooks — and washed it down with Cokes, just like they were champagne.

After the brief celebration I headed back to the *Seadragon*. I found the wardroom table taken over by a couple of officers and several crewmen busily rubber-stamping envelopes. Before leaving Hawaii, a couple of the men had drawn up a cartoonlike design depicting our submarine with a dragon on deck, moored to a barber's pole at the top of the world. It bore the name "*Seadragon*" and "August 1962." Everyone liked it, so we had it copied onto a rubber stamp that we planned to use on our outgoing mail. These fellows corresponded with some men on the *Skate*, and they jointly drew up a cartoonlike representation of two dolphins tied on either side of a similar barber's pole with the legend "*Skate* and *Seadragon* at the pole, August 1962." We wanted to decorate letters to our family and friends with these two stamps as a memento of the occasion. We knew we could not mail them until we reached port, but we waited to stamp them until we were actually at the North Pole. I had personally written many letters to the commanders and officers of various navy commands that had played a part in the operation to show our appreciation. There were hundreds of letters being stamped.

A couple of hours after lunch, we performed our planned ceremony in honor of the meeting of our two submarines and their surfacing at the pole. A color guard from each sub marched across the ice and met halfway between the two boats. Then Joe Skoog, with his exec and Dr. Lyon, and I with my exec and Walt Wittman, marched out and joined our color guards. We stood there face to face, with the two submarines clearly visible in the background. Pictures taken of this event appeared in newspapers all over the United States as well as abroad. We read aloud and exchanged letters from the commanders of the Atlantic and Pacific Fleet Submarine Forces and exchanged ships' plaques commemorating the meeting. All in all, it was a very successful public relations effort.

At the conclusion of the ceremony, Joe and I were invited to have our picture taken with Santa Claus. A crewman dressed as Santa was ready to have his picture taken with all of the fathers who wanted to show their children that not only had they reached the North Pole, but they had also met with Santa. We had rented the Santa suit in Honolulu just for this purpose. Our Santa was a rather robust sailor who had weighed only eighty pounds when he was released from a Japanese prison camp at the end of World War II. No one had the heart to tell him he needed to lose weight. The picture taken of Joe and I flanking Santa, all three of us laughing, ended up in quite a few newspapers.

On our way back to the ship I told Walt Wittman I wanted to get a lump of ice to take back to my two sons. I always tried to bring them something from the many ports at which I called, but here there was nothing but ice. I set about trying to break off a chunk with my hands, but Walt insisted that I wait while he went aboard and got a special tool he had so he could get a proper chunk for me — rather than packed snow, which was all I had managed to come up with. In short order he returned with a piece of true Arctic ice weighing about ten pounds. It was most unusual. It resembled a piece of petrified wood, which has a grain to it. I had a cook wrap it in aluminum foil, mark it for me, and put it in the freezer. It was a perfect gift.

It was now time to dive and head toward Canada. I went to the bridge early as we prepared to get under way. I was bundled up well, but it was easy to sense that it was getting colder. The sky was now overcast and the wind was picking up. It was definitely becoming darker as the cloud cover increased. We were fortunate to have had sunny weather for our visit.

The exec reported that all hands were accounted for, but I asked him to have the muster taken again. I did not want there to be any chance of leaving someone behind. When he again reported that all hands were present, I felt much relieved.

The *Skate* had finished backing out to the center of the *polynya* when, just as it started to dive, it started snowing. Seeing a submarine dive straight down was a most unusual sight. It was eerie.

Joe soon reported that he was clear and called for us to come on down. I maneuvered the *Seadragon* toward the center of the *polynya*. It was snowing hard now and the wind had really picked up — a great time to dive.

We reached the desired depth in short order and took position about

Joe Skoog and I pay a visit to a local resident.

five hundred yards on his starboard beam. We were off to rendezvous with an icebreaker at the edge of the ice north of Canada, about a thousand miles away.

We encountered no problems en route to our rendezvous with the icebreaker, the USS *Burton Island* (AGB-1). It was strange to surface in the open sea once again, but we still came straight up, slowly, just in case we missed detecting any stray chunks of ice.

Joe Skoog passed the word for me and those directly involved with shooting our torpedoes to join him aboard the icebreaker in about half an hour to make detailed plans for commencing our tests the next day. A boat from the icebreaker was alongside very shortly to take us to the meeting. After climbing a rope ladder to board the icebreaker, we were escorted to the wardroom where we were to meet. We waited about ten or fifteen minutes for the captain of the icebreaker to join us. He was a bit groggy because, to our embarrassment, it was still nighttime for them. We had failed to inform him of the time we were keeping. Although he assured us it would be no problem to set his clocks to match ours, I am certain he was somewhat put out.

We selected three of the shots planned for the next day that were the simplest to execute. We then worked out all the necessary details to insure everything went smoothly, including how we would coordinate having the helicopter in the right position to spot each torpedo as it surfaced following its run, and how the launch would retrieve the torpedoes and get them aboard the icebreaker. After about an hour and a half we were satisfied that all aspects had been fully addressed and that no questions were unanswered.

The captain invited us to tour the ship and we enthusiastically accepted. I had never been aboard an icebreaker and was anxious to see what it was like and to learn how it was operated.

We were impressed with the ship's rugged construction and power. Any ship can break through ice up to the thickness commensurate with its strength and power, but an icebreaker can plow through ice that is much thicker. To my surprise, it was designed so that the bow rides up over the ice until enough weight is applied to it that the ship falls through. If the ship rides up over the ice as far as it can and fails to break through, then water held in its after tanks is pumped forward until sufficient weight is added to break the ice. Water can also be pumped from one tank to another to rock the ship and help it break through. Sometimes the ice defies all attempts to break through and the breaker must back off and try another route.

On the second day of our torpedo shooting, the captain of the icebreaker came aboard the *Seadragon* to see how we operated. He was amazed that the ice was so thick. Now he understood why he was so often thwarted in his efforts to work in the Arctic.

Walt Wittman and Dr. Waldo Lyon swapped ships that day and we learned from Dr. Lyon that his wife had accepted a gold medal for him the day before from President Kennedy in the White House. The award was "The President's Distinguished Federal Civilian Service Medal" for outstanding service to his country. This was quite an honor, and he had to miss it. Moreover, because our mission was classified, there was no mention why he was not there or where he was.

My executive officer, Lt. Comdr. Wes Harvey, received orders that day to take command of the USS *Thresher* (SSN-593), a recently built nuclear-powered attack submarine — the most modern sub in the navy. He could not have been more pleased. It was quite an honor. He had been a junior officer in the commissioning crew of the *Nautilus,* our first nuclear-powered submarine, and therefore was highly experienced. He was raring to go, but we could not release him until we arrived in Seattle.

A jovial meeting aboard Seadragon *between* Skate *captain, Joe Skoog (center), my exec, Wes Harvey, and me.*

Three days later, we successfully completed the test shots with our torpe-does. The icebreaker did a wonderful job of recovering the torpedoes and had them securely stowed on its deck for delivery to a base where they would later be opened up and have their "black boxes" removed. A careful study was to be made of their performance data, along with our plots show-ing where we were in relation to one another from the time of firing to the time that the torpedo shut down. It appeared to us that all had gone well, but their performance could not be fully evaluated without a thorough study of all the recorded data.

I had enjoyed operating with Joe Skoog and the icebreaker's captain and felt a little sad when it came time to say good-bye and go our separate ways. However, I quickly recovered. We were all anxious to get back to civilization.

We headed west toward the Bering Strait, our only exit from the Arctic, proceeding on the surface until we were well clear of the ice field. I had no desire to go back under the ice and squeeze out the same way we had en-tered. It was a rather cloudy, dreary day. Visibility was poor, but we could see far enough ahead to proceed comfortably.

I had not shaved for several days, so I went to my cabin, stripped to my waist, and applied a thick coat of shaving soap. Should the officer of the deck ever find himself in a dangerous situation requiring immediate action to avoid serious damage or disaster, he is expected to start taking action and also to call out on the general announcing system "Captain to the bridge!" or, "Captain to the conn!" I hoped never to hear such a summons, but all at once it came, "Captain to the bridge!" I could feel the ship begin to shake as we backed down full.

I darted to the bridge ladder, which was only about fifteen feet from my cabin, and raced up it for all I was worth. Halfway up I realized I was going to freeze because the only thing I was wearing above my waist was shaving soap! Thank goodness I had not been in the shower!

The officer of the deck was pointing and looking intently ahead. Sensing my arrival, he said: "I shouldn't have called for you. That is undoubtedly a big iceberg."

Somebody behind me wrapped a large jacket around my shoulders. The man had noticed me racing for the ladder, grabbed the jacket, and raced up behind me.

It was a true iceberg. It was about 150 yards across and at least a hundred feet high. The low cloud cover was just beginning to reveal its top. Chunks about the size of a refrigerator were breaking off its sides from time to time and crashing into the water below with great noise. It was awesome.

The officer of the deck explained that, when he first spotted it in the poor visibility, with its top hidden in the low-hanging clouds, he had thought it was the trunk of an atomic bomb blast like the ones we had seen so often in movies. I could easily understand what a shock it was to abruptly see such a thing.

The officer of the deck, Lt. Arnie Johnson, had reported aboard as the chief engineer well before we completed our training for this operation and had proved to be outstanding in every respect. He had done the right thing by calling me to the bridge. I needed to see this unusual iceberg and try to avoid any other large pieces that might be in the area.

We continued on ahead in order to examine it a bit closer, but then gave it a wide berth. We were not supposed to see icebergs in the Arctic. Maybe there were more. Sure enough, in the next few hours we spotted several more. It was most unusual.

The following day I was on the bridge when a lookout announced: "Something out there broad on the port bow. It's brown. Can't tell what it is." The OD responded, "Jones, can't you recognize land when you see it?" It had indeed been a long time of seeing nothing but ice.

We soon submerged and reached the Bering Strait. After passing through

THE WHITE HOUSE

WASHINGTON

5 September 1962

Dear Commander Summitt:

I have received your letter, signed jointly with
Commander Skoog, commemorating the first rendezvous
of two ships at the North Pole -- that of the USS SEADRAGON
and the USS SKATE.

I followed with great interest your progress throughout
your voyage. You have demonstrated the superb qualities
inherent in our submarines and those who man them. It
gave me great pleasure to discuss your operations at one of
my recent press conferences.

Would you extend for me my best wishes, deep
admiration, and a hearty WELL DONE to the officers and
men of the USS SEADRAGON for this memorable and historic
performance.

With every good wish.

Sincerely,

Commander C. D. Summitt, USN
Commanding Officer, USS SEADRAGON (SSN-584)
c/o Fleet Post Office
San Francisco, California

Congratulatory letter from President Kennedy.

the strait, we headed for Adak in the Aleutian chain, where we were to post all of our mail from the North Pole and pick up the officer who was to relieve Wes Harvey.

It was after suppertime when we finally reached Adak and got moored to the seawall, but there was still plenty of daylight. Adak is notorious for its extreme tidal range, and our brow tilted up sharply to reach the level of the

THE VICE PRESIDENT
WASHINGTON

September 7, 1962

Dear Commander Summitt:

Congratulations to the officers and the men of the United States Ships SEADRAGON and SKATE for their unique meeting and surfacing at the North Pole.

The spirit that carried our forefathers into the wilderness in the early days of our country was never more in evidence than it was in your truly great adventure and feat.

I deeply appreciate your letter from the North Pole and wish you well as you continue to explore the possibilities that nuclear submersibles have opened for us. Best wishes.

Sincerely

Lyndon B. Johnson

Commander C. D. Summitt, USN
Commanding Officer
USS SEADRAGON (SS(N)-584)
Care of Fleet Post Office
San Francisco, California

Congratulatory letter from Vice President Johnson.

seawall. A fire truck was standing by, ready to rig a ladder when the brow could no longer be safely used.

A boarding officer from the base offered to take me to the base commander, to make the traditional call a captain makes when arriving at a base other than the ship's home port. The officer explained that it was after office hours and I would have a hard time finding the commander's quarters without his assistance. As we drove along, he explained that we would soon pass the Adak National Forest. A few minutes later he pointed to a pine tree about as big as a Christmas tree and said, "There it is!" It was the only tree anywhere around for miles.

The base commander and his wife met me at the front door. I was a bit taken aback at how they were dressed. They were attired as though they were in a tropical climate. They must have noted my surprise, because they explained that they had just recently arrived from Hawaii and that all the belongings they had shipped had been misrouted. It would be several weeks before they would have appropriate clothing. He insisted on helping me out of my heavy navy overcoat, which he obviously admired. We appeared to be the same size.

He was aware that we expected to pick up my exec's relief and reported that the navy flight he was on was scheduled to arrive in about an hour. The commander said he had arranged to have him met and driven to his quarters to join us. I assured him that his attention to all these details was much appreciated.

I enjoyed their company. They had many questions about our operation in the Arctic. An hour came and went. Although I was thoroughly enjoying our visit, I tried to excuse myself so as to avoid taking advantage of their hospitality. He called the base operations office and discovered they had just learned that my new exec's flight would be about an hour late. He insisted that I remain until the awaited officer, Lt. Comdr. Bob Weeks, arrived. As soon as Bob showed up, we made a hasty exit. I explained that we needed to get under way if we were going to keep to our schedule.

By the time we arrived at the boat, the tide had gone out and we had to climb ten or twelve feet down the fireman's ladder to board the submarine. We got under way without incident, eventually reached deep water, dived, and commenced our transit to Seattle.

The next morning at breakfast, something jogged my memory and I remembered that I had forgotten my overcoat. I had not worn it for a couple of years prior to our Arctic cruise and easily forgot it when we left the base commander's house.

I sent word back asking him to please send it to me in Hawaii. The coat arrived a couple of months later. I guess he finally got his household goods shipment.

12

HEADING HOME

We surfaced in the early afternoon just outside the Juan de Fuca Strait. The weather was good, visibility unlimited. We had been instructed to moor in Seattle by midmorning the next day. We had a good deal of experience in arriving at specific places at specific times. My navigator never failed to make it right on the button. You could set your watch by it. Lieutenant Bill Green was outstanding at everything he did. You are always concerned that your navigator is giving you the right answer, but there was never any doubt in my mind that he could be relied upon completely. We never wanted to allow ourselves to come skidding in, preferring instead to go to a point from which we could reach our destination on time, stay out of sight, and then steam in, arriving right on the dot. We still had a long way to go; well over a hundred miles. You could never predict what you might encounter that would cause a delay.

I had not been in these waters since going to sea on

my first ship, the destroyer *Stickell,* many years before. We had to sail this route a couple of times on sea trials before we finally completed our overhaul and departed. At that time I had been impressed by the number of huge logs we encountered floating here and there. The Pacific Northwest is a great timber producing area. Much of the timber is simply floated and then towed to its next destination. A few logs break loose now and then. I suppose some effort is made to retrieve them at a later time, but until then, they are a hazard to navigation. When our destroyer first encountered some of these logs, we were greatly concerned, but our pilot said there was nothing to worry about. He continued on course at good speed while we looked on in horror. Sure enough, our bow wave rolled the logs aside as we came within inches of hitting them. He pointed out that this always worked as long as your bow did not encounter their exact center of gravity, which it never did. I would never have believed this if I had not seen it.

I had a vague recollection that something had been done during the intervening years to prevent logs from remaining adrift. Nevertheless, I informed the officer of the deck to maintain a good lookout for logs and notify me if he spotted one, no matter where it was in relation to us.

A few hours later, after we were well within the strait, I was informed that a log had been spotted. I went to the bridge to take a look. Sure enough, we could now see several more logs scattered here and there. A submarine is different from a destroyer. At the speed we desired to run, our bow was under water; in fact, water flowed freely over most of the deck forward of the bridge. We thus had to move water around in our trim tanks to insure the bow stayed dry and we produced a proper bow wave. I stayed on the bridge until we encountered a log dead ahead, then held my breath as we successfully rolled it aside. I could now relax as we proceeded on our way. It is hard to beat experience.

Several times during the night I felt it necessary to go to the bridge when we encountered heavy traffic. A submarine's running lights are often mistaken to be those of a small fishing vessel able to get quickly out of the way. Knowing this always left me feeling a bit uneasy in the presence of large ships. Sometimes I thought it advisable to turn on our signal light and illuminate our submarine enough for lookouts on the ships around us to recognize it for what it was.

The next morning, I changed into my blue uniform after breakfast in preparation for entering port. It was good that I did, because I soon received a call from the officer of the deck saying that he had spotted a small craft — possibly a pilot boat — on a course to intercept us. As it got closer, we made it out to be an admiral's barge. To my surprise, it pulled alongside so the two admirals it was carrying could board the *Seadragon.* One was the commandant of the naval district and the other the commandant of the Coast Guard district. I quickly moved to greet them and then escorted them to the wardroom, where I quickly briefed them on our Arctic operation as we continued on our way. I glanced at my watch and saw we had about twenty minutes until our scheduled arrival time. The naval district commandant suggested that I leave them and go about my duties. The exec took over and gave them a brief tour of the boat, explaining the purpose of the various items of ice equipment they encountered. I made my way to the bridge and saw that we were about ready to make the final turn into our berth. We were right on schedule.

After completing the turn, I could see lots of people waiting to greet us. A platform large enough to hold a couple of dozen people had been erected and on it were our squadron commander from Hawaii, several local navy officers, a handful of civilians I did not recognize, some of our wives, and, last but not least, Joe Skoog! A band off to the side of the platform was playing loudly. It was quite a welcome.

A couple of men from the city and the World's Fair Committee gave welcoming speeches. The last speaker announced that Joe and I were to report to a nearby building for a meeting with the press. While en route to our media meeting, the COMSUBPAC public relations officer briefed us on the many things we were scheduled to do over the next three or four days and handed each of us an itinerary. Joe and I were amazed at how busy we would be. One event was a real shocker: We were to be flown to Los Angeles with our wives to appear on *Who in the World?* — a television show hosted by Warren Hull. We would remain overnight and return to Seattle the next day, all expenses paid.

The press meeting was held in a large conference room holding about a dozen reporters and six or eight cameramen. All seemed to go well. About an hour later we were whisked off to lunch.

It was midafternoon before we finally checked in at the hotel booked for us. The phone rang almost immediately. It was my sister in Alabama; she was very upset that I had not yet called my mother. She said President Kennedy had announced the successful completion of our Arctic operation several days before, then demanded, "Why haven't you called your mother before now?" I assured her I would call right away. As I hung up, I wondered how she had managed to locate me. I never did find out.

While placing the call to my mother, I recalled one of the most memorable spankings I had ever gotten. I was about six years old at the time and had gone with a couple of buddies to a school about two blocks away to play in the gym, which had been left unlocked. She had told me very emphatically that I was never to stray from home without her permission. When she answered the phone, I started by apologizing for not having asked her for permission to go to the North Pole. She assured me that I was forgiven and that she had known I would call her as soon as I could.

The following four or five days were packed with receptions, interviews, dinners, television appearances, and our trip to Hollywood. It was a wonderful time for all of us. As I mentioned earlier, it was most unusual for a nuclear-powered submarine to visit a large, nonmilitary port, and we were making the most of it.

I went to bed on our last night in Seattle knowing that a life like this could not last forever. It was time we got back to sea and headed for home.

We got under way again the next day. Our stay in Seattle had been enjoyable, but I think all of us were pleased to be heading for our home base in Pearl Harbor. I know I had been looking forward to the quiet, submerged transit. It meant getting five or six days of much-needed rest and having time to think about what we would be doing next.

I remained on the bridge until we were far enough from Seattle that traffic had died down. We had to remain on the surface — steaming the length of the Puget Sound and then passing through the Juan de Fuca Strait, about 120 miles overall — until we reached our diving point. It would take at least eight to ten hours.

Satisfied that everything was under control, I went below to the wardroom for a cup of coffee. I enjoyed chatting with several of the officers as they caught a few moments of relaxation, hearing some of their tales of the visit and also learning about the minor problems on which they were working. Although I resisted a strong urge to lie down and take a nap, I did retreat to my small stateroom to work through the hefty stack of mail and messages that had been accumulating. Throughout our stay in port, the exec had seen to it that I immediately saw anything that required my immediate attention. However, he had not troubled me with things that could be addressed later. I was pleasantly surprised at the number of congratulatory messages and letters — some official, some personal — we had received. Some of the letters and messages would require careful attention and maybe a response. I carefully put these aside to work on before we reached port. The rest was the normal administrative mail all units received to guide their policy making and planning. Again I felt the temptation to lie down on my bunk and again I resisted it. I wanted to be up and about until we were finally submerged and settled in on our long transit. Only then could I fully relax and get some good sleep.

Late that afternoon we passed Whidbey Island Naval Air Station, which was just to the north of us. During our stay in Seattle, the operations officer had contacted navy facilities in the area to offer whatever services we could provide during our transit back to Hawaii. It was customary for submarines to offer to help various facilities with their training effort. Submarine services were hard to come by and we all wanted to do what we could to increase overall navy readiness. The air station at Whidbey Island was the only installation to express a desire to participate. We had provided a position and time for a rendezvous that evening with one of their patrol bombers. Once the rendezvous was completed, we would submerge and the patrol craft would try to track us until it had to return to base. It was a very simple procedure for us. All we had to do was wait for them to report they had us on their screens and then we would take off submerged, without any further communication necessary.

It was dark as we approached our rendezvous and diving point. I went to the bridge to have a look at the weather. The sky was completely overcast and the sea was much rougher than normal. The wind was strong and undoubtedly the sea was to become even rougher. Waves washed over our deck and spray and splashes were hitting the bridge at the very top of the sail. It was a pretty bad night. Once we dived, we would go down a couple of hundred feet and move ahead swiftly and quietly. We could make more speed submerged than on the surface because we were designed to operate best when submerged. The diesel-electric boats of World War II were just the opposite. They had been designed to attain their best speed on the surface, running on their diesel engines, so they could skirt ahead of the ships they desired to attack and then come in submerged. The diesel engines were also required for long transits because their batteries could not carry them for long distances. Nuclear power gave us almost unlimited endurance, so we operated submerged practically all of the time.

I looked around us one more time and then went back below to relax while waiting for the rendezvous. The patrol plane arrived right on time as we reached the rendezvous point. They reported they had us, wished us well, and down we went. In no time at all we were at the ordered depth, in good trim, and moving at full speed. All pitching, rolling, and rocking had ceased. It was good to be submerged again.

We had been down for ten or fifteen minutes and I was having a final cup of coffee before turning in for the night when the communications officer came to me with a problem. He reported that we had received an incomplete message from COMSUBPAC just prior to submerging. It was a report stating that there was another submerged submarine entering our area and that one of us was to surface immediately. Unfortunately, the line specifying which submarine was supposed to surface had been left out. The message was encoded, so the omission had not been discovered until we were submerged. There was nothing we could do but immediately surface until we could determine who was to continue running submerged.

I went to the control room right away, ordered a reduction in speed and depth and assumed the conn. Sonar had no contacts in the area, so we went to periscope depth. I made a quick but careful sweep all around with the periscope as soon as it cleared the surface. There was nothing in sight — at least no ship lights were visible — so I ordered, "Prepare to surface." I then radioed the patrol bomber that we were going to have to surface for a brief period. "That's okay," he responded. "I've got problems of my own." He sounded somewhat worried, so I did not bother him with an explanation of our problem. I immediately commenced another search all around — this time more slowly — just to make sure I had not missed anything. A moment later I was shocked to see a light on a ship. The light was so clear that I was amazed that I had missed it the first time around. I was really upset that I had been so careless. At least it was not heading toward us. Instead it was passing across my line of sight, moving very fast. I was dumbfounded. It was moving faster than any ship or boat I had ever seen. How could it be making so much speed in this heavy sea? The sea was too rough for a hydrofoil, which can move fast, but not in this sea. Suddenly the light went out. Then the thought hit me: Maybe I had just seen the last few seconds of our patrol bomber making an emergency landing.

"Mark this bearing," I ordered. The diving officer reported that we were prepared to surface. "Surface!" I ordered. Up we started. I passed the word on the general announcing system that I might have just seen the patrol plane crash and that we would head down the last bearing to see if that was true. I asked the exec to assemble a rescue team and stand by. Up to the bridge I went. We were now headed down the last bearing to the light. The officer of the deck, the two lookouts, and I were searching ahead with our binoculars, trying to pick out something in the very dark night. Our surface search radar would easily have detected the object of our search, but its antenna had been removed and a special sonar head substituted for our trip to the Arctic. We had no radar.

The officer of the deck, Lt. (j.g.) Tom Meinicke, was the youngest officer aboard, but I had faith in his seeing the plane if anybody could. He was a most capable young man who, I felt sure, would have an outstanding career. After a few moments, Meinicke said he thought he could make out the sail of a submarine up ahead. I had the disquieting thought that maybe I had been a fool to jump up and race toward the submarine we were trying to avoid. Then I caught a glimpse of something, but it looked to me like the tail of the patrol bomber.

Slightly to the right of where we were looking we saw the trail of a small rocket race toward the sky and explode, leaving a parachute flare overhead that clearly lit up a big Martin P5M Marlin sitting in the water and a yellow life raft overloaded with men!

On seeing the plane and the life raft, I immediately ordered, "All stop." However, we continued coasting ahead. The raft had been blown about a hundred yards to the right of the plane, so I started twisting to get us as close as I dared to the raft and yet remain clear of the airplane. I ordered the rescue team on deck. The quartermaster had brought up our signal light, which could also be used as a spotlight. He kept it trained on the raft because the flare had burned out and we needed to keep a careful watch on its location.

I called out to the men in the life raft with an electric handheld bullhorn. The men on the raft said that all of the crewmen were out of the plane and on the raft. Learning this relieved me greatly since we would have a good chance of saving everyone. A quick look at the plane with the signal light showed that we were clear of it and that it was slowly sinking. I was right where I wanted to be to rescue the men, the problem would be avoiding getting tangled up with the sinking aircraft wreckage. Our swimmer, Motor Machinist 1st Class E. P. Quick, was now on deck and ready to go. I signaled for him to go in and get hold of the raft. We had a long heaving line tied to Quick so that we could haul him and the raft to the submarine. His long swim fins propelled him toward the raft like a well-oiled machine. He had not taken time to put on a wet suit and I wondered how he was able to stand being in that cold water. He was quite a man. Without his amazing performance we would probably have lost several of those flyers.

The sea was so high that waves were breaking across our deck. From time to time one of the half dozen or so men working on the deck would be swept off his feet. Each man wore a safety belt and chain attached to a track in the deck, so there was no danger of the fallen men being swept overboard.

When the raft had been pulled to within about twenty feet of the submarine I had them hold it where it was. I then used the bullhorn to explain to the men on the raft just how we planned to bring them aboard. From their short distance away they could clearly see the waves sweeping across the deck and how the submarine would ride up on the crest of a wave and then fall down into the trough. They readily understood that we had to keep the raft from touching the rounded hull to prevent it from being flipped over, dumping all of them into the sea. If that happened it would be most difficult to round them up individually.

I had the feeling that I had been here before. In my earlier days I had spent many boring hours on watch in the middle of the night passing the time by thinking of various disasters at sea and how a submarine could best

Three navy P5M Marlins. The crew that crash-landed near Seadragon *during our return trip to Honolulu had been flying aircraft like these.*

rescue the survivors. Imagining how to go about rescuing passengers from a downed commercial airliner was one of my favorite problems to think out.

In this case we had thirteen men in a seven-man life raft. Several were in the water, clinging to the raft. I instructed them to decide who would be the first to be taken off the raft and for the rest of them to remain in place. The designated man was to hold up his hand so we could see whom we would get.

We then started hauling in the line. As the water rose on the rounded hull, the men on deck pulled the raft closer and closer. When the wave crested, the man being rescued was told to jump and two of the men standing on the deck grabbed him and held him steady while the raft fell away, pushed clear of the rounded hull by Motor Machinist Quick. The two men then escorted the airman to a door in the side of the sail where he was met and taken below by others.

After a couple of more cycles by the waves we repeated the effort. From time to time I had the light swing around to look at the plane and make sure we were still clear. It was going to go down pretty shortly.

All was going quite well. The plane was ready to go under as we retrieved the last man. As soon as he was aboard, we secured the water soaked men on deck so they could get below and get warm and dry. Before going below the chief of the boat cut holes in the raft and pushed it over the side to sink.

I was most pleased with the outstanding leadership and duty performance displayed by our chief of the boat, Chief Torpedoman Phillip Le Clair. He oversaw all that went on down on the deck that night and never missed a trick. As the senior enlisted man, he was invaluable in keeping our crew headed in the right direction and working together smoothly. We were lucky to have him aboard.

At one point a terrific explosion that undoubtedly came from the sunken aircraft surprised me. The exec called up to the bridge to report that one of the pilots said the explosion had, in all probability, been the practice depth charges the plane carried to mark its attacks on us. Each was set to go off at a specific depth and they must have all gone off at the same time. It had been a thunderous explosion and I was much relieved to learn we had received no obvious damage.

I agreed with the exec regarding reporting to the P5M's base that we had found the crew, had them all aboard, and were returning to off-load them at some suitable port. The base was surprised to learn that there had been a problem. We informed our operational commander of what had happened and asked for his concurrence regarding our going back to a designated port to off-load the airmen. We shortly heard back that we were cleared to go to Port Angeles, located on the northern end of the Olympic Peninsula in the Juan de Fuca Strait. We had to proceed on the surface and it was going to be the wee hours of the morning before we got there. The air station planned to pick up the crewmen at around nine the next morning. It was going to be a long night.

Our new exec, Lt. Comdr. Bob Weeks, had been a tremendous help taking care of all the communications and arrangements we needed to make while I was busy on the bridge. It was as though we had been working together for years, because not only did he do everything we needed to do, he did it the way I wanted things done. He simply kept me informed of what he was doing and did not bother me with questions. He continued doing an outstanding job throughout my tour of duty.

I checked around to see how our newly arrived guests were faring. No one had been hurt, thank goodness. The doctor had administered brandy to each airman and member of our rescue team. The cook had been busy putting out good hot food. The aviators had removed their clothes and hung them all over the place to dry. Some of them wore clothes furnished by members of the crew; others were wrapped in blankets.

The happy crew of the navy P5M Marlin at Port Angeles, located on the northern end of the Olympic Peninsula in the Juan de Fuca Strait.

Bit by bit I learned what had happened. They had developed engine trouble, such that they could not remain in the air. Unable to see how the sea was running, they could only hope that they landed in the best direction possible. Apparently they had not, as the plane's hull had been badly damaged. They had two life rafts, but only one was accessible in the wrecked aircraft. After getting the single raft clear of the plane, they saw our running lights headed toward them. At first they thought we were going to run over them. They thought the lights were from a small ship and were truly surprised when they saw us. They had not been able to get off a "May Day" message before the crash landing and were truly concerned that no help would come. It was going to be tough to survive in the terrible weather and cold water. I told them about the incomplete message that had forced us to the surface just in time to see their lights. That incomplete message had been a lifesaver, because it turned out that ours was the sub that was supposed to remain submerged.

Entering a strange port in the dark of the night sort of makes you stay on your toes. When we were at last moored alongside our assigned pier, I dived for my bunk. I left a wake-up call for eight o'clock and it seemed like I had barely closed my eyes when I had to get up.

The squadron commander and a couple of other officers arrived on time to pick up the crew. We invited them to the wardroom for coffee and chatted about the events of the previous night. After giving the newcomers a quick tour of the submarine, we went topside in time to witness a group picture being taken of the P5M crew on the pier with the submarine in the background, just as they had requested. After many farewell handshakes, they all loaded on the navy bus the squadron commander had brought and off they went. We wasted no time in getting under way.

After clearing Port Angeles, I remained on the bridge to enjoy a bright, sunny morning. The sea was still rough, but the heavy wind had subsided quite a bit. As I drank my coffee, I could not help but think back to the time we observed the explosion of another navy patrol bomber ten years earlier. However, when we reached that plane's crash site, we found everyone dead. Being able to rescue this crew had given everyone an almost indescribable feeling of satisfaction. I could not help thinking that someone up above had caused us to surface when we did and made me look in the direction that I did. If we had not surfaced when we did, or I had been looking in another direction, I would not have seen that light speeding across the water's surface and the P5M crew would have been lost.

Our long submerged transit from the West Coast to Hawaii was quiet and relaxed. All of us caught up on our rest and took care of the many tasks we had put off until a quiet time. Our paperwork was done, everything was neat and sparkling clean, and we were all anxious to get home.

We had to surface to avoid passing through any active operational areas near the island of Oahu. In a matter of a few hours we would be moored at the submarine base in Pearl Harbor. I had gone to the bridge to spend a little time enjoying the beautiful weather. The sea was rather calm. I could see Diamond Head in the distance. I wondered if any of those who had explored the Arctic in ages past were looking down on us, scoffing at how easy it had been for us to do all that we had done as opposed to the horrible hardships they had endured, or thinking how strange it was that anyone would leave for the North Pole from Hawaii, of all places!

I recalled how excited I had been to leave. I had been given the chance to go to the North Pole and I could hardly wait to get going. Having done it, I

Seadragon *being welcomed by sailboats, fireboats, and aircraft as we pass close to the beach at Waikiki.*

now had no desire to return. If I *had* to do it again, I certainly would — but not with the same exhilaration.

It was going to be good to get home. I expected to see a good turnout of families and friends to greet us at the pier. Almost all of us would have someone there to greet us. I felt sorry for those crewmen I knew would have no one waiting to meet them.

We had already received our mooring time and once again would try to hit it right on the dot. The navigator came to the bridge to show me a message we had just received asking us to pass as close as we could to Waikiki Beach so people could get a good look at us. A tuna boat had run aground just offshore about a year ago and was still sitting there because it could not be pulled free. I sure did not want *Seadragon* to become a national monument. I told the navigator the minimum depth of water I would accept, and he departed to lay down a recommended track. I was blessed with having excellent officers and men. I knew he would do a good job.

View of the USS Seadragon *passing Hospital Point as we proceed to the submarine base.*

We had left Hawaii on July 12, 1962. It was now September 14. We had been gone two months. The majority of that time, about six weeks, had been spent in the Arctic, under the ice. We had traveled almost five thousand miles under the ice during that time.

A small private plane approached at low altitude. It circled overhead several times and we could see someone waving. The homecoming festivities had already started.

Enough of this lazy basking in the sun. It was time to go below and change into the uniform for entering port: tropical short-sleeved whites. We had to look our best.

I got back to the bridge in short order and set the maneuvering watch for entering port a bit earlier than normal because I wanted my most select group at the controls when we passed close to the beach.

We had started on the first leg of our pass in review off the beach when a

Being welcomed by the Commander-in-Chief Pacific Fleet Admiral Sides, Commander Submarine Force Pacific Fleet Rear Admiral Cleary, and Mayor Blaisdel of Honolulu.

navy helicopter flew alongside and hovered close to the water, just about eye level with the bridge. The large side door slid open and we clearly saw a navy photographer inside taking pictures. Various ships started closing on us from different directions. A couple of formations of navy planes showed up and made welcoming passes low overhead. Some of the vessels approaching us were fireboats and started spraying water high into the air. It was a most unusual homecoming.

Before we completed our run along the beach, the fireboats took up position behind us and stayed with us through the channel into Pearl Harbor. About halfway up the channel to our berth at the sub base, a boat came alongside and passed us a huge lei made of fresh flowers that was at least ten feet in diameter. The message accompanying it said that it had been made by the wives of the crew and asked that we hang it over the forward part of the sail, the same way you would place a lei on the shoulders of someone be-

Following an old tradition, here I am accepting a gallon of ice cream for each of the naval aviators we rescued when the P5M Marlin went down near us.

ing welcomed to the island. Amazing! We did as directed and instantly became the prettiest submarine in the fleet!

As we cleared the final bend in the channel our berth came into view: a navy band was there, playing rousing music as a cheering crowd of people waved at us wildly. When we got closer, I could make out my family and quite a few friends amidst the throng. I was rather surprised to see so many dignitaries: the commander in chief of the Pacific Fleet; the commander of the Submarine Force, Pacific Fleet; my squadron and division commanders; and many more, including the mayor of Honolulu. What a welcome!

I made my way ashore as quickly as we got the brow across and, after many salutes and handshakes, finally reached my family. A public address system had been set up for the various distinguished visitors to offer their congratulations and welcome us home. The mayor called me forward and presented me with a beautiful wooden salad bowl for the ship. It bore an engraved silver plate that said the gift was from the city to the *Seadragon* for her historic venture.

When the squadron commander got to the mike, he invited everyone to enjoy a piece of the big cake displayed on a nearby table, commemorating our safe return from a historic mission. All of us were overwhelmed and most appreciative of this wonderful, surprising welcome.

I was just finishing my cake when my navy aviator friend on the Submarine Force staff, came up and said, "Come with me, I have something for you." I had no idea what he was talking about. He led me toward the *Seadragon* and stopped by a heavy-duty, four-wheeled, pushcart stacked with five-gallon containers of ice cream. "Here, this is what we navy flyers owe *Seadragon* for bringing that downed aircrew back to port." He had a photographer there to take a picture of us shaking hands with the load of ice cream and the *Seadragon* in the background.

Our homecoming was full of surprises. I had forgotten the tradition naval aviators had of giving five gallons of ice cream to a ship for each flyer it pulls from the sea. We now had enough ice cream to last us several months.

As I set about getting the ice cream loaded into our freezer, I recalled the chunk of polar ice that I had brought back for my sons. I had it brought to me, found the boys, and made my presentation. They seemed pleased to get it and proudly showed it around to all who cared to see it. There were things I had to do before I could go home, so the boys found a ride back to our quarters and put it in our freezer.

Liberty commenced and those crewmen who were not on duty departed with their friends and families. The crowd started melting away and I got busy completing what I had to do. As soon as I finished, I headed home to try to get caught up on all that had happened while I was gone and to try to get acquainted with home life once more.

13

FINAL DAYS ABOARD *SEADRAGON*

We were in upkeep for the first two weeks following our
return from the Arctic. This gave us time to perform
corrective and preventive maintenance, reload stores
and supplies, transfer and receive personnel, and spend
some time with our families.

Shortly before departing on our polar operation I
was promoted to commander. I had been so wrapped
up in preparing for the mission that I had not had time
to reflect that I had reached the advanced age that came
with gaining that status, but I sure liked the looks of that
third gold stripe and the scrambled eggs on the bill of
my cap — not to mention the pay increase.

One day, I received a phone call from my former
skipper on the *Sargo,* now on duty in the Pentagon with
the submarine staff, congratulating me on our successful operation. Toward the end of his call he asked if I
thought I was going to like my duty in Washington. I
told him I had no idea what he was talking about and he

expressed surprise that I had not already been informed of my new assignment. I finally got him to explain what was going on: orders had been cut for me to go work for Admiral Rickover. I felt as though someone had turned off the lights. I was dumbfounded. I had never entertained any thoughts about leaving the *Seadragon*. Being captain of a submarine as good as the *Seadragon* had always been my dream; I never thought of doing anything else.

After we hung up, I sat there trying to regain control of my thoughts. How naïve of me! Command tours did not last forever. Of course I would have to move on. Had I given more thought to planning my future, I would have asked for another sea assignment, not shore duty — and certainly not working for Admiral Rickover. I really did not consider myself suited for such an assignment. My days aboard the *Seadragon* were obviously numbered. Figuring I had better enjoy them while I could, I turned my attention to making the most of every minute I had left. I had no idea when I would have to leave, but the day surely could not be too far off.

Our published operation schedule covering the rest of the year showed only operations near Hawaii, no long deployments. We would be involved primarily in exercises designed to benefit ships en route from the states to the western Pacific. They generally spent a week or two conducting realistic training exercises with locally based ships and aircraft as they passed through Hawaiian waters. A good portion of the effort was devoted to antisubmarine problems, with us generally cast in the bad-guy role. We enjoyed the work because it gave us an opportunity to try out new techniques for penetrating a formation and attacking the major targets.

Nuclear power significantly enhanced our capabilities. We could maintain high speed indefinitely and there was no need to worry about refueling because our nuclear fuel was good for about twelve years. We no longer had to surface or snorkel to charge our batteries and refresh our air supply. We could survive submerged for months. Our most significant limitation was the amount of food we could carry: the boats were designed to carry a three-month supply.

Now we could chase after ships rather than take up a position and hope they came to us. Generally, destroyers involved in antisubmarine warfare were placed ahead of the larger ships needing protection. With nuclear power, we could sometimes approach from behind. However, we generally approached from ahead, coming in at high speed. By the time the destroyers were able to obtain a second sonar echo on us, we had moved so far from the initial echo point that the second echo could not be correlated to the first. After successfully penetrating the screen, we would then go for the main target, swinging in to follow a short distance behind it. The sonar scope at the conning station would show a solid spoke caused by the noise of the propellers of the target ahead of us. As we drew closer, the spoke would broaden and finally break into individual spokes for each propeller. As we continued to close, the spokes would fan out. By adjusting our speed, we could cause the spokes to stop fanning out and stay steady, which meant that our speed exactly matched that of our target. We now had our fire-control (shooting) problem solved. The target's course was our course, its speed was our speed, and its range was zero. All that was left to do was pull off to an acceptable distance on his beam and fire back at him. The ships preparing to go to the western Pacific needed such demonstrations to make them aware of what they could be facing if they had to tangle with Russian nuclear submarines.

One of the exercises we were involved in was rather advanced and quite lengthy. A day or two after its completion, all of the participants assembled in a theater for a review of who had done what and how it all turned out. About midway through the training staff's presentation of graphs, charts, plot projections, and the like, the commanding officer of the aircraft carrier we had been tracking rose to his feet, interrupted the presentation, and raised a big stink about the submarine never coming close to them. "Why involve a nuclear-powered submarine that doesn't dare mixing it up?" he demanded. He continued on in this manner. I was just getting ready to interrupt him when a member of the staff projected a plot of where the task force had sailed during the entire exercise. They then superimposed the *Seadragon*'s track, which showed us right with them the entire time. The skipper said no more and sat down.

On one occasion we had to transit a good distance from one exercise group to another. Late that evening, as we were steaming along submerged, I took a walk through the boat to see how things looked and what, if anything, was going on. I did not get a chance to do this often, but I liked to visit with the men and see what they had to say. In the control room, the diving officer and his team had things well in hand. I struck up a conversation with the quartermaster of the watch, First Class Petty Officer Robertson. "Robby," as his buddies called him, had been in submarines since World War II and was a true and valuable professional. He had a warm personality and was well liked by all. He had only a short time left on the *Seadragon* because he was going to retire in a couple of years and wanted his last assignment to be with a reserve unit near his permanent home. We got to talking about his next assignment and he explained that he was really looking forward to the relatively calm, steady routine of a reserve unit that never moved. He said he was going to place a row of stones bordering a flowerbed on either side of the brow leading to the reserve submarine and then whitewash each stone to give it a "homey" look. We chuckled about that and then got on the subject of how submarines were changing. As an example, an electronic depth meter with a digital readout now monitored our depth, replacing the big depth gauge with an arrow that swung around and pointed at a fixed number. We were both concerned that the depth being reported was the true depth and that the mysterious electronic gadget had not developed an unknown electrical fault. Both of us found it difficult to accept the reading presented by the electronic depth meter. He showed me a steel support strap behind the nearby torpedo-data computer, which would bend as the submarine moved deeper in the water. The hull of a submarine actually compresses the deeper it goes. Subs are designed to insure this compression produces no undesirable results, such as buckling decks. The decks are supported by brackets that slide in and out so that the decks never actually touch the hull. Anyway, he had a habit of looking at this strap to see if the amount it bent coincided with the reading on the digital depth meter. I became fascinated with the possibility of calibrating the strap so that we could use it to determine our depth. Robby taped a piece of broom straw to the strap and placed a strip of masking tape on the piece of equipment immediately adjacent to the strap. He then marked the location of the broom straw on the tape and labeled it with our present depth. I had the diving officer change depth up and down until we had marked the tape at hundred-foot intervals. For the rest of that exercise, whenever I gave Robby the signal, he would look at our homemade gauge and give me a thumbs-up to affirm that the digital system's reading matched that of our jury-rigged gauge.

Later, after Robby shipped out on his terminal assignment, one of my neighbors came by to say that he had just returned from a trip to Texas. He said that while he was there he had visited a reserve submarine and met one of my former sailors. The man told my neighbor his name was Robertson and begged to be remembered to me. The neighbor added that he had seen something he thought was most unusual: the sub had whitewashed rocks bordering flowerbeds on both sides of its gangway.

Operating around Hawaii permitted us to be at home most weekends, so we had many opportunities to enjoy the social life. There were a number of receptions, dinners, and parties for us to attend. One weekend, my wife reported that she had met an attractive lady about her age at a tea given by the fleet commander's wife. The woman's husband was a musician and she told my wife they were both interested in touring a submarine. I arranged to accommodate them that Sunday. Later, she called to ask if the houseguest they were expecting might join them. Of course, I agreed. On Sunday we met the musician and his wife at the main gate. Their houseguest, it turned out, had been unable to make it to Hawaii. They were a delightful couple, and after a good tour of the *Seadragon* (excluding the nuclear-power section) we settled around a table in the wardroom for a cup of coffee. During our conversation, it came to light that the missing houseguest was movie-star Ava Gardner. I almost fell out of my chair. I had missed a chance to become the most envied sailor in port.

I was really out of touch with the entertainment world, being at sea most of the time. Our guests were Martin Denny and his wife, June. Martin Denny was very well known for his most unusual island music. He performed in Las Vegas during the busy season and retreated to their home on Diamond Head during the off-season.

We were invited to their home a couple of times and met many of their friends. I never did meet Ava Gardner, but I did get to meet Jon Hall, a retired movie actor, and Bob Crosby, who led an orchestra known as "The Bobcats" and was the brother of Bing Crosby.

It was nice to have a bit of social life.

The time for us to pull up stakes and head for Washington arrived much too quickly. My relief, Lt. Comdr. Doug Guthe, whom I knew well, arrived about five days ahead of my scheduled relief of command. We spent a few days at sea demonstrating the *Seadragon*'s capabilities, permitting him to get acquainted, and briefing him on upcoming operations.

The day after the change of command ceremony, the family and I would sail for San Francisco aboard the luxury liner *Lurline.* Our car would be carried aboard the ship, so we could immediately start our trek across country.

The *Lurline,* like many U.S.-flagged merchant ships, received certain benefits from the federal government to insure they would be fit to be taken over by the navy in wartime. The arrangement required them to carry a limited number of military persons and their families during peacetime. I was lucky enough to draw one of those passages for my family.

The day before the change of command was our move-out day. We would carry only the clothes we needed for the trip to Washington. A small air shipment would carry additional clothes and things that we needed to have to survive before moving into our new home on the other end. Everything else would be sent by ship. Our last two nights in Hawaii would be spent at the Royal Hawaiian Hotel.

The movers were doing an excellent job packing our household goods. Suddenly, I remembered the piece of Arctic ice in our freezer. What was I going to do with it? I wanted to dispose of it in a manner befitting a piece of celebrity ice, so I put it in a cooler and took it to the hotel.

The *Seadragon*'s officers and their wives gave us a great going-away dinner party that night. At the change of command ceremony the next day we

Relief of Command ceremony, while a crane operator continues the work of installing on Seadragon *newly designed propellors.*

all regretted having had such a big time the night before, but we made it through the ceremony successfully. Immediately following the change of command, my wife and I hosted a party at the Officers' Club for all our friends. We finally made it back to the hotel and spent the rest of the afternoon enjoying our last day at Waikiki Beach.

We boarded the *Lurline* an hour or two early the next day so we could get set up to entertain those who came down to see us off. Everyone looked forward to a friend sailing on the *Lurline* so they could come aboard for the final sendoff. When our luggage was taken to our stateroom, I asked one of the stewards to please take my ice cooler and put it in the ship's freezer. He told me that there was no need to bring ice aboard because they had tons of it. I told him that the cooler held a very special chunk of ice that I wanted to keep. I suppose he thought I was nuts.

As expected, a good-sized crowd showed up to see us off. I hated having to leave all of the people we had come to enjoy so much. Most of us tossed coins to the Hawaiian kids in the water alongside the ship. It was a tradition. They were good at recovering them.

Here I am with Lt. Comdr. Doug Guthe, who has just relieved me of command of USS Seadragon.

"All ashore, going ashore," rang out time and again, and our friends disembarked and stood on the pier to wave good-bye. We slowly pulled out.

This was going to be five days of absolute bliss. I was a bona fide passenger, no duties to perform, just relax and enjoy life. The water was gorgeous, and it did not take long to get acquainted with a number of other passengers because there were so many activities.

My oldest son's twelfth birthday was on the second day out. I finally saw a way to dispose of our Arctic ice. We threw a birthday party and invited all of the kids on board. We put the block of ice in a big punchbowl and filled it with Cokes. Salt water does not freeze, so it was safe for them to drink. It was a fitting end for our treasured chunk of ice.

The marvelous voyage finally came to an end. We loaded up our car and headed for Disneyland. We spent two days there having a great time. I rode almost all of the rides that my two boys took. When we left, I figured I had spent enough to make me a part owner of Disneyland.

It was a long, long drive, going from the West Coast to the East Coast. We broke the journey at about the midway point and visited our families in Mississippi and Tennessee.

We arrived in Washington, D.C., a couple of days ahead of my reporting date. Our friends Pat and Nick Nicholson (he had been my skipper on the *Sargo*) invited us to stay with them while we found a place to rent.

A few days later we rented a house in nearby Alexandria. Our air shipment had arrived, but the sea shipment to California, which included all of our furniture, was blocked by a dock strike and was now headed for the Panama Canal. It would be many weeks before it arrived.

I went to a nearby army post and managed to borrow four cots, a card table, and four folding chairs. It was like camping out, but in order to preserve our friendship with the Nicholsons, we needed to be on our own. Life in the military can be truly unusual.

14

WORKING AT NAVAL REACTORS

At last the day came for me to report for duty at Naval Reactors (NR). There was a bus stop about three blocks from my house, where I caught a bus that took me right to the front door of the main navy building. From my past days of study there, I was well acquainted with how to get to the office. Dressed in a civilian suit and tie (they never wore uniforms at NR), I presented myself to Capt. Jack Crawford, for whom I would be working. There was no organization chart, no job descriptions, and no titles, but I knew how things worked: Crawford would be my boss; he in turn answered to Admiral Rickover. It was good to see him again. I greatly admired, respected, and liked him.

After we exchanged a few words, he said that the admiral wanted to see me. Off we went. As we were admitted to the admiral's office, I was surprised at the warm greeting I received. Rickover looked up from his desk, pushed his chair back and stood up, walked over to where Crawford and I were standing, shook my hand, and invited us to sit at a table. I had not expected to be treated so civilly. He asked where I was living and if the family and I were settled. I mentioned that our household goods were on their way through the Panama Canal. He turned to Jack Crawford and asked a question. When Jack responded, all hell broke loose. They lunged out of their seats and stood there pounding on the table and yelling loud enough to be heard a block away. I had jumped to my feet when they did. I thought about making a break for the door, but my way was blocked. Then the two of them started moving toward the door, still yelling and hollering. I edged around them, finally got the door open, and Jack and I left.

As we walked down the hall, I shook my head and mumbled something. I was sure Jack would get his walking papers before noon. There was no way his career could survive an outburst like the one I had just witnessed. I am not sure just what I had said, but Jack could tell I was concerned for him. "Don't worry," he said, laughing. "We do that all the time." I could not help but dwell on the fact that I had only been in the building about fifteen minutes and that I could expect at least two more years of this.

After exchanging a few more pleasantries with Jack, I headed for Comdr. Frank Adams's nearby office. It would become my office when I relieved Frank at the end of the week. It was a small, partitioned space with no door in a large room with windows overlooking the Reflecting Pool in front of the Lincoln Memorial. Frank's desk was pushed up against the partition with a long table and two mismatched chairs between it and the window. The only other thing in the office was the phone on Frank's desk. That was it; no pictures, no curtains — only a few patches in the old linoleum floor.

Frank chuckled as I told him about my call on the admiral with Jack Crawford. "There will be lots of 'pleasant' episodes like that," he said. "You'll get used to it."

He briefly reviewed with me the things he wanted to cover in detail, the people he wanted to introduce me to, and the various places in the Pentagon and the Navy Annex he wanted to take me so I would know how to get there and where to go to find various people. He explained that although there were certain areas involving personnel selection, training, examining, and assignments with which I would always be involved, there was no telling what other tasks I might be given. After several days of this, satisfied that he had done all he could to acquaint me fully with the job, I relieved him. He floated out the door, smiling all the way.

At this point we were about midway through the program of building forty-one huge Polaris missile-launching submarines for our unique and powerful deterrent fleet. It was imperative to get this force fully operational

The launching of a Polaris-class submarine. Eventually there would be forty-one of these in the U.S. fleet.

at the earliest date. The effort was truly amazing. We were completing and sending one of these huge submarines to sea every month! Providing trained crews for these submarines was an almost impossible task, but we were doing it. What made it especially difficult was that our regular submarine fleet was to be maintained at its regular level, so it was not merely a matter of decommissioning regular submarines and sending their crewmen to the Polaris submarines.

Each Polaris submarine was to have two complete crews: one the "Blue" crew, and the other the "Gold" crew. They were to take turns taking a particular submarine out on patrol. This kept the submarines out on patrol for the greatest number of days possible. Each crew received some time off after spending (typically) two months completely submerged.

The normal crew size was to be 12 officers and about 116 enlisted, for a total of 128. As each sub had two crews, this meant that we needed 24 officers and 232 men per Polaris submarine. Manning 41 such submarines would require that a staggering number of people be trained in a very short time. Even though only a minor portion of these men would have to receive special nuclear power training, we nonetheless had a large number of acceptable students to round up and educate.

Well before the first nuclear-powered submarine became a reality, the navy had to become disentangled from the regulations set up for the safe operation of a nuclear power plant. The Atomic Energy Commission (AEC), by law, was responsible for the safe operation of nuclear power plants. To insure that the navy was fully in compliance with AEC regulations, the agency wanted one of its personnel aboard every nuclear-powered vessel at sea, armed with the authority to overrule the ship's captain on nuclear propulsion matters. Admiral Rickover, as well as everyone else in the navy, knew that this requirement was completely unrealistic. He took on the AEC personally, insisting that he be held personally responsible for the safe operation of each and every navy nuclear power plant. In turn, he demanded from the navy that he have final approval authority over the selection, training, and assignment of all officers and enlisted personnel involved in the operation and maintenance of these plants. This meant that every captain, every executive officer, every engineering officer, and all of the other officers and crewmen involved with the operation of nuclear power plants were clearly under the admiral's thumb. It was quite a huge responsibility for the admiral. If anyone made a mistake, he would be held personally responsible. It is no wonder that he was so strict in the selection, training, and assignment of these people. Of course, he was also responsible for the design, building, maintenance, and operation of the power plants. He thus became a key man in determining what ships and submarines would be built, accountable to the navy and Congress for the oversight of expenditures and involved in the politics of obtaining congressional approval for the navy's nuclear programs.

Rickover was extremely busy with all that had to be done in Washington, but he also spent a great deal of time making overnight trips to shipyards, training schools, and prototypes to gain firsthand knowledge of their progress and the problems they faced. He had a navy officer at every shipyard and other activities, making daily reports to him by phone to insure he was

Presentation of my Legion of Merit medal by Adm. Hyman Rickover, the "father of the nuclear navy."

on top of problems as soon as they arose. The commanding officers of submarines and other nuclear-powered ships had to write him often, keeping him abreast of developments and problems. Nothing out of the ordinary escaped his immediate attention.

He put in long hours doing all that he had to do and, since those of us on his staff were supposed to be assisting him, we did not dare go home until he left his office. The only time I was able to catch a bus home where I got off in the mornings was during the few days I spent relieving Frank Adams. From then on, the bus I wanted to catch was no longer running by the time we closed down. I had to walk about six or eight blocks to the transfer point where I could catch the bus I needed. It was a cold walk in the wintertime. There was no route to take that did not take you beneath many trees filled with starlings getting ready for the night. I finally started wearing a hat. My treatment by the birds usually typified how my day had gone. As I rode home on the bus, I would review how many times I had been chewed out that day. If it was an unusually active day, I worried that I might be fired. On unusually quiet days, I worried that my services were no longer desired and that I would be left sitting on the sidelines.

It was most unusual to have to go to work on Sundays. However, the other line officers and I were always expected to be there on Saturdays. The majority of the staff was made up of civilians and only a handful of them had to come in on Saturdays. I always drove my car on Saturdays because the buses ran a very limited schedule and also because I could generally find a decent place to park.

Saturday was the day the admiral used to get caught up on less urgent, oddball items. Saturdays could be very tiring. There usually were only a few of us on hand and you would no more than get started on a job when he would call you back and give you something else to do.

One Saturday morning I felt something crunch under my feet as I moved around in his office. I made a mental note to check on it the next time I was there. The next time he called for me, I was in and out without getting a chance to check to see what it was. He always demanded your undivided attention, so you concentrated fully on him and nothing else. The third time, I made myself look around to see what it was. I watched as he bounced back and forth between his desk and a table, carrying a large box of corn flakes. He would grab a handful and pop them in his mouth, but a good amount would miss and land on the floor. Crunch, crunch, crunch.

On another Saturday I pointed out that something he wanted to do — change navy regulations, I think — required the secretary of the navy's approval. He said he had no intention of going to him with the matter. When I persisted in making my point, he yelled at his secretary to get the navy secretary on the phone. She did. He picked up the phone and proceeded to chew out the service's senior civilian official up one side and down the other, just on general principle. When he finished, he slammed down the phone, turned to me, and said, "That's what I think of the Secretary of the Navy!" I obviously was not used to doing business this way.

On two occasions he had me phone captains (I was a commander) who were far senior to me and chew them out for something they had done or were doing that he believed was hindering his program. This was an awkward thing to do, but I did it. Some years later, one of them became the chief of naval operations — the most senior admiral in the navy — and I worried that he might remember the time I had given him a dressing down.

Several most unusual events occurred while I was on duty at NR. One was the loss of the USS *Thresher,* the submarine that my executive officer on the *Seadragon,* Wes Harvey, had been ordered to command. It went down during a test dive out of the Portsmouth Naval Shipyard. All hands were lost. It was a very sad blow to all.

Needless to say, Admiral Rickover immediately launched an all-out effort to discover just what had gone wrong. The *Thresher* lay deep on the bottom of the ocean, far out of reach for any firsthand inspection, but the answers were gleaned from what had been said on the underwater telephone from the submarine to the surface ship standing by. A pipe joint had failed under the extreme seawater pressure and sprayed saltwater all over electric control panels that shorted and caused the reactor to "scram." Power was lost to drive the submarine to the surface, and the crew's attempt to blow the main ballast tanks failed for some unknown reason.

In no time at all, the inspection programs for submarine construction were significantly increased and all high-pressure joints were X-rayed to ensure that proper welding had been accomplished. Tests of the main ballast-blowing system revealed that seawater pressure past a certain depth could freeze the valves shut so that no air could be blown. The valves were redesigned so they would not fail under such conditions.

Not only were improvements being made that would affect the submarines being built, necessary inspections and corrections were made on all operational submarines.

Submarines built after World War II were designed to operate much deeper than their predecessors had, and the water pressures experienced were far, far greater than ever before.

Another event that occurred during my tour in Washington was the assassination of President Kennedy. I was talking with someone on the phone and the line went dead. All of the phones in the building were out of order for hours. A few minutes later we heard on someone's radio that the president had been shot. Everything seemed to come to a standstill. On the day of his funeral, all government offices closed early. I went outside to watch the procession. Policemen with rifles could be clearly seen on the roofs of all the buildings along the route to Arlington Cemetery. As the column of vehicles approached, Secret Service men appeared on either side of the street walking so that they faced the crowds lining each sidewalk, intensely examining everyone, one hand buried in a coat pocket, ready to shoot. I do not think anyone moved a muscle. The line of limousines carrying the official mourners — both U.S. and foreign — seemed to go on forever.

I was also present the day Martin Luther King Jr. made his historic "I Have a Dream" speech at the Lincoln Memorial. Government offices were closed that day, but our "Saturday Team" was still expected to show up. I arrived at the office by bus without any unusual effort because the crowd had not yet started gathering. As time went on, I kept looking outside at the crowd gathering on either side of the Reflecting Pool. By midmorning I do not think there was enough room out there for anyone to fall down. Everywhere I could see from my window was solid with people. The admiral closed up his office at around one o'clock and left. I left, too, not knowing how I was going to get home. Streets were closed everywhere; there were no buses in sight. I picked my way through the mob, heading away from the Lincoln Memorial. I did not break clear of it until I passed the Washington Monument. Somewhere well beyond that point I caught a bus that took me across the river. I got off the bus not far from my neighborhood and walked the rest of the way.

One day I was informed that I had been awarded the Legion of Merit medal for my role in the *Seadragon*'s Arctic operation. It came as a surprise to me, and I remember feeling pride at the knowledge that my service was being officially recognized. I was also told that Admiral Rickover would be making the presentation, as he did not want the secretary of the navy to do it. I felt even more honored because he rarely participated in such ceremonies. Several days later, at the appointed time, the admiral, several other staff members, the prospective commanding officers at NR for training, and my family assembled in a small space whose only decoration was a chart of the periodic elements. There were no flags or anything else in honor of the occasion. After the citation was read, the admiral pinned the medal on my chest, shook my hand, and a photographer took several pictures. After the ceremony I was told to take the rest of the day off and go celebrate with my family.

The Bureau of Naval Personnel informed us that they were having a hard time finding volunteers for training who would be acceptable to the admiral and suggested that it might be helpful if a couple of us at NR would visit various universities that would soon graduate navy ROTC cadets who might like to volunteer if they knew more about the program. We quickly made arrangements with the commanders of NROTC units for one of us to come speak at each of their schools.

Each of us was scheduled to visit five or six universities. They were to be whirlwind trips, so I went in uniform rather than carry double the luggage by packing both civilian and military attire. One day I started on a trip to a couple of colleges in the Midwest. There was a bit of confusion at Washington National Airport — a substitution of planes, confusion at the gate, and so forth — but I finally boarded the right aircraft. As we taxied to the runway, the stewardess announced that our first stop would be in Charleston, followed by a couple of other places. I jumped up, sure that I somehow had gotten on the wrong plane after all: I certainly would not be going west by way of Charleston, South Carolina! The stewardess calmed me down as she ushered me back to my seat, explaining that we would be stopping in Charleston, West Virginia. I was much relieved. The idea of landing there intrigued me. I had never been there before, but I had read that the city's airport was built on top of a mountain. There was concern that planes might come in short of the runway and crash into the side of the mountain. There was also concern that a plane might not be able to stop before reaching the end of the runway and go over the other side of the mountain. I was going to watch this landing closely.

Eventually the "fasten seat belts" sign lit up and we began to prepare to land. We were still at a pretty high altitude. I looked out the window, caught a glimpse of the side of a mountain, and then felt the shock of the landing gear hitting the runway. The plane shuddered as the pilots reversed the propellers to slow us down. It seemed like it was taking longer than usual for the plane to stop when we abruptly turned and headed toward the terminal. Outside I could see the end of the runway right there — with a beautiful view down the other side of the mountain. What a landing!

As we pulled up to the terminal, it was announced that we would be there about twenty minutes while they refueled the plane. We were free to get off and go in the terminal, but if we did, we could not get back on until the refueling was completed. Most of us climbed off the plane, walked through the gate in the fence, and set about looking at magazines, drinking coffee, and the like. Eventually I walked back to the fence and stood there, enjoying the weather. An elderly fellow at least in his late sixties stopped beside me and started talking. I commented that this was the first time I had ever flown in here. He looked at me with raised eyebrows and a rather astonished expression but said nothing. I went on to say that I had thought we were not going to stop before running off the runway and going down the other side of the mountain. By now the man's legs were unsteady and his face had an almost horrified expression. He looked nervously around, obviously searching for a place to sit down. Suddenly it dawned on me that he thought I was the pilot, what with my dark-blue uniform, gold stripes, and white cap. I hurriedly explained that I was a passenger like him, a naval officer who knew nothing about flying. He looked relieved, but continued his search for a place to sit.

I believe our trips to the universities were useful because there seemed to be real interest in the navy's nuclear power program. However, I do not know if our visits actually inspired anyone to volunteer.

The deeper I got into my work, the more strongly I agreed with Frank Adams, Jack Crawford, and many others that we simply had to increase the number of officers being accepted for nuclear training. Admiral Rickover, however, stubbornly refused. He was concerned that graduates of his training program who were not immediately assigned to duty aboard a submarine or ship might decide to leave the navy as soon as possible and accept a job with civilian nuclear power enterprises. The admiral did not want to waste time or money to become a training institution for civilian endeavors. Unlike the heads of other service schools, he did not provide anything in writing to graduates of his program that certified they were qualified to operate and maintain nuclear power plants.

A friend of mine in the Pentagon had completed a computer analysis of the numbers of personnel in the various job categories that would be required from year to year to man our nuclear-powered ships and subs, but Rickover dismissed his findings as being ridiculous. I decided to graph out the manning requirements through the time that the last Polaris submarine (number forty-one) put to sea. I restricted my chart to just submarines, not including any surface ships. Using four-foot-long sheets cut from a roll of plotting paper, I first sketched it out in pencil and then used colored crayons to make it easier to read. I considered only the officers of various ranks and experience that would be required, using the official navy percentages for anticipated losses due to resignation, medical discharges, shore duty, and so forth. I worked on it for weeks. The end result clearly showed that we needed to start pumping out a good deal more young officers than Rickover had originally planned.

Bill Wagner had relieved Jack Crawford by this time. I was discussing with him just how this could be presented to the admiral so that he would take time to study it. He said he had an idea and told me to leave the graphs with him. He was confident he could get the admiral's attention. I wished him luck.

Several days later, Bill sent for me. He said the admiral had looked it over and agreed that it was time to increase the number of personnel being trained. I could not help but ask how he had gained the admiral's attention. He explained that Rickover had a habit of taking a fifteen- to twenty-minute break at about two o'clock each day. He would go to Bill's office, spend a few minutes getting briefed on the latest happenings, and then go to the office next door and have a cup of coffee with the two women yeomen who managed the administrative office. After relaxing for a few minutes, he went back to work.

One day, Bill laid the big sheets of colored graphs on a long table near his desk and then covered all but one corner with a bunch of other papers. Sure enough, Rickover noticed the corner of the graph and asked, "What's that?"

"Just a study," Bill answered. "You wouldn't be interested."

The admiral would not be denied. "Let me see it!" he demanded.

"You wouldn't want to waste the time," replied Bill.

The Admiral again demanded to look at it. Bill gave in, uncovered it, and Rickover studied it.

A couple of days later, the admiral sent word for Bill; Jim Watkins, the other line officer; and me to be in his office in an hour. We expected it had something to do with the training numbers. The admiral announced he had an appointment with the chief of naval operations (CNO, the navy's head admiral) and that he wanted us to accompany him. He then asked us to sit down around his large table with him. He started asking us questions, and then we asked him questions we thought the CNO might address to him. After he was all warmed up and focused on the problem, he said, "Let's go."

We went out and piled into his car. The admiral sat up front with the sailor who served as his driver, in addition to being a strong hand in the administrative office. All of us, including the driver, wore civilian clothes. His car was an old Chevrolet. Although it was a navy vehicle, it was nothing like the staff cars given to most admirals. It was really a heap, and intentionally so.

We got out at the main entrance to the Pentagon. Inside the doors was a large lobby with a handsome, square wooden counter enclosing several desks. Two attractive middle-aged ladies were there to assist visitors. Several vases spaced along the countertop held fragrant fresh-cut flowers, adding beauty and dignity to the place. Rickover greeted the ladies, picked up one of the flower arrangements, and headed for the CNO's office. Upon reaching the CNO's secretary, he presented the flowers to her as if he had brought them all the way from his office.

After exchanging greetings with the CNO, he told us to wait outside for him and closed the door. He came out about an hour later and went to the secretary's office to dictate a directive the CNO had agreed to sign. Another half-hour passed. Rickover came out of the secretary's office with the finished directive in hand, got the CNO to sign it, and off we went. Our "limousine" was waiting for us at the foot of the steps outside the entrance. We piled in and headed back to our office, still with no idea what the directive said.

The admiral eventually showed it to Bill Wagner, who informed the rest of us what it contained. It was nothing like what I had expected. It gave Rickover the power to consider for nuclear-power training any officer in the navy, whether or not he had volunteered for such training. Nor did Rickover care if they were submariners. They could always undergo submarine training later — *if* they volunteered for submarine duty. Rickover would not be able to make them serve on submarines unless they requested it. We suddenly realized what a huge task this was going to be.

Within a few days I was spending the majority of each day at BuPers screening service records to identify candidates for Rickover to consider for nuclear-power training. I sought officers with excellent fitness reports who had performed well in college. Rickover did not seem to care what a person had studied in college as long as he had been a good, dedicated, and serious student. He was also more interested in seeing someone who had earned good grades at a small college, but would consider candidates with less impressive grade-point averages who came from colleges he knew to be difficult and demanding.

Selecting candidates based solely on the strength of their records was not enough. He wanted to interview each and every one to see what they were made of and if he thought they had what it took to successfully qualify. He saw no sense in wasting time and money on anyone he did not judge capable of being successful.

Several times a month we provided BuPers a list of officers he wanted to interview and a schedule. It was up to BuPers to make sure the schedule was met. Upon arrival, those to be interviewed were assembled in a room with sufficient chairs and I would explain the routine.

Five or six of us would interview one person each for fifteen minutes, then write down our observations and whether we recommended selection or rejection. Three different people interviewed each candidate. Our comments were typed up for easier reading and given to the admiral. He would read our reports and then call in one man at a time. He made his decisions as he saw fit, regardless of what we recommended. He had so much other stuff to do that he rarely completed these interviews by the end of a normal business day.

He also interviewed all of the midshipmen who were about to graduate from the Naval Academy. Those groups always came in on Saturdays.

This big effort went on for months. I had to review literally thousands of records. We then interviewed hundreds of officers and midshipmen. We succeeded in filling the training pipeline with sufficient candidates to fill not only the submarine requirements, but also those for the nuclear-powered carriers and cruisers being built.

Sometime during all of this I learned of the death of the wife of one of the submarine officers Rickover had selected in the early days of the nuclear-power program. When it had become known about a year earlier that this officer's wife was terminally ill with cancer, he was ordered to shore duty in New London so that he could be with her and help take care of their children. It was all very sad and on everyone's mind. I drafted a letter of condolence for the admiral to send to the fellow. When his secretary gave it to him to sign, he called me to his office. He handed it to me unsigned and said he was not going to send it, that he had been sending out too many personal letters. I suggested that it would mean a great deal to the young man and that it was the right thing to do. After arguing briefly, he threw me out. I left the letter on his desk.

He called for me again about an hour later. As I entered his office he held out a letter written in his own handwriting, including the envelope, and said, "A letter of condolence should have a more personal touch than a typewritten letter." I was truly touched. I reiterated that the letter would mean a great deal to the young man. I could not get over his doing this.

His writing that letter in his own hand caused me to reassess my feelings for, and understanding of, him. I was beginning to appreciate the tremendous workload he carried and the great responsibility he bore. No wonder he was constantly driving ahead, seemingly unconcerned for others' feelings. He did not have time for pleasantries. He wanted straight, honest, and brief answers. When he asked your opinion about something he had already thought out, it seemed that he always opposed any answer you gave him, but the sly old fellow simply wanted to make sure he had not overlooked any aspect of a given problem. He did not want any "yes men" around. He was tough on accepting personnel for training. He was not looking for grade-A students, he was interested only in those men he believed would seriously concentrate on learning and could be relied upon to produce desired results. All my life I had wondered what it would have been like to work with various famous, historically significant men. I believe I did work with a man who occupies an important place in our nation's history. He deserves full credit for successfully fighting through many virtually insoluble technical problems, political and administrative roadblocks, monstrous training and production problems, and the traditional personnel selection and assignment problems. He gave the United States one of the most valuable technological advantages imaginable.

After having spent almost two years at NR, I heard one day that the captain of one of our Polaris submarines had unexpectedly submitted his retirement request. I mentally noted that it was a good illustration of the types of unexpected losses we were going to incur. To my surprise, I was informed the next day that I was going to have to relieve him because I was the only officer in the navy who was qualified and not already serving as the captain of a Polaris sub. It took great self-control, but I firmly resisted letting out a joyous "whoopee!" and doing cartwheels down the passageway. Instead, I remained somber and uttered something like, "Well, when you have to go, you have to go." I could hardly wait to be detached and be on my way.

The timing was surprisingly good. It would take a couple of weeks to obtain a replacement for me. Then I would have about a week during which to move to Charleston, South Carolina, where my crew, the Blue Crew of the USS *Alexander Hamilton* (SSBN-617), was home ported. I would then have to attend the Polaris Missile School in Dam Neck, Virginia, for about two months. My graduation would be just in time to relieve the *Alexander Hamilton*'s skipper, "Buzz" Bessac, when he returned from his last patrol.

15

PREPARING FOR COMMAND OF
USS *ALEXANDER HAMILTON*

Our move from Washington to Charleston, South Carolina, went pretty smoothly. There were no dock strikes to contend with this time, but we did have one minor problem. As the packers completed a very smooth and professional job, one of the young men discovered he had lost his wedding ring. We searched every room, but it was nowhere to be found. The logical conclusion was that it had come off as he was packing one of the many boxes, barrels, or crates. I assured him I would carefully inspect each and every crumpled piece of packing paper, do my best to find it, and mail it to him as soon as I did.

Luckily we were able to find an affordable home in a beautiful neighborhood. I was fortunate to have a couple of days to help my family get settled before I had to report to Dam Neck, Virginia, for the Polaris Missile School. The course would last several weeks. During that time I would stay in the BOQ there and go home on the weekends.

Carefully examining each wadded-up sheet of packing paper for the packer's wedding ring seemed to be taking forever. I had no such luck finding it quickly. The ring finally turned up as I unpacked the next to last container.

We were beginning to get settled in pretty well after a couple of days when the first of our neighbors called on us to welcome us to the neighborhood. It was nice to be in such a friendly group. As I opened the front door to welcome our caller, her dog, waiting there with her, bounded inside and proceeded to make himself at home. I wished she had left her dog at home. From time to time I caught myself, fighting off the urge to drag it out of a chair or off the sofa. I did not want to embarrass her by correcting it, but she sure did not seem to mind what it was doing. It was all over the house. I finally asked her how old her dog was, and she said, "That's not my dog, I thought it was yours." I think I heard it utter a smart-aleck chuckle as I ushered it out the door. It had enjoyed a great visit.

I had just come from a job related to the massive effort of providing the navy a completely new and different type of propulsion system and the trained men to operate and maintain these amazing power plants. Now I was entering the world related to a completely new and amazing weapon system requiring highly trained personnel to maintain and operate it. In order to deploy our forty-one Polaris missile submarines in record time, we had to train the missile-related personnel from the ground up in short order. Although the commanding officers would not be personally involved in the maintenance and checks of the missiles, they would need to understand all aspects of what made a missile work and what was needed to successfully launch it. Many hours of lectures, reading, discussions, and practice with sophisticated training devices were required. I found my time at this school to be extremely interesting and thorough — to the point that I had complete confidence in my ability to do all that was required of me.

One night in my lonely BOQ room I got to thinking about the Polaris missile fleet. The fact that such a fleet was even being considered had not become known until only a short while before. All of us in submarines were acquainted with the Regulus guided-missile system. We had only a couple of subs capable of launching those primitive cruise missiles. The Regulus submarines were equipped with a large tank on the afterdeck capable of carrying four Regulus I missiles with nuclear warheads. In order to launch a missile, the sub had to surface so crewmen could open the big door at the end of the tank, pull a missile out, and mount it on a track that they then elevated to about a thirty-degree angle. As soon as the crewmen were clear, the missile would be fired and off it would go. It had a range of only a few hundred miles. The idea of building a submarine that could carry and launch sixteen nuclear-tipped missiles capable of reaching targets at least a thousand miles away while remaining submerged was incomprehensible. I had never encountered a submariner who thought such a thing possible. A missile capable of going a thousand miles had to be huge. How could a submarine carry even one, much less sixteen? How could you fire a missile while submerged? If you did fire one submerged, the sudden weight change would surely cause the submarine to lose depth control. It is a law of nature that for each action there is a reaction. How could you launch a heavy missile straight up without forcing the submarine to go straight down? I did not think it would work. However, considering the amazing feats with the atomic bomb and nuclear power I had witnessed in my short life, I did not rule it out as impossible. I had been somewhat stunned to learn that Vice Adm. William Rayborn, an aviator, had been made head of the Special Projects Office and given the mission of developing and building such a fleet. The more I thought about it, the more sense it made to pick someone who did not know enough about submarines to think it would not work! I am sure he has earned his place in the history books for successfully accomplishing the task of producing forty-one Polaris missile submarines in record time, which helped keep us safe for the remainder of the Cold War.

My completion of the missile school program tied in quite nicely with the Blue Crew's return to Charleston to commence their off-crew routine.

It did not take too long for Buzz to go through the turnover procedure with me, introduce me to the officers and crew, and for us to work out plans for the formal change of command. He suggested that the ceremony be held in a small auditorium rather than outside as was normally done when the submarine was nearby.

When I asked why, he explained that our new off-crew training building was right next door to the navy's firefighting school. From time to time, a big pit filled with oil was set afire for the students to practice the techniques they were being taught. The huge cloud of thick, black smoke that was always produced discouraged outdoor gatherings. One crew had planned an outdoor ceremony after first obtaining an agreement from the school that no fire would be started during their ceremony. Sure enough, someone started an oil fire after the ceremony was under way. Heavy, black smoke completely engulfed the reviewing area and everyone scrambled to get clear. The ceremony was reorganized in a new location clear of the smoke. As soon as it was completed, everyone dashed off to the Officers' Club for the cocktail party that followed.

The cocktail party was going great when strange things started happening. The smoke had caused a chemical reaction that destroyed certain clothing material. Ladies' stockings started unraveling and falling to their ankles, seams opened up, sleeves fell off, all sorts of unusual things occurred.

Our indoor change of command ceremony went off without a hitch, and all who attended the cocktail reception that followed made it through in good shape.

When it was all over, there I was, in command of a crew, but with no submarine. I had yet to even see a Polaris submarine.

I had taken command of the Blue Crew just after completion of their leave period, which lasted about three weeks after their return to port. Now we were in our training period, which would last for about two months there in Charleston. After completing a patrol, about 15 percent of a crew would be lost. Some were ordered to a new submarine that needed to build its crew around a nucleus of experienced men, or to an operating submarine requiring an individual replacement. Others were assigned to much-deserved shore duty, retired, or left the service at the completion of their enlistment. A well-trained crew needed to work as a group of teams — missile group, navigating group, nuclear-power group, and so on — so this training time was necessary for them to learn to work together and, of course, improve the knowledge of the newly assigned men. Training was a very important part of this business.

All of the equipment needed for training, which duplicated what we actually had on the submarine, was in place. Our offices were still under construction, however, so we had to make do with space that was available in the existing buildings. Having to use borrowed office space was a reminder that getting the missile fleet operating was very high priority and that making do was necessary until all the pieces were in place.

The exec and I shared a small office with two yeomen. The activity in that small space was distracting, but I was able to learn the problems we were working much more quickly while being exposed to the officers and men of the crew more readily, which helped me get acquainted.

A day or two before our scheduled flight to Scotland, I was provided an aluminum chest in which to pack uniforms, clothes, and personal articles I wanted to take to the submarine. It was large, but narrow enough in width to fit through a hatch.

The uniforms worn aboard Polaris submarines were unique and not worn on other subs until several years later. They were one piece, coverall type suits, fairly lightweight, and very comfortable. They came in small, medium, and large sizes and were worn with a belt. There were no buttons or zippers, just Velcro strips. They were lint-free to protect all of the electronic equipment, and no pressing was required. Each person was issued three of the dark-blue outfits. Each bore the person's name stenciled on a white strip on the chest. A quick run through the washer and dryer and you had a clean, ready-to-wear uniform. Two of these suits took up very little storage space. The only complaint about these suits was that after spending two months undressing by ripping the Velcro strips open, you went home and unconsciously ripped all of the buttons off the first regular shirt you put on.

On the day of our flight to Scotland, we assembled at the Charleston airport at the terminal used by the military. Our heavy luggage was trucked over from the base. At the appointed time we loaded aboard a big four-engine passenger plane chartered from one of the major airlines. Any seats not taken by our crews were then made available to other military personnel flying space available. Our crews took up almost all of the seats.

This was my first of quite a few flights back and forth across the Atlantic. The exec and I were seated up front near the flight deck. After getting airborne and settled down for the journey, the pilot came back and introduced himself. After exchanging a few pleasantries, he said, "Where are you all going?" I was shocked! Didn't he know where he was going? I could only answer, "Where are you taking us?"

He saw my consternation, laughed, and said, "I see what you mean, but we're changing crews in New York, and I don't know where you're going from there." We explained that we were on our way to Scotland.

We spent a short time in New York, changing the plane's crew, loading food, and topping off the fuel. Once more we were airborne and got settled down for about a seven-hour flight.

We landed in Prestwick, Scotland, in the wee hours of the morning. The terminal was practically deserted, but the navy transportation officer stationed there to arrange the comings and goings of military personnel met us and directed us toward two double-decker buses that normally provided public service in some nearby town. They were big and red, just like the ones you see in movies with scenes in London. I had never been in this part of the world before and was pleased at the chance to ride on one of them. The exec and I took a seat on the top deck of the first bus. I wanted to see all I could, even at that late, dark hour.

Soon we were on our way on a two-lane road through the countryside. I was surprised to see that no one drove with their headlights on, just their parking lights. I learned that they thought it was much better that way because no one was blinded by oncoming headlights.

From time to time we drove through small villages that were all shut down for the night. Eventually we passed through the industrial area in the outskirts of Glasgow. All was dark and quiet.

Our destination was the waterfront in Greenock. There were two large personnel boats awaiting us when we arrived. The crew and most of the officers took their seats in the enclosed cabin space, but the exec and I entered the pilothouse so we could again see all that we could. Soon we were under way again, this time headed for the Holy Loch, where the squadron of Polaris submarines and their big tender were based. We had to cross the Clyde River to reach the Holy Loch, and it is very wide at that point. We were under way for nearly half an hour getting clear of Greenock, crossing the Clyde, and then into the Holy Loch to the tender. I could see a couple of submarines tied up alongside the anchored tender, but could not tell which of them was the *Alexander Hamilton.*

We boarded the tender on the clear side and the officers were escorted to the cabins in which we would spend what was left of the night. I had our escort take us by an out-of-the-way route that would get us to the far side of the tender so I could look down on the two submarines tethered alongside. They were immense! I knew they were 425 feet long, but you had to see them to appreciate their huge size. Think of it this way: a football field is only three hundred feet from goal line to goal line. (The *Seadragon,* by comparison, was only 278 feet long.) I was truly excited about taking command of this huge submarine. I wanted to go down and board my submarine right then, but it was a very inappropriate time to go aboard.

From there I was taken to the captain's cabin. The tender's skipper lived ashore and made his cabin available to all of the arriving Polaris sub captains. I was amused. It was a very spacious cabin with a double bed rather than a bunk. What luxury! It did not take me long to climb into that bed. It had been a very long day, but I did not intend to sleep late. I wanted to see that submarine!

I awoke at about 7:30, still anxious to see my Polaris sub. Although I had gotten only a couple of hours sleep, I felt refreshed. I quickly put on my uniform and made my way to the squadron commander's office to introduce myself. The commodore, Captain Eubanks, was at his desk in his office space, which was in a large compartment located several decks above the main deck. The compartment ran from one side of the tender to the other. Captain Eubanks's office area was on the port side, and the tender's commanding officer, Capt. Bob Black, occupied a space on the starboard side. In between their office spaces was a long dining table capable of seating at least fourteen guests. I was welcomed by both the commodore and the captain and invited to join them at breakfast. Several officers from the squadron staff and the tender's executive officer soon joined us. I already knew a couple of the officers and quickly ascertained that I would be happy serving with all of them.

After eating a hearty breakfast, I excused myself. One of the staff officers offered to show me how to get to my submarine. We went down several decks, made our way through several passageways, then through a machine shop to a large door that opened through the side of the ship. It accommodated a large gangway leading to the first submarine moored alongside the tender. The *Alexander Hamilton* was the next sub over. I made my way over to it, introduced myself to the deck watch, and explained that I was going to look around topside before going below. I simply could not get over how huge she was!

One of the missile hatches was open. I knew the missiles were big, but I was still amazed at just how big they were. The missile had been off-loaded, so I could clearly see down into the huge launch tube. The Polaris missile was thirty-five feet tall, so I was looking down at least that far — three, possibly four, stories below. The *Alexander Hamilton* carried sixteen of those monsters! I forget the exact diameter of the Polaris missile, but I would guess it was seven feet or so.

I spotted an open deck hatch nearby and headed below. I thought I could find the wardroom on my own, but finally gave up and asked a passing sailor for directions. I was on the wrong deck — imagine *that* in a submarine — but at least was headed in the right direction. I finally found the wardroom and went inside. Commander Ben Sherman, captain of the Gold Crew, was there and welcomed me aboard. We had a good laugh about my getting lost, after which he introduced me to those officers of his crew who were busily working with their counterparts from my crew. They had not wasted any time in getting started on the turnover.

Although I had never served with Ben, I knew and admired him greatly. He was several years senior to me. After a cup of coffee, Ben took me on a guided tour of the ship. I was determined to pay close attention so that I could get from one place to another without getting lost. My stateroom was one deck above the wardroom. I was surprised at how much space I would have. There was a desk with plenty of cabinets and drawers, and a chair. The bunk swung back out of the way, exposing two benches underneath with a small table that folded down from under the bunk. I had my own washbasin, a nice closet for hanging clothes, and shared a shower stall and toilet with the exec, whose stateroom was next door. The control room was about twenty-five feet down the passageway. I would spend the majority of my time in these three spaces — my cabin, the control room, and the ward-room — all of which were fairly close together.

I continued to be absolutely amazed by the size of everything. The crew's mess was at least ten times as large as the crew's mess on the older submarines I had served aboard. On the old boats, the ship's office had been big enough for only the yeoman to squeeze into. Sometimes, to get to a hard-to-reach drawer, he would have to move himself and his chair into the passageway. The ship's office on Polaris subs accommodated two yeomen, lots of file drawers, and a photocopier.

There was a space for a library that was pretty well stocked with books for education and relaxation. There was even a small barbershop.

A large space housed all of the sophisticated navigation equipment, and another good-sized space served as the missile control room. The missile compartment was so big that you could barely see the bulkhead at the far end.

It was natural to think that all of that space had been designed for the crew's comfort. However, the reality was that you needed all of that space to carry all of the missiles and equipment needed for the sub to perform its mission. If the hull had been any smaller, it would have sunk straight to the bottom. It was necessary to displace the weight of water equal to the weight of the ship in order for it to float. The result was that the crew got to enjoy the comfort of this necessity.

At about 9:30, Ben told me we were due to attend the daily briefing in the squadron operations room on the tender. The commodore and a few key members of his staff, along with key members of the tender repair team, met with the submarine skippers and two or three of their officers. A quick review was made of the status of upkeep of those submarines present and any major problems they had. Immediate decisions were then made to solve those problems.

About once or twice a week it was discovered that a particular repair part or component needed was not available on the tender. The tender was well stocked with parts that were routinely used, but it was physically impossible to carry every single item that might possibly be needed. A system had been established that ensured absolute top priority was given to shipping any item needed to keep the Polaris force fully operational. A priority message was sent to the supply depot back in the United States. The required part was immediately obtained from a central warehouse or the manufacturer — sometimes even taken off an operating submarine — and delivered overnight via a special courier flight. Amazing attention was paid to maintaining the absolute readiness of the Polaris force.

At the end of the normal workday, Ben and I and a few others shifted to civilian attire and caught a boat ashore.

Our boat landing was in a little village named Sandbank. The area was well known for its small shipyards, which had built some famous racing sailboats and ships.

We took a couple of taxis a few more miles along a road paralleling the shoreline toward the Clyde to a small town named Dunoon. It was the principal town in the immediate area — small, but very friendly and cozy. The nearby U.S. Navy activity had increased its tourist attraction, so the four or five small but comfortable hotels in town were always pleased to have us visit. We had drinks and dinner that night at the largest of these hotels. A monthly dance was being held in the dining room. We enjoyed watching. Several of the men were wearing kilts. I had smoked salmon for dinner. It was the first time I had ever eaten smoked salmon, and it was absolutely delicious. The salmon was caught and smoked locally.

As we left the hotel and reached the asphalt pavement, we experienced great excitement. First one, then another, and finally all of us were slipping and falling. It was cold, but no ice was apparent. One of the old-timers explained that this was what was known as "black ice." You cannot see it, but it is there, not thick enough to notice, but enough to cause you to slip and slide. We newcomers finally got the hang of how to stay on our feet and finally made it to the taxis. Thank goodness the cabbies were experienced at driving on it.

We completed the turnover on the fifth day and relieved the Gold Crew. There was no ceremony except my signing a stack of papers acknowledging I was taking custody of the missiles and power plant and the overall ship. Ben and I reported this to the commodore, and Ben and the Gold Crew loaded onto the boats that would take them to Greenock for their trip to the airport.

Finally, after much preparation, I was in command of the *Alexander Hamilton*. How fortunate I was to have such a wonderful ship! I sure hoped I would measure up to the responsibility.

16

COMMAND OF USS *ALEXANDER HAMILTON*

As soon as we finished moving aboard we focused on successfully completing the ship's upkeep mission.

I spent my time reviewing the progress of work; studying ships' orders, directives, and operation plans; poking around, learning more and more about the submarine; and watching the crew work, trying to learn the men's names and something about each of them.

My good friend Commander Paul Early was also in command of a Polaris submarine undergoing upkeep in Holy Loch. I invited him to lunch one day and he responded with an invitation to come with him in the early afternoon and watch as they moved his submarine from one side of the tender to the other. It was the only chance I had to observe the operation of one of these big subs before I had to take mine to sea.

The tug, which was always present when a vessel was under way near the tender, did a very professional job of assisting Paul in moving from one side of the tender to the other. However, in the final stages, Paul needed to move his stern toward the tender, and the tug was tied up to his bow. Paul ordered the "outboard" to be lowered and trained so that it pointed toward the tender. He then ordered it started and the sub's stern swung neatly until it snuggled up against the tender. I really enjoyed having the opportunity to see the outboard in operation. The Polaris submarines had only one propeller, which made it difficult to maneuver them in tight spaces. Because they were so big, they were built with a unique, electrically driven propeller that could be lowered from its housing near the stern and then trained in any direction desired. You could not regulate the propeller's speed, but you could readily turn it on or off as desired to move the sub's stern from one side or the other or forward or astern. Although it was rarely used, the outboard sure came in handy when you needed it.

I became better acquainted with SSBN-617 with each passing day.

The upkeep period lasted roughly three weeks, with the work following a well-planned schedule that included corrective maintenance, preventive maintenance, loading, checking, record keeping, testing, and the like. The tender's workforce and the ship's crew were well coordinated to ensure that all was done within the prescribed time. An effort was also made to give the officers and men time off for occasional half-day tours of nearby places of scenic or historic significance. During my five patrol periods there I got to see such places as Sterling, Glasgow, Edinburgh and several lesser-known but most interesting places. I was fortunate to get to know many of the local residents and to attend a number of functions given by them.

We repaid our social obligations by occasionally inviting two or three couples out to the submarine for dinner and a movie. They seemed to particularly enjoy seeing our movies.

Scotland is very rugged and appears sparsely settled. There are few large farms because it is so mountainous. However, there are lots of sheep. Each flock bears particular colored markings to distinguish who owns them. I also saw a breed of cattle that I had never seen before: Ayrshires. The cows were very hairy, almost scary looking. No matter where you went, the scenery was breathtaking. It was not unusual to pass two or three beautiful lakes, called lochs, no matter where you drove. I saw Loch Ness many times, but never caught sight of the monster.

The weather always felt chilly to me, if not really cold. I wore heavy suits or tweed jackets no matter what time of year it was. I always had my raincoat with me — not just for rain, but also for added warmth when needed. It rained quite a bit, but you became used to it. In the summer, the locals would complain of the heat if the temperature reached seventy degrees or more.

The food was good no matter where you ate. However, I steered well clear of such things as haggis and black blood pudding, as did most people. One evening my meal came with boiled potatoes. I could not believe how good those potatoes were. I had never tasted potatoes so good. I offered the owner my compliments and asked what kind of potatoes they were. He stated that they were "Ayrshire Potatoes." He said they were only grown locally and were available for only a short time each year. I hope to enjoy them again someday.

One afternoon I went into town to shop for a couple of gifts to take back to my family. It was already dark. Dunoon, Scotland, is much farther north than any of the big cities in Canada. Sunset is as early as 3:30 in the afternoon in the winter and as late as ten at night in the summer. In addition to being cold and dark, it was also quite rainy that evening. After finishing my shopping, I was ready to sit down in a warm, cozy place and have a cup of coffee. I spotted a popular tearoom and went in hoping they also served coffee. They did. There were only a couple of people there at that time. I took a seat at a small table and started enjoying the warmth and cozy comfort. In the middle of each table stood a several-tiered piece holding a variety of fancy cookies and cakes. I could not resist helping myself to one of the dainty offerings even before my coffee arrived. The coffee was very good and tasted even better with each pastry I ate. I wondered how they could remain in business giving away such delectable goodies. When I went to pay my bill, I could not help telling the cashier how much I had enjoyed the treats. The lady smiled, thanked me, and asked how many I had eaten. I replied that I enjoyed them so much that I had eaten quite a few. "Goodness!" she replied. "Can you remember how many you had?" I shook my head and said, "No, but quite a few; they were so good." Again she smiled and said, "I have to know how many you had so I can charge you for them." It suddenly became clear to me how they stayed in business.

It seemed that I learned something new or observed something unusual every time I went ashore. One evening I experienced a near tragedy that left me laughing.

The evening began with one of my officers and me enjoying a good dinner at my favorite hotel, the Tornadee. We were seated alone in the bar enjoying a quiet after-dinner drink. It was a weeknight, and we were about the only guests. Two Scots came in a short while later and we asked them to join us. They had spent a few hours at their local pub but wanted one more drink before calling it a night. Eventually they finished their drinks and headed out, leaving us all by ourselves. There was no one else around except the help. A few minutes after the Scots left, one of them came back in and asked if we had seen his buddy. When we told him we had not, he stated that the fellow had simply disappeared. He said he could not imagine what had happened to him and left.

A little while later he came back to report that he had looked everywhere and still could not find his friend. He was worried. He said they had walked together to their car in the parking lot, that he had climbed in, and then all at once his partner was gone. The two of us hopped up and went with him to the parking lot. Theirs was the only car there. The Tornadee was well outside of town on a hill overlooking the Clyde River and there was complete silence. You could have easily heard a car from a good distance anywhere around. It was eerie. The Scot said his friend had simply disappeared. We started shouting his name, but there was no response. The fellow assured us he had made a thorough search of the hotel, and it was easy to see he was nowhere around outside. Where could he have gone?

We were standing there quietly, each trying to think how next to proceed, when we heard a low moan. We bellowed the man's name again, waited, and then heard the low moan once again. The moaning continued; it was coming from bushes down the side of the steep hill falling to the Clyde. We finally spotted some bushes moving. It was going to be difficult reaching him. You could get down to him, but it would be very difficult, if not impossible, to get back up without some assistance. I sent my companion in to get a couple of staff members to help us.

He returned with several helpers and we formed a human chain. First one and then another of us went over the side to go get the man. It was slow business, but we finally got to him and brought him up. When we were all safely back on the parking lot, the man explained that when he reached the car, he had stepped back to open the door and fallen down the side of the hill. Thank goodness the bushes had broken his fall. I could not help but laugh. I wish I had been there to see it happen.

I saw the fellow a couple of more times during my visits to Scotland and always inquired it he had fallen down any mountainsides lately.

It was not unusual for me to be invited to a couple of cocktail parties when I went to Scotland. I enjoyed getting to know the local people; it was very refreshing and enjoyable. Being in their homes in the wintertime always gave me a chuckle. Central heating was a rarity. The people depended upon a coal fireplace to heat each room. They were used to the cold weather, however, and I was not. We would stand around talking, each of us producing a cloud of vapor whenever we spoke. It was what I would expect to see outside the house on a very cold day. To them it was very natural. I always made a point of dressing warmly.

One Christmas holiday period I was invited, through the commodore, to attend a ball being given by the Duke of Argyle in his ancient castle. The duke was very gracious in recognizing the presence of the U.S. Navy and made a habit of including the commodore and the commanding officers of the ships that were present in the Holy Loch.

The castle was a very impressive, rugged stone edifice that was hundreds of years old. It sat close to a large loch on a small plain and was surrounded by mountains. It was visible for miles in every direction. We were admitted through the main entrance and led directly to a large hall with a ceiling several stories high. At each floor level there was a walkway all the way around. Several large chandeliers hung from the ceiling. I fully expected to see Errol Flynn come swinging in to rescue a damsel in distress. The duke and duchess personally welcomed the guests. The ladies wore attractive evening dresses and the men were clad in kilts, formal jackets with shiny brass buttons, and fancy white dress shirts — a level of dress comparable to our tuxes and tails. There were well over a hundred people there already.

In spite of the hall's grandeur, a majestic fifteen-foot Christmas tree standing off to one side immediately caught your attention. It was most unusual. About every foot and a half up the trunk, branches stood almost straight out in every direction. I am pretty sure it was a Scotch pine. What else? It was decorated in a conservative but attractive manner with brightly colored balls. To my amazement, sturdy red candles adorned the branches rather than electric bulbs. The spacing between the branches was sufficient that the needles hanging down from the branch above each candle would not catch fire. The candles had not yet been lit. Later on, I was relieved to see abundant firefighting equipment, along with men to use it, in a nearby alcove.

About midway through the party, a butler using a lighter on the end of a long pole lit the candles. The tree was spectacular. We sang a few Christmas carols after it was fully lighted. It was a most impressive and memorable occasion.

There was dancing, drinking, and eating. A large buffet had been laid, presented in very beautiful silver dishes, in a nearby room. I particularly enjoyed one meat dish that I could not identify. I did not learn that it was venison until I had finished, thus missing out on being impressed as I ate it.

I was very fortunate to be able to see some of Scotland, visit some its historic sights, and meet a lot of delightful people.

We conducted a "fast cruise" during the last week of our upkeep period, right before our sea trials. I do not think I had ever heard the term *fast cruise*

before, even though I had participated in such a thing several times. The word *fast* in this case means fastened snugly to the pier and cruising in place. It is wise, when your ship has had a lot of work done on it, to take time to check it out as fully as possible without leaving your berth. We believed we were ready to go to sea, but we wanted to be as sure as possible that we could before actually trying it.

The scheme that was used with the Polaris submarines was to get the whole crew aboard, close the hatches, and then spend twenty-four hours as though you were at sea. The crew stood regular watches, meals were prepared and served, all equipment was checked and operated, and the crew performed general drills such as fire, collision, and so forth from time to time.

This period helped me become more familiar with the *Alexander Hamilton* and its officers and men. A few hours before completing our fast cruise we received word that a good-sized-storm was approaching. The wind velocity was rapidly increasing. I became so concerned about the increasing wind that I ordered an interruption to our training to go topside and ensure that we were securely moored to the tender. After a quick inspection I decided that we needed to double our mooring lines to the next submarine and suggested to the captain of that sub that he might want to increase his lines to the tender. He considered his mooring to be adequate, but I went ahead and doubled our lines to his vessel.

We were scheduled to get under way for two days of sea trials that evening. I was not at all pleased with the prospects of taking my big submarine to sea for the first time during a heavy storm. I was not familiar with these waters, and no one else on board was either. The *Alexander Hamilton* had first been assigned to the U.S. Navy base in Rota, Spain. Each crew had made a patrol from there, but the Gold Crew was ordered to complete its patrol in Holy Loch, Scotland, where we relieved them. Holy Loch was to remain our base for the foreseeable future.

As the time to depart for our sea trial neared, we prepared to single-up our mooring lines. At the appointed hour, the officer of the deck asked me for permission to bring in all lines and get under way. I granted his request and the lines started coming in — with one exception: a line at the bow could not be taken from the cleat on the inboard submarine. The captain of that sub had finally decided to add additional lines to the tender and one turn on top of our line held our line fast to that submarine. Meanwhile, the strong wind at our stern was going to swing us around if we did not free the bow line. The exec, who had taken charge of freeing the line, realized it was going to take too long to get it untangled and asked, "Request permission to cut Number One."

Officers of the USS Alexander Hamilton, *following my third patrol:* (front row, left to right) *Lt. Comdr. Tom Hopper, Comdr. Dan Summitt, Lt. Comdr. George Halliday;* (back row, left to right) *Lt. Jack MacKinnon, Lt. (jg.) Tom Jones, Lt. John Shrum, Lt. Dan Smith, Lt. Walt Wynn, Lt. (jg.) Gene McDermott, Lt. (jg.) Tom Bragg, Lt. (jg.) Jack Reed, Lt. Carl Schubert, Lt. (jg.) Jim Foster, and Lt. Charles Stuart.*

I had never seen a line cut. I had heard of it, though, and I could not help but think what a new line would cost. We had to do something quickly, however, before we found ourselves completely turned around. "Cut the line!" I responded, expecting a delay while they got something to cut it with and then spent time hacking away at it. One of the sailors had a diver's knife hanging on his belt. He whipped it out and cut through the line in a single swipe, just like it had been butter! Off we sailed. I was pleased with the immediate, professional action. I also gained a healthy respect for a diver's knife.

The night could not have been any darker. The wind was whistling down Holy Loch from the northwest, funneled between the mountainous hills on either side, blowing very close to hurricane force. It was raining hard. The raindrops stung your face. We had difficulty being clearly heard even though we were shouting at men standing right next to us. Our bridge was a small, open cockpit that provided none of the protection normally afforded by a pilothouse. I could not make out the landmarks I had studied and had to depend heavily on the navigator, who was working in the control room below, where he had access to the radar. It was a short run out of the loch to the Clyde. As we neared the point where we were to make our turn into the Clyde, the navigator informed me that the large buoy that would confirm we had reached the turning point had apparently been blown out of position. I would have to turn on his signal. I kept my fingers crossed, hoping he had it right. After making the turn I started picking up lighted buoys as anticipated. There was no traffic to contend with; who in his right mind would be out voluntarily on a night like this? Satisfied that all was well, I dropped below to study the chart and check the radar. The navigator had done a good job getting us on our way. It would be several hours before we reached the open sea. Those who were not on watch went to their bunks. I needed to stay up and about in case we encountered any traffic. I did not plan to sleep until we were at sea and running submerged.

Several hours later we lost the protection of the land mass and began to experience much heavier seas. We were still some distance from the prescribed operating area where we were scheduled to submerge when we spotted the lights of a ship we suspected to be the Russian intelligence ship that was always present to observe our comings and goings. We could not see the ship clearly, but judging from the way it maneuvered and followed us, there was little doubt it was the Russian. The sea was too bad for him to be very fancy in harassing us. I felt a little sorry for him, knowing he would have to ride out this storm for its duration, while I would soon be submerged and free from its fury. We all wished that we did not have to contend with this ever-present Russian nuisance, but we realized that its presence was needed to convince the Russians that we had this mighty deterrent force and meant what we said about having it steadily deployed and ready to respond should they ever launch their missiles at us. They must have been impressed with our unrelenting effort to keep such an impressive retaliatory force at sea day after day. They undoubtedly realized that they would be annihilated if they ever attacked, because no one had the ability to destroy our submarines running submerged at sea. Each of our Polaris subs could destroy up to sixteen of their cities all by itself.

I finally made my first dive in a ballistic missile submarine. We quickly gained a good trim and started working on the schedule of events designed to check out our many systems. The heavy weather had caused us to reach our diving point a few hours late, but we figured out a way to overlap several events so we could get everything done and return to port on time.

It was necessary for us to come to periscope depth from time to time. Our ability to hold a steady depth near the surface was rather poor. It seemed

The USS Alexander Hamilton *at sea, making full speed on the surface.*

that all Polaris submarines handled poorly at periscope depth. The diving officers were all performing properly, but the results were poor. I attributed much of our problem to the heavy sea, but things just did not feel right. I intended to improve our handling at periscope depth, but could not afford to take the time from our busy schedule. We would have to work on this problem during our patrol period. I was determined that *this* Polaris submarine would eventually perform like a thoroughbred.

It was well after midnight and I had just decided to go get some sleep when one of the officers announced that the baker was about ready to pass around a fresh batch of sweet rolls. For weeks I had been hearing about the *Alexander Hamilton*'s sweet rolls. All hands had been telling me what a great baker we had. The baker did his baking at night. He would bake the bread and desserts required for the next day and always made doughnuts or sweet rolls for breakfast. He also made enough to fill a large tray that he carried around the ship in the early morning so that everyone who happened to be up could enjoy his wares fresh out of the oven. I had to admit that the sweet roll I ate that night was absolutely the best I had ever tasted.

Later, before leaving on our second patrol, I told the exec I wanted someone else to do the baking. At first the exec thought I had lost my mind. However, I pointed out that our baker could be ordered to another submarine at any time and before that happened I wanted him to teach several others to bake as well as he did. There was a lot of grousing, but sure enough, his students not only learned from him, they strove to surpass him. I was vindicated.

Our sea trials were progressing well the next morning when the exec came to me and reported that the engineer wanted to make a full-power run for an hour at the same time the navigator was scheduled to run a "P point." This presented a problem, because running a P point was always done at slow speed. In preparation for deployment of the Polaris missile system, our survey ships had carefully surveyed many small areas along the ocean floor in order to provide us a means for accurately determining our position. Of course, we had several other means of determining our exact position. You cannot shoot a missile with great accuracy unless you know precisely where you are. Recording the water depth as you pass through one of these P points enables you to fit these measurements to the chart with pinpoint accuracy. You do this at slow speed to get a maximum density of soundings for a very exact position. I told the navigator to be on his toes because we would be running his P point at flank speed. He looked a bit horrified but swore to do his best. As we raced through the P point, the navigator got an excellent fix. It just shows what you can do when you have good people.

For me, the highlight of our sea trial was the test of our missile-launching system. The thirty-five-thousand-pound missiles are launched from the submarine by a blast of high-pressure air. The submarine needs to be dead in the water so that there is no shear force on the missile as it exits the tube. The push of air is strong enough to shoot it to the surface, where the missile fuel ignites, and off it goes, guided to its target a thousand or so miles away by a complex guidance system.

Immediately following the blast of air, seawater floods the empty launch tube and the outer door automatically shuts, trapping only the amount of seawater needed to compensate for the weight of the missile fired. This all happens in a matter of seconds.

As I mentioned earlier, one or two missiles are removed from the submarine when it returns from patrol. These missiles are then shipped back to the United States, where they are carefully examined, tested, and made ready for further use. This method of regularly rotating missiles helps ensure that perfectly tuned missiles are carried on patrol and that none have deteriorated due to age or some other factor.

The effect on submarine depth by launching one of these heavy missiles is unnoticeable because the weight change is immediately corrected by the weight of seawater immediately filling the empty tube. However, blasting the missile from the tube makes a pretty loud *Baa-wham* sound and the submarine jolts up and down as the hull recoils from the shock of the launch. There is absolutely no doubt that a missile has been launched.

When the missiles being shipped stateside are unloaded upon return from a patrol, their tubes are left empty. Just before going out on sea trials, the empty tubes are loaded with an amount of water equal to the weight of a missile. The tubes filled with water are then fired, just as you would a missile, to test the launching system. To take full advantage of this opportunity, we go to General Quarters and go through the whole process, as if missiles are actually being launched.

Upon receipt of the order to launch, the officer of the deck proceeds to the desired depth and at the same time kills the way of the submarine and finally orders the hovering system into play. By the time everyone reaches his battle station, the submarine should be at the desired depth, dead in the water, with the hovering system pumping or flooding as necessary to maintain that depth. I was very impressed with how well this computerized hovering system performed. It is not an easy task to hover without such a machine.

Launching water from a missile tube is termed a "sabot (pronounced "say-boh") launch." I can never think of a sabot shot without recalling a story told to me by another fleet ballistic missile submarine skipper. Soon after the first SSBN became operational, the Joint Chiefs of Staff went to inspect one of the SSBN's in port somewhere on the East Coast. It was quite an honor to have the top officers of each of our armed services — the army, navy, air force, and Marine Corps — visit one of our members of this awesome missile fleet.

The SSBN was moored to a pier for easy access. Every phase of the visit had been well planned, and according to the carefully observed schedule, the time had come to execute the launching system test, which had been fully explained. My friend, who at the time was the SSBN's executive officer,

Test firing a Polaris missile from the USS Alexander Hamilton *on the Atlantic Test Range.*

had guided the admirals and generals back up to the pier so that they could clearly observe the launch. Something momentarily distracted the exec's attention and at that time the flag officers decided to move farther down the pier closer to the missile tube so that they could observe more closely. When the marine sentry, who had orders not to let *anyone* go beyond him, tried to stop them, the admirals and generals paid no attention to him. The marine, who was pretty sure he was not supposed to shoot them, stood still. When the exec turned to check on his entourage, he was horrified to see them moving toward the launch tubes and raced toward them, trying to get them to come back. He was too late. *Ba-boom!* Thirty-five thousand pounds of water roared upward. The senior officers immediately realized they needed to get the heck out of there. A news photographer got a picture of them: wide-eyed, desperate expressions on their faces, running for all they were worth. In less time than it takes to tell, the water was pouring down, almost driving them to their knees. It was as though a swimming pool had been dumped on them. They could not have been wetter if they had fallen overboard. Some wild language was heard and then they all started laughing as they looked at each other.

The exec led the drenched group below decks to the wardroom, where they peeled off their uniforms and donned borrowed underwear, blankets, and whatever else could be found. A special team carried their soaked uniforms away, to be restored as soon as possible. Meanwhile, they traded verbal jabs, describing what reactions each had observed, arguing who was the wettest, who looked the silliest, and all declaring that this incident would never be forgotten. From time to time they commenced trying to discuss one of the many serious problems they needed to solve, but then one of them would start giggling and they would enjoy another round of laughter at their predicament.

Finally, their restored uniforms were returned to them and they once again became the serious, dignified group that befitted their office. When it came time for them to depart, they all remarked at how much firsthand knowledge they had gained and said they would never forget their visit. I would be willing to bet on that!

After successfully completing our sea trials on schedule, we surfaced and headed back to port. It was midday, the sea was reasonably calm, visibility was good, and eventually, as anticipated, we encountered the Russian spy ship. As we closed on him, he maneuvered several times, causing us to alter course, as required by international rules, in order to safely pass him. It was obvious that his actions were deliberate. I quickly developed a dislike for this bird, as well as a growing determination to get even someday.

As soon as we moored, we commenced final preparations for going on patrol in about two days. We would have to load a missile into the empty tube, correct whatever small deficiencies we had discovered during our fast cruise and sea trials, and top off our load of food, spare parts, and whatever else we might need. We had to take with us everything we might need for three months. We planned to be gone only two months, but we had to be prepared to remain at sea a month longer if conditions required. We followed an established load list so that nothing would be overlooked. I reviewed the load list and was quite surprised at the amount of kinds of supplies we required.

As an example, we carried ten thousand ice cream cones! We had a soft-serve ice cream machine similar to the kind you see at a Dairy Queen. Submarines carry all sorts of little luxuries like that to make the crew's life more pleasant, but you still have to remain within the daily allowance per man or the captain has to pay for any overage. You can bet we keep good records!

≈≈≈

After receiving orders to command a Polaris submarine, but before actually setting foot aboard one, I labored under the impression that most of my days would be boring, far different from my time spent on "go get 'em" fast-attack submarines. I would be spending two months traveling submerged and undetected, patrol after patrol, simply to be available to launch missiles if ordered to do so. I had thoughts of getting a rocking chair, some fleece-lined slippers, and plenty of good books to read during my two months of inactivity.

As I became more involved with the Polaris program — attending missile school, experiencing an off-crew training period ashore, and certainly when I finally arrived aboard the *Alexander Hamilton* — my first impressions completely evaporated. I was impressed with the huge responsibility I had been given. The unit I commanded in this awesome deterrent force had cost hundreds of millions of dollars. My country entrusted it to me and had faith that I would successfully carry out my orders if ever directed to do so. I was determined to be worthy of that trust and ensure that I would be fully ready to act if called upon to do so. I had no doubt that I would be fully occupied each time we put out to sea.

Life on patrol was different in many ways from the life at sea to which I had earlier become accustomed. The first good surprise I got was that the officers and men preferred to stand six-hour watches rather than the traditional four-hour periods. You have probably heard of the tradition of ringing the ship's bell every half-hour, each time adding one more bell until it reaches eight, and then switching back to one bell again. That tradition started back in sailing-ship days with the changing of the "watch" every four hours. The watch was the team of men assigned the task of sailing the ship. A fresh team took over every four hours. Wristwatches and pocket watches were rare in those days, but everyone was always interested in how much time they had left on their watch. The system of sounding bells every half-hour was developed to satisfy that curiosity. At the completion of the first half-hour of a watch, the ship's bell would be struck once. At the end of the next half-hour it was struck twice, then three times, then four times, and so on until it was struck eight times, marking the end of the fourth hour and the completion of the watch. The bell was always struck eight times at 12, 4, and 8 A.M. and P.M. The system makes no sense at all unless you know it.

Anyway, as skipper of the *Alexander Hamilton,* I learned that everyone aboard believed that the longer periods between watches permitted them to work and sleep longer during off periods and that things ran much smoother with less frequent changes. Another habit they had adopted was to serve an additional meal at midnight. The midnight meal was usually a fast-food type such as pizza, hamburgers, chili, and the like. It was quite popular with the younger sailors. I quickly discovered I was the only one not included in that group.

Only two or three officers ever joined me for breakfast, about half the seats would be occupied at lunch, and there was always a full house at dinner. Several weeks of this pattern of attendance caused me to be unconsciously guided as to what time of day it was. There eventually came a day when the cooks served something special for lunch, I cannot remember what it was, that resulted in a full turnout. Everyone was there. It was just like suppertime. When I finished eating, I went to my stateroom and shortly thereafter turned down my bunk and climbed in for a good night's sleep. The next thing I remembered was the steward tapping on my door announcing that it was suppertime. I was shocked. Good Lord, I had slept for a full twenty-four hours! As I stumbled around trying to get dressed, I finally came to my senses and realized what had made my mental clock go haywire. It is sort of difficult to keep track of night and day when you never see the sun. Although I felt a bit foolish, I could not resist telling everyone about what I had done.

Ever since World War II, when our cooks were trained at the Royal Hawaiian Hotel while in port at Pearl Harbor, the submarine force had a reputation for serving excellent food. I was surprised to learn that Polaris submarines were afforded some very unusual food items to bolster that reputation. We carried turkeys that had been dressed and cooked almost to completion. A bag of ready-made gravy was included in the sealed plastic bag containing each turkey. You could then carry the turkeys unrefrigerated wherever you had space. All you had to do was open them up and finish cooking them for about an hour. We also carried large cans of freeze-dried vegetables such as carrots and peas. When you shook the cans it sounded like they were filled with pebbles, but once you opened them and soaked the contents for a couple of hours, you had delicious food that tasted like it was fresh from the garden. We also carried freeze-dried shrimp that was the equal of the best you ever had.

We carried sixty movies on each patrol and showed one every night in the wardroom and the crew's mess. Some were new, but most had been around for quite a few years. Whatever it was, you watched it, because it was the only entertainment available.

From my earliest days in submarines I was impressed by the fact that I seemed to learn something new every day. One day, the weapons officer reported that he was having trouble running a required missile test that could be done only if the sub was stable. We were experiencing a very noticeable roll caused by heavy seas above. Other submarines were built with bilge keels — long fins running almost the full length of the hull on both sides of the bottom — which helped minimize rolling in heavy seas. The hull of a Polaris submarine was completely circular in cross section. For a bilge keel to be effective, it would have to be unusually big and thus would add too much drag. On the earlier subs, once you reached a depth of about a hundred feet you were not affected by the waves above. However, a Polaris submarine seemed to roll at almost every depth when there were heavy seas above. Of course, the deeper you went, the less roll you experienced.

To try to accommodate the weapons officer, I maintained the same course but increased our depth in increments of ten feet, measuring the amount of roll at each depth. As expected, the roll continued to diminish. Then it suddenly started increasing. It finally reached a maximum that was less than it had been when we started before once again decreasing. This happened several times. It was a phenomenon I never would have expected. I knew that wind caused the water to roll, and that this roll continued unbroken until the depth of water decreased to less than the roll. That is what causes breakers on a beach. I never expected to find multiple layers of rolling water that decrease in size as the depth increases.

We finally went deep enough so that the amount of roll was acceptable for the test. Several days later I played around changing depth, recording the roll, and plotting it. I ended up with a very disciplined sine-wave graph of ever-decreasing amplitude.

As I explained earlier, we shot our trash and garbage out just about every night through a "garbage gun" that was similar to a torpedo tube, only pointed straight down. It was flushed out of this tube to avoid creating bubbles that would rise to the surface. Trash containers were located throughout the ship, lined with porous plastic bags made from plastic similar to the mesh used in a screen door. The bags were collected and loaded into a compressor that was loaded with a much larger mesh bag. The whole thing was compressed as a complete unit, then weighed and, if necessary, loaded with enough extra weights to ensure that it sank. One night, shortly after shooting a load of trash, the officer of the deck informed me that they had heard an explosion astern, but did not know what it was. He suspected it was a charge dropped by an aircraft. We went to periscope depth to have a look around, but found nothing. A couple of nights later another explosion was heard. We finally hit on the idea that something going out in the trash was imploding when it reached a great depth. Eventually we discovered that the engineers had disposed of two metal flasks that had been emptied of their compressed contents. Later, when another such flask became available, we shot it out. Sure enough, it imploded with a load bang. We made a rule that, in the future, all empty flasks would be kept until we returned to port. Setting off a loud bang was not in keeping with our intent to remain undetected.

While out on what was at least my second patrol, I was still trying to figure out how to maintain good control of the sub at periscope depth. Despite excellent performance and reaction by all the diving officers, we still were unable to keep the desired amount of periscope exposed. Up and down, up and down. During daylight hours, when I could see both the wave direction and the swell direction, I tried to take up a course that would permit optimum depth control. This helped a little, but our control still was not satisfactory. However, believing that every little bit helped, I struggled with how to see what the sea was doing on a dark night. Finally, I arrived at what I thought was a good idea. We had two periscopes. I got on one and had the other scope constantly trained in the same direction in which I was looking. When I requested it, a crewman would turn on a flashlight he was holding against the eyepiece of the second scope. I figured the flashlight would illuminate the waves enough so that I could see them. "Turn it on," I commanded. A light suddenly appeared that was so bright it scared me. It not only illuminated the waves, it no doubt could be seen from miles away. I immediately ordered the crewman to turn it off. I gave up on the idea for the moment, but I believed the scheme of shining a light through the periscope had merit and might someday come in handy.

My first patrol was anything but boring. I was fully occupied learning more and more about the submarine, the officers and men, how we could improve our performance at every turn, and became accustomed to responding to Weapon System Readiness Tests (WSRTs).

We constantly received coded messages via a very-low-frequency radio system that covered the world. Every week or ten days or thereabouts, our headquarters, following no set pattern, would send a missile-launch message. We never found out until the end of such a message whether it was a

WSRT or the real thing. As soon as we began receiving a launch message, we scrambled to man our stations and get the submarine in a hovering state. Only then would it be announced whether it was a WSRT or an actual launch. We still went through every single step for launching the missiles without actually doing so. Our performance was recorded in a black box and the tape would be analyzed at the end of the patrol to see if we had performed properly and how long it had taken us to do it. Our control was so positive that it was impossible to launch a missile without a bona fide launch order. Needless to say, it kept us on our toes. Everyone breathed a sigh of relief each time we learned it was a WSRT. We all knew that if we were ever ordered to shoot, it would mean that our homes and our families were being attacked. Potential enemies knew full well that they would be destroyed if they attacked us. There was no way to stop us.

At the end of two months, we surfaced and headed for port. Ten or fifteen minutes after surfacing, we invited off-duty crewmen to the bridge — a couple at a time was all that could be accommodated — to get a look at the outside world once again.

As we approached Scotland's inland waters we encountered the ever-present Russian spy ship and permitted him to check us off his list, just like clockwork. This time the weather was calm and visibility good, so he maneuvered closer to us and kept up his harassing efforts by trying to make us change course to get past him. We welcomed his presence because it proved that we were maintaining constant coverage and were ready to knock them out if they dared attack. However, he was a real pest, and the more patrols I made, the more I wanted to do something to pester him.

I came up with what I thought was a great idea, but could not get authorization to carry it out. I wanted to go out on our next sea trial with the empty missile tube filled not with 35,000 pounds of water but 35,000 pounds of wet grits. I would let the Russian get in close to us, maneuver to get him downwind and at just the right distance, and then execute a surface launch of the 35,000 pounds of wet grits. He would not know what hit him. What a mess! What a great idea! We would both remember it for the rest of our lives. I truly regretted not being able to get clearance to do it.

While I was on duty in Washington, and later at the missile school, I heard a few tales about relationships between some Blue and Gold Crews that were rather disturbing. I do not know if the problems were caused by jealousy or laziness, or if they were mischievously intentional. In any event, I became intent on cooperating fully with the other crew when I got command of an SSBN.

When I returned from my first patrol, Capt. Harvey Lyon, who had re-lieved Ben Sherman as skipper of the *Alexander Hamilton*'s Gold Crew, was there to greet me. Harvey, who was a few years senior to me, and I had served briefly together a couple of times. During our five-day turnover pe-riod I developed a real liking for him. He was topnotch in every way, profes-sionally and socially. Just prior to my departure from the ship, we vowed to always turn it over in better condition than we received it, if at all possible. That was the type of competition that Blue and Gold crews should have.

Cooperation between our crews was most important in giving a helping hand ashore. Those ashore needed to help the families of those at sea in time of need. The families of those at sea knew that they merely needed to let someone at the ship's office or on the command staff know if they had prob-lem. Also, those ashore and those on the command staff needed to be alert to recognize things that might occur that could be problems for those at home alone. This type of attention was a great relief to those at sea.

Each officer and crewmember was permitted to receive several brief mes-sages, called "Family Grams," while out on patrol. The messages were closely screened for any disturbing news that could adversely affect a crew-man's duty performance. There were exceptions, however, to accommodate special requests if it was believed that a crewman truly needed to know about and could handle knowledge of a problem.

I was involved in one such incident. One day I received a "for your eyes only" message reporting that the father of one of the officers had died. I had already known that his father was very ill and that he wanted to know right away if his father died, rather than wait to be informed of his death at the end of the patrol. I informed the exec and the engineer officer (for whom he worked) so that they could observe his behavior following receipt of this bad news. Informing him was my responsibility. I dreaded it, but it had to be done out of respect for his wishes. It was not proper to simply hand him the message. I called him into my stateroom and revealed the sad news as gen-tly as I could. There is no such thing as an easy way.

Soon after surfacing at the end of another of my patrols aboard the *Alexander Hamilton,* I received a message from Harvey Lyon. He said he wanted to inform me directly, before I reached port and heard it from some-one else, that my home had burned down a few weeks ago, that no one in my family had been injured, that they had been moved elsewhere, and that our homeowner's insurance had covered almost everything! I knew that mem-bers of the Gold Crew had undoubtedly done all that they could for them, and I had to agree that it was good that I had not been informed before we completed the patrol.

Harvey met me shortly after we moored and filled me in on the details.

The Gold Crew had moved all of the salvageable furniture to a refinishing shop, taken all the smoke-damaged clothing that was still usable to the cleaners, and moved everything else to a storage barn where they had cleaned up all of the items that they could. A number of people had donated such things as a coffeepot, pans, dishes, blankets, and the like for us to use to get somewhat reestablished. I will be forever grateful to that wonderful Gold Crew.

Harvey worked hard at subtly trying to comfort me. He said he just had to tell me about something that had happened to him. One day, he said, he went to the office knowing that he had a lot of things to take care of, knew he would be working late, and wondered how he would find the time to get some things done to his car that were truly needed. One of his stewards heard him grousing about having so many things to do and wondering how he could find time to service his car. The steward had things he had to do near the base gas station, and figuring he could save himself a long walk, offered to take care of his car for him.

Harvey gave the man his keys, told him it was a Ford Fairlane with California tags, and handed him enough money to cover the service charges. The steward said he knew which car was Harvey's. When he returned, the steward gave Harvey the car keys, leftover money, and a detailed receipt.

That evening, when Harvey finally finished work, he headed home thinking how lucky he was not to have to spend even more time getting his car serviced. He looked down and was shocked to see that his gas gauge still read what it had that morning. The gauge undoubtedly was stuck. When he got home, he dipped the gas tank and, sure enough, found that it was almost empty. He then went to the front of the car and opened the hood. To his amazement, he still had the same dirty air filter. Moreover, the dirty oil on the dipstick meant the oil had not been changed! He could not wait to go to the service station the next day and raise Cain. Somebody was going to get it!

The next morning he drove straight to the service station, showed the manager his receipt, let him know quite plainly that he was not going to be taken like that, and demanded that they do what he had paid them to do. Harvey was not a man to back down when he knew he was right. The manager, realizing he had no leg to stand on, made sure that everything Harvey had paid for was done.

After getting to the office, Harvey started wondering if there was some other explanation for what had happened. He got hold of the steward and had him accompany him to the parking lot. Stopping in plain view of his car, he asked the steward to point out the car that he had taken to the service station. "Sure, that's it over there," the steward said, pointing to a Ford Fairlane station wagon with California tags. It was not Harvey's car. He was pointing at the station wagon belonging to Comdr. Stan Smith, another SSBN skipper.

Harvey thanked the steward and headed for Stan Smith's office. Stan was a delightful, slow-talking fellow with a marvelous sense of humor.

"Stan, have you noticed anything strange about your car lately?" Harvey inquired.

Stan leaned back in his chair, carefully considered the question, and responded, "Yeah, it's making gas."

Harvey broke out laughing said, "Tell me about it."

"Well, last night when I left here I went by the gas station because it was time to fill it up. Can't trust the gas gauge, but I knew I needed to get gas. I asked the fellow to fill it up. I heard him take the gas cap off and bang the nozzle in, and then I heard the sound of something splashing on the ground. The fellow came to my window and said, 'What does your gauge say?' I looked down and said, 'It says it's full.' The fellow was visibly upset and said, 'Well, it *is* full!' I drove off scratching my head. I don't know how it happened."

Harvey was able to control his laughing enough to tell Stan his side of the episode, and then they went out to the parking lot and discovered that their keys were interchangeable! One car had been built on the East Coast and one on the West Coast.

I think Harvey got Stan to take him to lunch to cover the full tank of gas and all the other work.

Harvey's story gave me something to laugh about.

≈≈≈

I spent my first patrol trying to improve our depth control but made no significant headway. Now, here I was on my second patrol, at it again. While we were ashore, one of my sons bought a model kit of an SSBN and put it together. I had borrowed it and brought it along on patrol. It was very true to form. I thought that perhaps studying it in comparison to all of the other submarines I had served aboard might help me solve the problem. The other submarines had all been equipped with bow planes. The SSBNs, on the other hand, had planes that were mounted on the sail and much higher than bow planes would have been. The stern planes were configured as on all other submarines.

Because of the SSBN's huge missile compartment, the control room — and therefore the periscopes — was, relatively speaking, much closer to the bow. On other submarines the periscopes were not too far forward of the center of buoyancy and center of gravity. This meant that the relative position of the periscopes to the center of gravity and center of buoyancy on an SSBN was quite different from the other submarines we were accustomed to, while the method of control of both types of submarines was nearly the same.

I had the exec and several diving officers examine the model and then asked them if they thought there was anything we might do differently, such as apply more pitch on the sail planes, that would give us better depth control. At some point I made the comment that our depth gauges measured the depth of the boat at the periscopes. The exec interrupted me to say that was not so, that depth was measured back at the center of buoyancy for the sake of the hovering system. I was stunned by his revelation; but, by golly, that explained what was wrong with our depth control at periscope depth! We were trying to control the precise amount of periscope exposed above the surface. If the boat carried no angle, then we had it like we wanted it. However, we had to be able to hold the exposure exactly, regardless of angle. Even a slight up or down angle would throw us several feet off of the depth we wanted at the periscopes. It was also true that we needed to observe the depth at the center of buoyancy in order for the hovering system to perform properly.

I asked the exec and the engineer to examine our seawater systems to see if there was a hull penetration in the area of the periscopes that we could use for our depth measurement during normal operations and then quickly switch back to the original system for missile launching. They quickly pointed out that we should make no alteration without first obtaining authorization to do so from the proper authority. I was pleased that they had taken the stand that they were supposed to, however, I explained that I was responsible for operating the ship to the best of its ability and that I was willing to take full responsibility for implementing what appeared to be a workable and safe solution.

They came to me the next day with a proposal that was simple and could be very safely accomplished. The modification took only a few hours and resulted in a tremendous improvement. It took the diving officers only a couple of days to fine-tune their techniques for maintaining depth control. I was much relieved with our improved performance. Now we were operating more like a thoroughbred.

I considered it a good idea to be in the control room, practically at the elbow of the officer of the deck, whenever it was necessary to go up to periscope depth. We spent our sixty- day patrol completely submerged, coming up to periscope depth for a few minutes a couple of times each day when it was necessary to expose any one of several antennas or scopes. Our mission was to remain undetected throughout the patrol, and our chances for detection increased whenever we exposed anything above the surface. Although I had complete confidence in my officers of the deck, I wanted to be near at hand in the event anything unusual occurred during this period. As I had done on the *Seadragon*'s Arctic cruise, I kept a small, comfortable folding lawn chair in the control room. Whenever we went to periscope depth I would open it up and sit quietly in a corner near the periscope stand so that I was right there if needed.

Running submerged for two months made it necessary to pay close attention to our atmosphere. We had equipment that closely monitored the atmosphere's contents, as well as equipment with which to correct any out-of-specification problems that might occur. On one occasion, we found a small Freon leak in our refrigeration system and repaired it. However, the only way to reduce an excessive amount of Freon in our atmosphere was to purge the submarine with fresh air. To accomplish this we had to go to periscope depth, raise the snorkel mast, and start ventilating the ship. The process of ridding our air of the excessive Freon would take about an hour.

It was a very dark night. The sea was running pretty heavy. The head valve on the snorkeling mast was shutting and opening quite frequently as waves came in over the snorkel's head and then fell away. Sensors on the head valve automatically caused a small needle valve to open or close, which in turn caused the head valve to shut or open. This system prevented seawater from being sucked inside and flooding the ship.

Keeping our big submarine at a steady depth while running this shallow, particularly in a heavy sea, required excellent performances by the officer of the deck, the diving officer, and the diving-plane operators. All of them were performing beautifully.

We had been ventilating for about twenty minutes when I was startled at the sight of small water droplets being blown from our air-conditioning vents. This was not normal at all. I was already aware that we were beginning to lose good depth control and were headed deeper than desired. There was no reason for strong measures, but I found myself springing out of my chair and leaping onto the periscope stand. I could not believe it when I heard my voice call out, "Ahead standard." With more speed I figured we should have been able to get back to proper depth. It is well understood that when the captain gives an order to the helm, he has the conn of the ship until he formally relinquishes it to the officer of the deck. Something was not right. We were still going down. "Ten degrees up angle," I ordered. Again I appeared to be overreacting, but something was telling me to do it. We were still going down. "Shut the main snorkel valve," the officer of the deck ordered. Good man, I thought, that needed to be done to isolate the snorkel system. Closing that valve produced a whale of a noise: *Wham!* The whole ship shuddered. It had produced an unbelievable water hammer. We were now down to about a hundred feet. I had already increased our speed to full and had us at a ten degree up angle, yet we were still going down. "Blow Main Ballast!" I shouted. That was an extreme measure to take. We continued downward as compressed air started emptying the tanks. We reached a depth of 380 feet before we finally started up. It was unbelievable. Something truly serious had gone wrong! I decided to surface and find out what had happened. Whatever had gone wrong would have carried us straight to the bottom without all of the extreme measures we had taken.

Just before blowing the main ballast tanks, the weapons officer had called from below the control room to report that the fan room was flooded and water was pouring out onto the deck. He recommended maintaining an up angle to keep the water away from a hatch leading to our big battery room. I had the after main ballast tank vents opened before we reached the surface and then shut them again after a brief period so that we would maintain a small up angle after reaching the surface.

We were all by ourselves there on the surface. There was no sign of anyone else in the area. Within fifteen minutes the submarine had been well inspected. The only thing we found out of order was that the snorkel's head valve no longer shut automatically. The main snorkel valve was shut tight; the severe water hammering we experienced upon shutting it during the flooding had not damaged it. We pumped a total of seventy thousand pounds of water from the fan room and bilges. No wonder we had such a hard time getting to the surface.

We finished exchanging our atmosphere while sitting on the surface and submerged as soon as we determined it was safe to do so.

It would not be possible to discover what had gone wrong with the snorkel's head valve system without sending men topside to swarm all over the piping, fittings and controls. I figured we would just have to forgo repairs until we completed our patrol in three or four days.

A few hours after returning to our tender in Holy Loch, we found that a needle piston about the size of a nail had corroded enough to become bound in its cylinder, thus preventing the snorkel's head valve from shutting as it was supposed to do. The wrong metal had been used in its manufacture. It should have been made from noncorrosive steel. The force commander was notified of this problem, and an urgent inspection of the valves in all similar systems was conducted.

It is amazing to think that such a little part almost caused us to lose our lives. It reminds me of the line: "For want of a nail, a shoe was lost; for want of a shoe, a horse was lost;" and so on. Just think how many little parts there are on a submarine.

~~~~~~

You would think that the crews of Polaris submarines would just about go out of their minds after spending sixty days fully submerged on each patrol. No radio transmissions were permitted, so a person could not communicate with anyone off the ship. We were fully isolated from the outside world except for what was reported to us in radio transmissions. All Polaris submarines had the means to receive radio transmissions without coming to the surface. It was absolutely necessary to maintain this reception capability so that we could receive orders to launch our missiles at any time. Since World War I, military foes have kept close tabs on their opponents' radio traffic, even when in code, because a radical change in the number of transmissions, regardless of whether they can be clearly read or not, is a sure sign that something unusual is about to happen. To deny our foes this tip, the special coded transmissions to the Polaris submarine fleet were continuous. Along with the transmission of required operational and administrative traffic, other fill-in type traffic was used to keep the transmissions constant.

The "Family Grams" mentioned earlier filled in a lot of this empty space. Personal messages of limited length could be passed to the squadron offices for transmission to individual crewmembers. Each man was limited to about five messages per patrol. The majority of the fill-in effort was accomplished by the transmission of material provided by various news services. The transmitting station made no attempt to edit the news, so the same stories would be transmitted several times during a twenty-four-hour period. Most Polaris submarines assigned their doctor the task of taking all the news copy that came in each day, sifting through it, and preparing a daily newspaper that could be copied and distributed to the crew each morning.

We all looked forward to seeing the paper each day. It satisfied the natural desire to know what was going on in the rest of the world. One day I was shocked to read that Princess Margaret had appeared at a topless beach in England clad like everyone else. I could not believe it. Surely it was a case of mistaken identity. The whole crew was discussing this item. Most believed as I did: it certainly could not be so.

The next day there was a follow-up article emphatically stating that the story about Princess Margaret's immodest activity was indeed true. The Royal Family refused to comment. Princess Margaret responded to questions with a big smile and a cheery, "No comment!" I was very disappointed by Princess Margaret's actions. I knew her behavior would upset my friends in the Royal Navy. Most of the crew felt as I did. Others thought it was great, that there needed to be more women like Princess Margaret.

The next day, before I had a chance to read the paper, the executive officer informed me that the doctor had admitted to having inserted the story in an effort to combat boredom. He had printed an admission of his indiscretion that morning to set the record straight. I could not help but chuckle. The doctor swore to never mess with the news again.

The prize-winning act of news generation occurred on another Polaris sub. About three weeks before the end of its patrol a story about "Big Foot" appeared in its paper. Several people had reportedly discovered tracks in the snow somewhere in the Alps that could only have been made by Big Foot. Several days later a story appeared in the paper about a small party of three or four people in the Alps claiming to have seen Big Foot at a distance, just before sunset. After sunrise the following day they located tracks leading to a small village several miles away. Two more days passed and then a story appeared about several search parties being formed in the general vicinity. Several days after that there was a story about one of the search parties catching a brief glimpse of Big Foot and later locating his tracks, which were now headed into the wilderness.

The submarine's captain was a bit skeptical and closely questioned his doctor. The doctor strongly denied that he was generating the story. The captain, still not satisfied, had his communications officer question all of the radiomen. The radiomen denied any part in doctoring the news. Half an hour later, one of the radiomen ran to get the communications officer so he could witness the receipt of a Big Foot story that was being received at that very moment. The communications officer did not realize that the story he saw coming out of the machine was being fed to that machine from another machine in the radio room. After that, the skipper and everyone else aboard accepted the Big Foot news as the real thing.

The stories coming in were increasingly dramatic. A huge effort was being made to capture Big Foot. Each day brought another account of the operation. About a week before the patrol ended the crew learned that Big Foot had been cornered, that there was no way he was going to escape, and that he would soon be captured. A number of people were involved in trying to keep television cameramen and news people out of the way so they would not confuse the people involved in the operation. The next day's headline screamed that Big Foot had been captured! He had been shot with a medicated dart and loaded into a specially built cage while he was unconscious. It would take a few days to get him out of the mountains to the nearest village, where cameramen and news people would at last be permitted to view the creature. By coincidence, the date set for this occasion was the same day the submarine was scheduled to return to Holy Loch. Excitement reigned. Everyone who expected to go on liberty soon after arrival planned to head for the nearest pub in hopes of seeing Big Foot on the house TV. The major newspapers might already carry photos. All the talk was about Big Foot. The whole world was undoubtedly just as excited.

The submarine had been surfaced for some hours and was now approaching the big tender at their base in the Holy Loch. The tugboat that would assist the submarine in mooring alongside the tender was already on its way out. The squadron commander was always aboard that tug because he wanted to get with the captain as soon as possible to learn how the patrol had gone. He wanted to know if there had been any unusual problems, if any notable events had occurred, if anyone was sick, and so forth. It was also a great morale boost to know that the commodore was keenly interested in their welfare and accomplishments.

The captain met the commodore as he stepped aboard and gave him a quick briefing on the patrol's highlights. A typed patrol report would be presented to the commodore later. That report would cover everything in detail and fully address all facets of the operation for the benefit of the staff and the other Polaris captains.

With his briefing completed, the captain could not resist asking, "Have you seen him yet?"

"Seen who?" responded the commodore.

"Big Foot!" the captain said excitedly.

"Big Foot?" responded the commodore.

"Yes, Sir. Has he been on TV yet?"

"What are you talking about?" The commodore was beginning to think the captain had been out on patrol too long.

"You know, Sir," the captain replied. "We've been following the search for and capture of Big Foot for two weeks and we're all anxious to see what he looks like."

"I suppose I must have missed the story. I haven't heard anything about it," the commodore stated.

The two officers stood there facing each other, their eyes locked.

"Commodore," the captain finally said, "I know I haven't lost my mind. I believe I've been had!"

As soon as the submarine was moored alongside the tender and the commodore had departed, the captain met with his exec, the communications officer, and several others. They untangled the mystery in pretty short order.

I never did hear all the details, but I doubted that anyone would ever pull a similar stunt again. In any event, everyone aboard that sub agreed that the

Big Foot hoax had added a lot of excitement to their lives and was enjoyed by all.

I was on my last patrol when I received orders to report to the Commander Submarine Force Atlantic Fleet (COMSUBLANT), to serve as deputy chief of staff for Polaris submarines. It was an excellent assignment, but I did not look forward to leaving my command. I liked going to sea. I would still go to sea for a couple of days from time to time in my new job, but it would be as an inspector, really just a passenger.

We had completed our patrol and another SSBN had taken over the responsibility of covering our target package. As we neared port, we spotted the Russian spy ship coming over the horizon up ahead. He eventually spotted us and took up a course to intercept. Wanting him there to prove to the Russians we meant business was one thing, but his habit of harassing us served no other purpose than to satisfy his bullying nature. It really bugged me that I always had to let him get away with it.

The weather was good, the sea rather calm, and visibility excellent. I stayed on the bridge. This was my last chance. If I could not blast him with wet grits, then I was determined to do *something* to let him know we had had enough of his bullying.

He had maneuvered ahead of us such that it was now time for us to change course in accordance with the International Rules of the Road in order to avoid him. I made my turn, not away from him, but toward him. He held on as long as he dared but finally turned away to avoid us. I turned toward him again. We continued to close. I increased our speed to full. He had obviously increased speed and now he turned again. I again turned toward him and continued to close the gap between us. We were not expected to have much speed on the surface, but we were now making more speed than he was. It was all he could do to get away from us as we followed close astern.

The exec was down below watching him through the periscope. Thanks to the periscope's magnification he was able to observe the activity of the Russian personnel. He called up to report that the Russians were very agitated, running about and putting on life jackets!

We were now so close that I had to turn to avoid running into him. Just as I was about to order, "Left full rudder," the Russian started a tight turn to the right. I immediately gave the order to turn left and waved to him. I think I saw a horrified look on his face. Well, I thought, now you have something to remember us by. I will never forget the pleasure of that moment.

When we reached Holy Loch, the squadron commander boarded us from the tug, as was his practice. I told him of the incident. I expected no rebuke and got none. Months later I learned that the Russian spy ships were not as bothersome as they had been in the past.

It was good to get together with Harvey Lyon and his crew again. He passed along all the news of what had been going on in the navy as well as back home. Thank goodness he had no major problems to report this time.

We passed the few evenings we had together calling on all the Scots I needed to say good-bye to and wish well. They had been most friendly and hospitable.

The weather was very bad the morning we conducted the official change of command. It was raining hard and the wind was very strong, just as it had been the first time I had put to sea from there. I was concerned about our boat crossing to Greenock. It was going to be rough, but we had to get across in order to catch our chartered flight home.

Our party of about 125 people was being carried in two personnel boats that were rather small for such heavy weather. I boarded the lead boat and took up a position in the pilothouse rather than going below. I wanted to keep my eye on things. We were being thrown about quite hard, but when we cleared Holy Loch and started across the Clyde, we lost some of the protection afforded by the high hills bordering the loch and it really got bad. To ease the extreme rolling we were experiencing from the strong wind on our port side, the coxswain changed course about forty-five degrees to the right, which caused us to head on down the Clyde. He said he planned to go on downriver a bit and then make a ninety-degree turn back to the left so that the wind would not be broad on our beam except during the time of the turn. I agreed with him, it was exactly what I would have done.

Before the time to turn came, one of the waves crashing over the bow broke through the glass window in the front of the pilothouse. The boat simply was not built for such heavy weather. I held my breath as we made our turn because our chances of rolling over were greatest during the brief period in which the wind was directly on our beam. We managed to make it, but I had my doubts for a couple of moments.

The boat following behind us had made its turn before we did and was now up ahead. It seemed even worse, watching someone else being thrown about. Soon we started to close on the second boat. I could not imagine him slowing down so much without a problem. We pulled alongside and learned that one of his mooring lines had washed over the side and become tangled in the propeller. We managed to take it in tow and finally made it to Greenock. It was an experience I never want to repeat.

Two double-decker buses were waiting for us when we landed. Before boarding, I made sure the two boats would remain there until the storm was over.

It was good to sit down in a warm, dry, stable bus. The roads and villages we drove through were deserted. Nobody in his right mind wanted to be out in this weather. Broken tree limbs were down here and there; there were even a few uprooted trees. As we passed a wide-open area, we saw a double-decker bus lying on its side just off the road. The wind had blown it over. It must have happened some time earlier, because there was no one anywhere around.

The local navy transportation officer met us at the air terminal in Prestwick. He reported that the airport was closed because of the bad weather. It would be at least the next day before our plane could land there. A barracks that had been built there to house Polaris personnel facing a delay in transit had been closed in the most recent round of budget cutting. It was going to take some effort to find a place for us to spend the night. We were able to stay in the terminal building while the transportation officer went to work out the details.

We had been in Prestwick's terminal building enough times to know our way around, so we made the best of it. I recalled having to wait there several hours for a flight back home some time before and had paused to watch a live horse race on TV that was about to start. Shortly after the announcer cried, "They're off!" all of the horses disappeared in a dense fog. The announcer did a pretty good job of filling the dead time because absolutely nothing of the horses could be seen until they approached the finish line.

The transportation officer returned after a couple of hours. He had made sure that our headquarters in Charleston knew the details of our delayed arrival so that our families could be notified. There was no single place in the area that could house our entire crew, but he was able to arrange for spaces for everyone in several different establishments. The exec worked out who would stay where and arrangements were made to get us to our various abodes and back to the airport the next morning. The transportation officer handled payment for our rooms.

Some of the men were a bit upset at the delay, but no one complained about the lodging, and all had words of praise for the hardworking transportation officer.

We made it safely home the next day.

17

DUTY WITH COMSUBLANT STAFF

Just prior to the completion of my last patrol, I was promoted to captain and ordered to report to the commander of the Atlantic Fleet's Submarine Force, headquartered in Norfolk, Virginia, for duty as the deputy chief of staff for Polaris submarines.

The staff was manned and organized to run a submarine force. With the advent of the Polaris missile and the submarines designed to carry it, it was necessary to add personnel to cover the unique items such as the missile weapons system, the complex navigational system, and a few other things requiring special attention. It was this new section of that staff that I was assigned to head. I had an assistant who, acting as my right-hand man, oversaw the daily problems experienced by the others and stood ready to tackle any special tasks I might assign him. My staff also included an officer who was primarily responsible for items related to the missile system, one for the navigation system, and a civilian on temporary assignment from the Applied Physics Lab at Johns Hopkins University, which was responsible for analyzing our weapons system's performance and advising us on any matters that might improve it. That lab had played a significant role in developing and perfecting the Polaris missile.

One of our primary tasks was to review all of the SSBN patrol reports to ensure that all was going well and to try to spot problems. We learned from the information recorded during WSRTs if performance was what it should be in terms of the fleet's readiness to launch missiles.

About a week before departing the United States to relieve the crew coming back from patrol, the skipper, exec, navigator, and weapons officer of each SSBN came to Norfolk for a briefing on their next patrol. Not only was this necessary for them, it also gave us a chance to hear directly from them of anything that they needed to make the program even better.

When construction of an SSBN was completed, the ship went through a shakedown cruise topped off by a trip to Cape Canaveral, Florida, where it launched a missile to prove its readiness for patrol. It was specially outfitted for this cruise with equipment that monitored the proper operation of its various systems. One or more members of my staff would go along and return with a firsthand report on how it all went.

The commander of the Atlantic Fleet's sub force was responsible for and in complete control of all SSBNs until they went on alert. At that time, control automatically shifted to the commander in chief, Atlantic (CINCLANT), who had overall responsibility for all naval operations in the Atlantic. As they completed a patrol and went off alert, command automatically shifted back to COMSUBLANT. It thus was important for us to work closely with those members of the CINCLANT staff whose primary interest was SSBN matters. Since our headquarters was within a hundred yards of CINCLANT headquarters, we spent a lot of time walking back and forth. Both staffs needed to keep in touch with what an SSBN was doing, regardless of who had control.

To ensure operational security was maintained, nobody had any idea where an SSBN was while on patrol, although a few of us knew which huge area of the ocean they were assigned to operate in at a particular time. It was necessary that *no one* be able to pinpoint an SSBN's position.

When I began working on the COMSUBLANT staff, about half of the planned forty-one Polaris submarines had been built. As their numbers increased, they took over more and more target coverage. The U.S. Air Force's Strategic Air Command (SAC) had been in this business for quite a few years and had the responsibility of ensuring that all of the desired targets were continuously covered by the weapons systems best suited to the task. Individual targets required the assignment of particular weapons in order to achieve the best results. It was one whale of a planning effort. Computers were utilized for much of it, but the submarine force had none, so it was up to my section to manually perform the required scheduling of our assets.

It is rather difficult to recall the constant tension of the Cold War days. It was a way of life to which we all became accustomed. Yet, always lurking in the back of our minds was the knowledge that we might one day have to launch our missiles and hope that we could survive the attack on its way from the Soviet Union. I felt a tremendous sense of relief years later when the Soviet government fell apart. It is a blessing that nuclear warfare never erupted during the Cold War, but we labored under the constant threat that it might for a very long time.

One afternoon I learned that one of our nuclear-powered attack submarines, the USS *Scorpion* (SSN-598), was overdue. It was a Submarine Squadron 6 ship, based there in Norfolk, returning from a long deployment to the Mediterranean. No reported change to its time of arrival had been received. Families and friends of the crew had been waiting on the dock for hours, their anxiety rising. Ships and aircraft operating in the area had been asked to report if they spotted the *Scorpion,* but no reports of sightings had yet been received.

All of us openly hoped that there was some unusual reason for their delay which also prevented them from reporting and that we would soon hear from them. However, most of us silently feared that something disastrous had occurred.

An air-sea search had been initiated, but darkness greatly inhibited our efforts. A special watch was established to receive and handle all incoming messages and information relative to the search. Everything reported was plotted on a large wall chart. I drew the midnight-to-four watch for several days. Despite the intense search, no solid clues had been found. We stood down after about a week and let the special search vessels take over.

Everyone was saddened, not only for the crew but also for the families and close friends.

The *Scorpion* was discovered several months later by special deep-sea search equipment. Its position indicted that the loss had occurred about two days before the ship's scheduled arrival. *Scorpion* was the second nuclear-powered submarine to be lost. The first was the USS *Thresher,* which had gone down while I was working for Admiral Rickover.

Despite these losses, I never heard any submariner express a desire to leave the service. I did, however, observe an intense desire in everyone to ensure there were no more such losses.

It was interesting to me that Great Britain joined the effort to deter a nuclear attack by also constructing a Polaris missile force. Agreements were made that specified the amount of cooperation they could expect from the U.S. Navy. They were to design and build their own submarines, while we helped them with the missiles and passed along the operational know-how we had developed. Our association reached its peak during my tour of duty with COMSUBLANT. I became well acquainted with their key submariners involved in this effort. In addition to hosting their visits to our offices, I made several trips to Cape Canaveral to observe their missile tests.

About midway through my tour on the COMSUBLANT staff, I was informed that the Royal Navy had invited me to come to England for several days to explain how we scheduled upkeeps, sea trials, and patrols, and the various things we desired to accomplish when an SSBN was in port. The invitation specified that my wife and I would be their guests. They would take care of all the arrangements and pay our expenses. It was most unusual; I was truly surprised and pleased. I was authorized to accept the invitation, made the trip, was well received, and developed strong ties with the Royal Navy. From then on I worked with the British from time to time and assisted them however I could.

Several months before the completion of my tour of duty on the COMSUBLANT staff, I received orders to join two other captains from the staff on a routine inspection of Submarine Flotilla 8's staff in Naples, Italy. I was delighted to be given the task because I was greatly impressed by the very thorough, professional, and exciting work they did.

The commander of Submarine Flotilla 8 (COMSUBFLOT 8) reported directly to COMSUBLANT on matters of submarine policy, administration, and maintenance, but to the Sixth Fleet commander and commander in chief, U.S. Naval Forces Europe (CINCUSNAVEUR), on operational matters. As part of the Cuban missile crisis settlement, the United States had agreed to dismantle some missile sites in Greece and Turkey that threatened the Soviet Union. This loss of target coverage was made up by the covert deployment of Polaris missile subs in the Mediterranean. Once a Polaris submarine entered the Mediterranean it came under the operational control of CINCUSNAVEUR, whose staff was in London. Meanwhile, attack submarines assigned to COMSUBFLOT 8 were under the Sixth Fleet's operational control. The COMSUBFLOT 8 staff kept very busy responding to requirements from these three different headquarters.

In addition to all this, COMSUBFLOT 8 wore a North Atlantic Treaty Organization (NATO) hat and had a small NATO staff located adjacent to his headquarters consisting of one U.S. Navy officer, two British officers, an Italian officer, a French officer, and a Greek officer. It was COMSUBFLOT 8's task to coordinate all NATO submarine operations in the Mediterranean. This meant reporting to a *fourth* headquarters: that of the commander in chief, Allied Forces Southern Europe (CINCSOUTH), who was always a U.S. Navy admiral based in Naples. The two submarine staffs worked together closely, but none of the foreign officers were ever admitted into the U.S. command center. We informed them of U.S. operations only when we wanted them to know something. There was never a dull moment on the staff of COMSUBFLOT 8.

The three of us spent two and a half days probing every aspect of the staff. At the end of that effort, we got our heads together and determined that their performance was superb. The only thing they needed was some more personnel; they were clearly overworked. Our inspection report clearly addressed the need for additional people. We did our best to paint a clear picture of the problem and hoped that they would receive some relief.

Several weeks after completing my inspection trip, I received orders to report to COMSUBFLOT 8 for duty as chief of staff. I nearly turned cartwheels I was so happy. I could not have asked for a better job. I could hardly wait to get there.

During my final days with COMSUBLANT, as I was saying my good-byes, I was told that soon after I reported to COMSUBFLOT 8 they were scheduled for a 30 percent staff cutback as a result of a recent budget reduction. Man, I sure had my work cut out for me!

18

COMSUBFLOT 8

Our move from Norfolk to Naples, Italy, was handled like any other move except that it would be at least six weeks or more before we would see our furniture again.

The first leg of our trip was a flight from New York to London, where we spent a couple of days visiting some of the many historical sights. Then, by train and ferry, we made our way to Germany. I had expected to see evidence of the vast destruction rendered during World War II, but instead saw reestablished cities and hustle and bustle that belied the fact that there had been horrendous bombing attacks.

Our visits to various cities were rather brief as we worked our way south to Rome, where we planned to spend most of our time. The staff at COMSUBFLOT 8 had made reservations for us, so we lost no time hunting for suitable accommodations. They had even arranged for a guide with a car. He spent several days taking us to points of interest we otherwise would never have known about.

On the final day of my leave, we took a train to Naples. Members of the staff were on hand to greet and drive us to the hotel where we would live until our furniture arrived and we had a place to live. The hotel was very good and was priced to fit my budget. Our rooms overlooked the Bay of Naples. A driver picked me up in a staff car each morning at a specific time and brought me back in the evening whenever I was ready to go.

After much effort we found an apartment we liked. There were two bedrooms, two baths, living room, dining room, den or parlor, large breakfast room and kitchen, and a good-sized patio. The only windows were in the kitchen and bathrooms. All of the other rooms had French doors opening out onto small balconies. The main rooms had inlaid marble floors designed to look like oriental rugs. The workmanship was amazing. All of the rooms had high ceilings.

Across the street, running hundreds of yards downhill to the bay, was a large, well-kept vineyard. To the right of the vineyard was a large field planted with row after row of flowers that were picked each morning and carried off in armloads to be sold at the market. It was quite a beautiful sight.

A good distance across the bay we could see the isle of Capri, which we visited many times. To our left, also at a good distance, was Mount Vesuvius. We could plainly see all of the ships entering and leaving the port.

It took about two months from the time we left Norfolk for our furniture to arrive. We remained in the hotel throughout that period. It was nice to again have a place to call home. Although I had started my job the day after we arrived in Naples, it was good to finally get settled so I could concentrate even more on all that I had to do.

It was only about a ten-minute drive from our apartment to the NATO base where COMSUBFLOT 8's headquarters was located. The base was a large fenced-in compound consisting of five or six large three-story buildings. It was nicely landscaped, with a parade ground in front of a central building that housed the NATO commander's office. The gate was manned by a couple of Italian policemen.

When I first visited the base and headquarters on my inspection trip, we had entered a building off to the left of the main NATO headquarters. I was surprised to find myself in what looked like a shopping mall. There were all sorts of shops, a coffee and snack bar, a bank, and a number of people milling around. We headed for a wide stairway and climbed to the second floor. There I saw a travel office and a couple of NATO offices. We continued up the stairs to the top floor, which appeared to be abandoned. We went to the end of the passageway, turned right, and there was the NATO submarine office. We passed it, went to the end of that passageway, and stopped in front of a steel door that was closed and locked. My escort lifted the lid on a small box, punched in a few numbers on a keypad, and unlocked the door. We went inside and were greeted by a sailor sitting at a desk with a phone on it. We were now inside COMSUBFLOT 8's headquarters. I had seen nothing in the passageway to indicate that there was a submarine headquarters at the far end. To the uninitiated, the locked door could have led to a storeroom.

After a brief welcome by various members of the staff, we were led to the operations center for the morning briefing. Ten or twelve armchairs had been arranged so that they faced a huge chart of the Mediterranean that went from floor to ceiling and stretched about twenty feet across. Magnetic markers were used to indicate the location of any ship or submarine of any possible concern. It was an amazingly comprehensive presentation. The watch officer, armed with a five-foot-long pointer, reviewed the status and gave pertinent comments concerning the U.S. attack submarines (SSNs), the Polaris submarines, the Sixth Fleet, NATO submarines, Russian ships and submarines, and other items of interest. After answering any questions that arose, he relinquished the floor to the chief of staff, who made any necessary special announcements, reviewed the status of any ongoing special projects, and commented as necessary to insure that everyone was well focused on what had to be done that day. The briefing lasted about half an hour and was of great value in keeping the staff work headed in the right direction.

We had then spent a little while reviewing the headquarters' communications system. In addition to the worldwide broadcast to submarines, COMSUBFLOT 8 produced its own broadcast for submarines in the Mediterranean. A secure "hotline" telephone setup provided direct lines to all major operational points worldwide. It employed a scrambler system that made it completely secure so that conversations of the highest classification could be conducted.

It was interesting to learn that the Sixth Fleet commander would show up there to get a full and complete picture of operations from time to time. A helicopter landing site was located atop a hill about two blocks away. It was not unusual for a helicopter to arrive to take a SUBFLOT 8 officer to Commanding Sixth Fleet flagship. The U.S. Navy admiral who headed the NATO headquarters would also stop by now and then to get a full U.S. briefing on a hot situation. We took great pride in maintaining a very fresh and fully detailed picture of all that was going on in the region.

My job was all that I had anticipated it would be — and then some. Our objective was to very professionally direct and support all U.S. submarine operations in the Mediterranean. Everyone had to be on their toes to insure that every submarine was kept informed of everything that we learned that might affect their particular operation: weather changes, changes in ship movements, changes in other operations, anything to assist them in performing their tasks well. We had to stay on top of, and follow through on, the procurement of parts, supplies, or even personnel that they unexpectedly required. It was a twenty-four-hour-a-day, seven-day-a-week responsibility. It was not unusual for any of us to be called in the middle of the night by the watch officer for guidance on a particular problem. If the subject was classified and could not be discussed on the phone, we had to jump out of bed, dress, and race to headquarters. We did an awful lot of work during our off-duty hours.

I had been on the staff for only a couple of weeks when the first of several wives called on me in my office. They all had the same complaint: their family lives were in turmoil. The fathers had little time for their children. Plans for recreational activities such as side trips, movies, and the like were usually disrupted. As far as they were concerned, the wives thought they would be better off living back in the United States — at least there the family could be with relatives. One wife simply broke down crying. I needed to do something, and the sooner the better.

The thought occurred to me that all of the wives who had come to see me were married to radiomen. I called for the communications officer and worked with him to see if we could make some changes that would reduce his men's workload without affecting the superb performance of that department.

The communications officer agreed to lower his standards for qualification requirements from "highly qualified" to "sufficiently qualified" to avoid doubling up on certain watch stations with the understanding that, if our level of performance dropped even close to being unacceptable, we would return to the old scheme. It all worked out well and soon the strain on their home lives was closer to normal.

I continued to encourage everyone to come to me if they truly believed a task was not required to maintain our high level of performance. There was no reason to spend time on unnecessary tasks when it could be better spent on truly important things.

In the early part of the 1970s, the Sixth Fleet was placed in a rather high alert status due to a crisis involving Jordan. One of our nuclear attack submarines was given a large area in which to operate that was in close proximity to the concentration of Sixth Fleet ships in the eastern Mediterranean. If its services were desired, then it would be there, ready to go. Using a series of area assignment changes, we then worked the patrolling Polaris submarines westward, away from that area.

The crisis passed after a couple of weeks and we brought the attack sub into Naples before it commenced its scheduled transit back to the United States. While it was in port we were surprised to learn from the skipper that they had picked up a Russian submarine following one of our carriers wherever it went. They had trailed the Russian submarine constantly and tried several times to notify Sixth Fleet what it was doing, but they could never get through. The operation order had designated that a certain VHF frequency be used for communications between the submarine and the ships of the surface force. This high-level frequency had only a line-of-sight capability, which means that it was effective only in the local area. We had no desire for such communications to be picked up by monitoring stations ashore. The sub skipper risked losing the Russian whenever he came to periscope depth to transmit, so he dared not spend a long time trying to raise the surface ships.

He was always able to receive our low-frequency broadcast and knew we would alert him if fighting broke out, but the Sixth Fleet needed to know immediately of the presence of such intruders without alerting the Russians that we had detected them. We had to solve this communication problem fast.

I called the Sixth Fleet operations officer and told him that I had something very interesting to report; that we had a problem we had to work out as soon as possible. He called back shortly and said that his admiral and several staff officers would meet with me in Naples the next day. The Sixth Fleet commander did not walk around sniffing for problems but jumped on them right away when reported. That was what I liked about working with the Sixth Fleet.

The admiral was naturally pretty upset to learn that our attack submarine found it impossible to notify someone in the fleet that a Russian sub was trailing one of his carriers. However, he quickly recovered and said we needed to learn quickly how we could establish good, clear, secure, tactical communications among planes, ships, and submarines. Boy, was I pleased to hear that. Enough of this interforce rivalry!

We immediately started discussing various ideas that might work. All three forces — ships, planes, and submarines — were represented in our group of four or five officers, and it appeared that we could come up with some schemes pretty quickly. The admiral emphasized that we had to use equipment that was already available to us because we needed immediate results. Designing and manufacturing new equipment could come later. We had to come up with workable schemes now!

He turned to me and said that I had two weeks to gather all the workable ideas, write up test procedures for them, and devise a schedule. He then would give me a destroyer and some airplanes to work with one of our submarines for a week so that we could identify which of the ideas worked best. I briefed the rest of the staff on the assignment and soon ideas came pouring in, most of them very worthwhile, although many expressed the same suggestions.

One of the more interesting suggestions involved the use of transmitters that could be launched from the signal guns with which every submarine was equipped. These transmitters were carried for use in emergencies to help surface ships searching for a downed submarine. You recorded your message and shot the gadget out of your signal gun, which is like a small torpedo tube. It went straight to the surface and floated there, transmitting your message over and over again.

I recalled the time I experimented with shining a flashlight through the periscope with the hope of illuminating the sea to observe wave direction. I had never used the technique again because the beam of light was so bright. It was also very directional, which meant that it might be a good way to pass a message to a ship because only the ship you aimed at would see it.

Another idea was to create a list of simple code words having more complex meanings. In this way, a lengthy message could be reduced to only a couple of words — as long as everyone concerned had a copy of the list of code words and what they meant.

I quickly gathered a surprising number of good ideas, prepared detailed tests for evaluating them, and developed a schedule for getting the job done within a week. That accomplished, I boarded the destroyer the admiral had provided because it was the best place for me to be to keep things coordinated and to best judge the degree of success of each test.

I was particularly pleased to be aboard the destroyer when we reached the test of how well a flashlight could be seen through a periscope. We moved out to a range of about six miles from the sub, which was the maximum distance at which the line of sight between the bridge of the destroyer and the head of a periscope could be maintained. It was an average night so far as the level of darkness. The light was visible only when aimed directly at the destroyer and we could easily see it at that distance.

Most of the schemes we tested proved successful and were soon being routinely used in our normal and special operations. We were now able to provide much better support to the Sixth Fleet. At the same time, ships and aircraft operating in the region were much better able to support our submarines.

The number of SSNs steadily increased until about half the submarines provided to the Sixth Fleet were SSNs. Their everlasting endurance, their improved sonar, and their silence greatly increased our ability to detect and track any Russian submarine entering the Mediterranean. In one instance, one of our SSNs had secretly trailed a Russian submarine for weeks and weeks, right up to the time that it was due to depart the Mediterranean and head home. The Sixth Fleet commander did not want to lose track of the Russian when our SSN broke contact, yet he did not like the idea of holding the sub beyond its scheduled departure date. He therefore directed us to relieve the SSN with one that was just reporting to SUBFLOT 8. This knocked us back on our heels because such a thing had never before been attempted. We had anticipated the need to know how to go about doing such a thing, though, and our boss back in the United States, COMSUBLANT, had ordered our development group to come up with the best and safest method for accomplishing it. However, the details had not yet been worked out. They said it would take them at least another month to do that and get the method approved. When we informed the Sixth Fleet commander of the status of this effort, he pointed out that he had complete confidence in us and insisted that we go ahead with the relief as desired.

We got our heads together and in a very short time developed a simple, positive, and very safe method to accomplish the turnover. We incorporated some of the tricks we had learned during our search for better communications and, to our delight, it all worked beautifully. The new SSN continued to secretly trail the Russian sub until it left the Mediterranean. It was things like this that made my job so exciting.

About six months after I returned stateside for an assignment in the Pentagon, another crisis broke out and the work of the submarines was outstanding. The commander of SUBFLOT 8 was ordered to the Pentagon to brief the submariners there on all that had transpired. I attended the briefing and was most pleased to learn just how well the submarines had supported the Sixth Fleet. The new means of communicating made a big difference.

Some years later, after I retired from the navy, I saw the movie *The Hunt for Red October* and was greatly surprised to see the two very modern submarines using a flashing light built into the periscope to talk to each other!

In August, 2000, it was reported that a Russian submarine suffered severe damage and was lying on the bottom of the Barents Sea at a depth of about 350 feet. Some 116 men were trapped in the sunken submarine. Four days passed and the men still had not been rescued. Russian submarine or not, I remember thinking that every living U.S. Navy submariner was hoping and praying for their rescue. Heavy seas and strong wind, coupled with the fact that the submarine was listing twenty degrees or so, all hampered the rescue effort. In the end, none of the crew survived.

Why would anyone want to be a submariner? Why had I wanted to be a submariner? One of our submarines, the USS *Squalus,* sank in peacetime while conducting sea trials following overhaul in Portsmouth, New Hampshire, in the 1930s. I was about ten years old at the time and closely followed the news reports for several days until the survivors, about half the crew, had been rescued. In spite of all this, I remained steadfast in my desire to join the navy and become a submariner. I was drawn to submarine duty because I thought it would be unusual, exciting, and that we would operate as an independent ship rather than a member of a large task force. It definitely promised to be more adventurous.

I experienced a few very close calls in the course of my career. At the time such things happen, you usually are so busy trying to take care of the problem that you do not have time to think about the consequences. It is not until the crisis has passed that you have time to think about it and realize how lucky you are to have survived.

It takes all kinds of people to do what has to be done in our country. Thank goodness people are different. For example, I would never jump out of an airplane — regardless of what incentive was offered me.

Well, back to the subject at hand.

The Sixth Fleet commander informed us of an interesting discovery made by one of our destroyers equipped with the latest sonar. While transiting the Strait of Sicily it had picked up a strong contact from something right in the middle of the strait. This is a very narrow part of the Mediterranean. Some time later, as the destroyer passed back through the strait, it encountered the contacts in the exact same place. It appeared that whatever the sonar contact was, it was in a fixed position — probably on the bottom. Since no one had ever reported such a contact before, it was not known whether the contact was something just recently placed there or whether it was something only the improved sonar could pick up. Whatever the object was, it was a possible threat to our security. The intelligence community in Washington wanted to examine it thoroughly. A couple of Sixth Fleet staff officers and I flew to Washington and spent a day with the intelligence group devising a plan. It was obvious that a small, two-man, deep-diving submarine would be required to locate the target, illuminate it in order to examine it, and take pictures so that we could learn all that was possible. We wanted to do all this without it being known to anyone else.

The two-man submarine we needed was located on the East Coast. We would quietly load it aboard a seaplane tender, which would carry it to the area to be examined. The seaplane tender was built so that it could load and off-load seaplanes at sea. It had a big well deck large enough to hold a seaplane. A large gate at the stern could be opened so a plane could be floated into the well deck. The gate would then be closed and the water pumped out. This would be perfect for picking up and off-loading the submarine. The sub could be covered so that it would not be visible from the air. The unloading and loading would be done in the dark of night.

It took several weeks to prepare the submarine, get the tender on scene, load the submarine, cross the Atlantic, and arrive at the Strait of Sicily. A time was set two or three days hence for the tender to rendezvous with the submarine. The submarine would signal the tender by shining a light through its periscope. Zeroing in on the beam of light, the tender would move in close and pick it up. There would be no use of radio communications at any time. When all was ready, the submarine was off-loaded and the tender continued on its way.

Of course, we were most anxious to learn the outcome of the investigation. However, as agreed upon in the operation order, we would learn nothing until the captain of the two-man submarine showed up at our headquarters and personally briefed us.

The night and the time for the rendezvous finally arrived. The tender arrived at the rendezvous point and, seeing no other ships were around, began looking for the signal from the sub. Right on schedule, the tender spotted the small flashing light about half a mile away. They closed on the spot where they had seen the light, opened the stern gate, and in sailed the submarine. They immediately headed in a westerly direction for the trip back to the United States. The next morning, a Sixth Fleet helicopter picked up the sub's skipper and brought him to Naples.

The captain related how they had very carefully searched the whole area and found absolutely nothing but some large boulders where the contact had been reported. I remember being disappointed that they had not located some sophisticated detection system, but my thoughts drifted to the large boulders I had seen up in the mountains. I asked him to describe what the boulders looked like and his detailed description clearly fit what I had seen in the mountains.

At this point I need to double back and relate an adventure I had a couple of months before.

A fellow church member in Naples, an Englishman, had finally persuaded me to go with him into the mountains outside Naples, just beyond Pompeii, to see something very unusual. He had already persuaded two other couples, but he refused to tell any of us just what it was we were going to see.

We loaded into his van and off we went, finally leaving the main road not far beyond Pompeii, and headed up a steep road into the mountains. After about fifteen minutes we had climbed pretty high and the rarely traveled road finally ended. We got out of the van and hiked up and up, farther and farther — for what seemed to be an eternity, but was at least an hour and a half. There was no trail; we simply picked our way through the thick woods until we were almost at the top and came to a clearing in which there were four or five immense boulders. There were no stones, rocks, or outcroppings anywhere around — just these huge boulders measuring about fifteen feet in diameter. They were not perfect spheres, but looked like huge balls of bread dough that had relaxed a bit. How had they gotten on top of a mountain?

He led us around to the far side of the first boulder. By George, there was an entrance in it! The entrance was about a foot thick and the inside of the boulder was hollow. People had lived inside it sometime in the distant past. The entrance had to have been man made, but no one could have hollowed that boulder out. It had to have been formed that way. A huge stone bubble!

The other four boulders also had entrances cut in them and were hollow inside.

Now, back to my meeting with the two-man sub's captain.

I described the big hollow boulders I had seen in the mountains above Pompeii and said that if the ones he had seen were also hollow, they still should contain the gas that had made them into huge bubbles, which would indeed have caused them to reflect a strong echo on the destroyer's improved sonar. You always get some sound reflected off the bottom, but the hollow stone bubbles would have produced a much stronger echo.

It was a relief to learn that we did not have a new detection system with which to contend, but it also left us with a big question to ponder: How had these strange boulders wound up only on the top of a mountain and at the bottom of the sea?

As the end of my three-year tour of duty in Naples approached, I reflected on how fast the time had passed. I knew I would not be permitted to serve there for more than three years and that I could expect orders for my next assignment to arrive pretty soon. I hated the thought of having to leave. I would never find a job more demanding, more exciting, and more satisfying than this one had been. Whatever my new job turned out to be, my life in the navy would be downhill from this point onward.

I enjoyed looking back at the problems we had faced and how well we had fared. I considered myself most fortunate to have been able to travel around Europe and the Mediterranean as I had. The social life in Naples also was superb. I had never attended so many top-notch cocktail parties, dinners, and dances. Some of these events were in beautiful homes, some in clubs — some had even been in the Palace of Naples. I became acquainted with almost all of the English-speaking people living there permanently.

I particularly enjoyed the church we attended. It was an Anglican Episcopal church. The building was medium sized, made of beautiful stone, and had cathedral-like architecture. The congregation was just the right size for everyone to feel very much at home with everybody else. I thought it rather unusual, however, for a Protestant church of such long standing to be there. I eventually learned that Garibaldi had deeded the land for the church to the English because they had helped him pull all of Italy together many years before.

The anticipated reduction in the number of personnel on the COMSUB-FLOT 8 staff never came about. Instead, we had carefully managed our personnel and streamlined our administration so that people now enjoyed reasonable hours, short periods of leave, and adequate time with their families — all of this despite a substantial increase in the complexity of our operations and the number of submarines assigned.

My orders came through about a month before my scheduled rotation date. I was going to a job in the Pentagon dealing with nuclear and chemical warfare. How depressing! I was sad to have to leave my job and sad to be leaving Naples. My detachment date inevitably arrived. We sadly departed.

19

THE PENTAGON AND RETIREMENT

We arrived in Washington about a week before my scheduled reporting date. The idea was to locate a place to live and try to get settled, which we did.

After reporting for duty, I learned I would head a group of about five officers whose duty was to provide support material for use by the chief of naval operations in all matters he needed to act upon in the field of nuclear and chemical warfare. Thank goodness my officers were all as sharp as tacks and needed practically no guidance and directions. very top notch officers. I was assigned the additional duty of dealing with certain matters related to the Polaris program, a job usually reserved for an admiral. The job had either lost its importance or never had any real significance. They kept it on the books, however, which meant it had to be filled. The office they gave me for this task was far removed from my primary office. I logged quite a bit of mileage walk-

My simple retirement ceremony. My expression shows that it was not a joyful moment.

ing back and forth between them. Sometimes I wrote a letter in one office and answered it in the other.

After several months passed, I realized that the time had come for me to retire. My seagoing days were over, and what I had wanted to do in the navy was go to sea and enjoy the adventure. I enjoyed serving my country and doing all that I could to improve the navy, but I had at last reached the point where I could leave and never be missed. There were plenty of capable people who could do what I was now doing. I would be leaving the navy in good hands. I was almost fifty years old and knew that my chances of launching a second career decreased exponentially the longer I remained on active duty.

I submitted a letter requesting retirement despite having no job prospects. My request was approved several weeks later and my retirement set for a date in June, just a couple of months away. I set about trying to find work I thought I would enjoy and got lined up with a large corporation headquartered in Houston that was principally involved in drilling offshore oil wells.

A couple of weeks before my retirement date, I began doing the myriad administrative things called for in the retirement process: getting a complete physical exam, obtaining a new identification card showing that I was retired rather than active, and all sorts of other things — including scraping the parking permit decal off my car's windshield and turning it in the day before I formally retired.

On the scheduled day, my boss conducted a brief, rather informal, retirement ceremony in his office. Most of my fellow workers attended. Admiral James L. Holloway, then serving as the chief of naval operations, signed my retirement orders. I had gotten to know him pretty well while I was working for Admiral Rickover because he had to take the Prospective Commanding Officer Course there before taking command of the huge nuclear-powered aircraft carrier USS *Enterprise*. What most pleased me about having his signature on my retirement orders was that his father, as superintendent of the Naval Academy, had signed my diploma when I graduated.

I left the Pentagon without remorse and took the normal long walk to my car. There on my windshield was a ticket for parking without a permit. It cost me ten dollars. Oh well, just one last thing proving that it was time for me to move along.

APPENDIX

USS *SEADRAGON* (SSN-584)
SAILING LIST FOR ARCTIC OPERATION

CDR Charles D. SUMMITT, USN

LCDR John W. HARVEY, USN

LT Bobby D. MATHEWS, USN

LT Arne C. JOHNSON, USN

LT George W. GREENE, Jr., USN

LT Robert B. PIRIE, Jr., USN

LT James P. RANSOM II, USN

LT Roy W. ADLER, USN

LT Arthur L. REHME, MC, USN

LTJG Thomas A. MEINICKE, USN

ENS Robert L. WITTEN, USN

ARCHER, Delmer L., QM2, USN

ARINGTON, Dennis (n), SK2, USN

ASHLEY, Robert E., MM2, USN

BARLOW, Paul A., ETR2, USN

BOYARCHURCK, Joseph R., YN2, USN

BREAULT, George O., Jr., ETC, USN

BURDICK, David J., EMFN, USN

BURGE, Robert W., ENCA, USN

CABE, Phillip A., SM3, USN

CARLSON, Owen D., SOS2, USN

CLARK, James M., EN2, USN

CLARK, William G., IC2, USN

COLLINS, Patrick B., ENCA, USN

CONSER, Herbert R., EN1, USN

COOPER, Irwin E., Jr., ET1, USN

CORNWELL, Lewis L., MMC, USN

CROWLEY, Earl J., III, TM1, USN

DANIELS, David A., EM1, USN

DAVENPORT, Ray A., Jr., CS2, USN

DAVIS, James P., IC2, USN

DEPOY, Meredity B., TMSN, USN

DORSEY, Charles E., HMCA, USN

DITTO, Kenneth W., IC2, USN

EDENBURN, Calvin E., ETC, USN

EVANS, John K., RMCS, USN

FERGUSON, Robert E., SA, USN

GOIN, Jerry "A", MMFN, USN

GUARNES, Mauro (n), SD2, USN

GUNN, Andrew J., HM1, USN

HAINES, Harold R., EN1, USN

HARVEY, Franklin D., MMCA, USN

IRVING, Don K., EM1, USN

KABLIN, Spencer L., ETN3, USN

KEPNER, Edward L., III, SN, USN

KNOEDLER, Clair L., EN1, USN

LAUGHRUN, Floyd L., CSCS, USN

LE BEAU, James J., SN, USN

LE CLAIR, Phillip L., TMC, USN

LEMBERGER, Richard R., ETR2, USN

LESCHIUTTA, Harold L., EN1, USN

LLOYD, Thomas H., EN1, USN

LOYD, Eugene G., ETR2, USN

MARTINEZ, Gerald S., EM2, USN

MC MURRAIN, Wendell G., ETRSN, USN

MEGAW, Kenneth A., ICFN, USN

MORRIS, Thomas E., YN3, USN
MUNSTER, Marvin E., TM2, USN
NORMANDIN, Frederick L., ETR2, USN
NORRIS, James H., EM1, USN
MC MICHAEL, Richard L., EN2, USN
ODEGAARD, Michael H., CS2, USN
PAYNE, Patrick J., EM2, USN
PERRY, Clyde M., RMCA, USN
RAYNER, Edward C., QM3, USN
ROBERG, Lyle S., SOSSN, USN
RODDY, Wilton J., Jr., ICFN, USN
ROESKE, Lee W., RM2, USN
RUSH, Donald R., TM3, USN
RYAN, Patrick D., ETN2, USN
QUICK, Edward P., MM1, USN
SANDS, William G., ENFN, USN
SAUNDERS, Thomas H., ET1, USN
SCOTT, Harold T., SOCS, USN
SCOTT, Lawrence D., EM2, USN
SHRADER, James W., TMSN, USN
SHUGART, Charles D., MM1, USN
SIEBERT, Arthur E., III, IC1, USN

SLOAN , Henry A., ETN2, USN
SMITH, Alfred G., FTG2, USN
SMITH, Austin E., QMCM, USN
SPENCER, Arthur D., EM1, USN
STALLO, Norbert G., YN1, USN
STANIS, Raymond W., SOS2, USN
STAUFFER, Everett A., MM2, USN
STEIN, Robert J., FTGSN, USN
STUBBS, Ronald E., EM1, USN
TETERS, Tomas N., SOS3, USN
TRUNKHILL, Lee W., EMCA, USN
TUCKER, Loren B., RM3, USN
WANNAN, Donald T., ENC, USN
WARNKE, Larry J., TM3, USN
VENZON, Ernesto M., SD2, USN
WESTHOFF, Stanley M., MMFN, USN
WHITMER, Thomas E., IC2, USN
WILLIAMS, Jerold W., MMFN, USN
WILLIAMS, Lee A., EMC, USN
WILLIAMSON, Robert L., IC2, USN
WORTHEN, Eules K., EN1, USN
ZANE, Robert L., MMCA, USN

The personnel below are civilians who were passengers on board for the cruise:

Walter I. WITTMAN—Hydrographic Office, Washington, D.C.
Keith W. NORLIN—Hydrographic Office, Washington, D.C.
Roger MERRIFIELD—Hydrographic Office, Washington, D.C.
John B. VAN VOORHIS—Sperry Gyroscope Company

INDEX